Conklin – Marinković

Family History

by

David G. Conklin

Please direct all correspondence and book orders to:

David G. Conklin
965 Ranch Lane
Kalispell, MT 59901
Tel: 406-210-4989
conklind@hotmail.com

Library of Congress Cataloging-in-Publication data is available

ISBN 978-0-692-07579-1

Printed for the author by
Moore Graphics
11200 W. Wisconsin Ave. #6
Youngtown, AZ 85363

Cover photos:

Front: from Left to Right-
Charles William Conklin; Caroline Lingren;
2nd Lt David G. Conklin; Evelyn Conklin
Back: Top-David G. Conklin; from Left to Right-
Betty Marinković; Seaman Bogdan Marinković;
Ana Marinković; Stevan Marinković
Bottom-Conklin Coat-of-Arms

Acknowledgments

I would first like to thank my mother and father Betty and Charlie, my aunts Alice, Louise, Dorothy, and my cousins for giving me permission to interview them, capture their memories on tape, and to use their family memories and photos. These recollections provided almost all of the information on Charles W. Conklin, Francis and Caroline Lingren, and Stevan and Ana Marinković that did not come from official government records available in the public domain. I also want to acknowledge the work of my wife Mary, who as always, is my editor-in-chief and biggest supporter. I also wish to thank my good friend and college roommate Arnold Browning, who co-authored the very interesting family history "The Descendants of Emory R. Wilder" (Browning, 2009), and provided the format for this family history.

Thanks to all of you that have provided me with your family information, stories, and photos. All photos not credited were provided by the author. In a way, you, members of the Conklin, Lingren, and Marinković families, are the authors of this book. I am just the recorder of the information that was provided. You encouraged me by your interest in learning more about the origins of the family. Any errors or omissions, however, are mine alone. Please send me your corrections and any additional information and I will try to include them in a future edition of this book.

The focus of Part I of this book begins down one generation from Abraham John Conklin, since I have not been able to find much information about him, to his son, Josiah Conklin, born in 1838. Josiah married Theresa Stockman for whom my Aunt, Louise Theresa Conklin, is named. The focus of Part II is on Francis Lingren, since I have not been able to find any record of his mother or father in Finland. Francis married Johanna Dalstrom for whom my sister Joanie is named. Their daughter, Caroline Lingren, married my grandfather Charles W. Conklin and so is discussed in their chapter in Part I. The focus of Part III begins down one generation from Josif Marinković, since I have not been able to find any record of him, to his son, Stevan Marinković, born in 1885. Stevan married Ana Marinković (not related), for whom my sister Joanie's daughter, Anna, is named.

It is my hope that this first edition will spur someone in our family to update this book in the future. Perhaps one of the cousins or their children will want to update their branch of the family. I would be happy to provide files and advice to any family member that would like to write a book and extend the Conklin, Lingren, or Marinković family history.

February 2018

About the Author

A Montana resident for more than forty years, David G. "Dave" Conklin is a retired park ranger who lives in the Flathead Valley. Although he has B.S. and M.S. degrees in Forestry and Wildlife Management, and an M.B.A., one of his first professional assignments was writing the *Montana Historic Preservation Plan* (Conklin D. , Montana Historic Preservation Plan, 1975) and nominating historic sites to the National Register of Historic Places. As a park ranger, he worked to preserve historic parks associated with people who made the country what it is today. While in Helena, Montana Dave built a log cabin where he lived with his family near the old mining town of Unionville. After retiring he published his first book, *Montana History Weekends* (Conklin D. , Montana History Weekends: Fifty-two Adventures in History, 2002).

Dave began gathering family information in 1978 while still working in Helena, Montana, to include local and family oral histories on audio and videotape as well as photos, documents and notes. After retiring he trained as a Broadcast Journalist for the Army National Guard and served two years in Iraq during Operation Iraqi Freedom, where he was awarded the Bronze Star during combat operations. In 2015 Dave retired again, began taking genealogy classes, and started work on his memoirs and family histories. He is a member of the West Valley Genealogical Society, Youngtown, Arizona and splits his time between Kalispell, Montana and Sun City, Arizona.

The Author: David Gene "Dave" Conklin, Nov 2013

CONTENTS

Part I. The Descendants of Josiah Conklin

Josiah Conklin

With information on his ancestors
to the 850s in Great Britain

Introduction

My purpose in compiling this information is to promote an appreciation of the Conklin family history and appreciation of both those born into the family and those married into the family. I have centered this part of the book on my paternal great grandparents, Josiah Conklin and Theresa Stockman. Although I did not know even their names until I began this project, I am thankful that I knew my paternal Grandfather and Grandmother Charles W. Conklin and Caroline Lingren who were still alive when I was a child.

When we look at our parents and grandparents we often catch glimpses of ourselves, and it's not just from shared DNA. The people who raise us shape us, almost invisibly, through the values they convey, their convictions, and especially through their actions. I hope that this book will cause you to think about the legacy that you leave your children. Our grandparents passed on to us a strong work ethic, moral values, self-discipline, concern for neighbors, the importance of hospitality, and the importance of family and love.

I have included brief information about each person's education, occupation, military and public service when that information was available. I would hope that Josiah and Theresa would be pleased to know that many in the family seek to honor their parents, their communities, their country, and each other.

The findings presented here are based solely on my research, primarily over the past three years. The discovery of additional sources or interpretations may affect the conclusions.

The Format

The National Genealogical Society Quarterly (NGSQ) generation numbering system format is used in this book in order of descent from the oldest paternal ancestor (William Conkling, 1533) to the thirteenth generation (Isabelle Conklin, 2004). I only show the direct lineage for each of the ancestors of Josiah. I list all of the children for each ancestor, but only the ancestors of Josiah are listed in the next generation. Details of ancestors' lives are mentioned when available. I included all the descendants of Josiah Conklin that I found. Even with this book going back thirteen generations, it has still been a challenge as there are more than 40 descendants of Josiah Conklin and Theresa Stockman and the number continues to increase.

Chapter 1 is about the Conklin ancestors. Practically all the information about Josiah's ancestors was obtained from published sources describing America, northern Europe, and their ethnic history due to the lack of both written and oral sources from family ancestors themselves.

Chapter 2 is about the lives of Josiah Conklin and Theresa Stockman, the focus of this book and the parents of Charles W. Conklin, my grandfather.

The remaining chapters list the descendants of Josiah Conklin and Theresa Stockman with a separate chapter for each of Josiah Conklin and Theresa Stockman's children who lived to be adults, beginning with the oldest, David (Chapter 3) to the youngest, Charles (Chapter 5).

Each descendant is assigned a number. Also, for both ancestors and descendants, a small number appears after their first name, or after their middle name if they have a middle name. This number indicates what generation of descendant this person is relative to the person listed at the beginning of the chapter. For example, in Chapter 5 the 5 after Isabelle signifies that she is the 5th generation descending from Charles W. Conklin who is listed at the beginning of Chapter 5 as person number 1. This is true except for Chapter 2 where the 8 after Josiah Conklin signifies that he is the 8th generation descending from William Conkling who is listed in Chapter 1 as person number 1.

Each of Josiah's ancestors' names appears in parentheses after his name. First, his 5th great grandfather William Conkling is followed by 1 indicating that William Conkling is the 1st generation that I have any information on. If we someday find William's father, he would become the 1st generation, and so on.

For descendants that married a person that already had children, I have included these children and their families in the book. Although they are not descendants by blood line, they are part of the Conklin family through marriage. Similarly, adopted children are included when their information was provided.

The book was developed with the "Family Tree Maker" computer application. Each of the chapters of the descendants of Josiah Conklin and Theresa Stockman was developed from a separate "Descendant" genealogy report file built with "Family Tree Maker." Each file has a number for each descendant of the primary person starting with "2," When there is a plus sign in front of the number, it indicates that the descendant also had children and will be listed again under the next generation farther along in the book.

This methodology is used to keep all of the descendants of each of Josiah's children in one chapter. If we had just used one file for all the descendants, the family members would appear mixed throughout this section of the book, because the report file lists all descendants by generation. You can also use the index to find the name and page with information for that individual. Josiah's ancestors are also listed by name in the index.

Conklin Family Movement

We assume that the Conklin name came from England, but one opinion believes the name could also be an English corruption of a continental name and that William Conkling may be a first or second generation English whose forbearers were skilled tradesmen in the glass business in Italy, Lorraine, or Normandy (Mann, The Family of Conklin in America, 1944, p. 49).

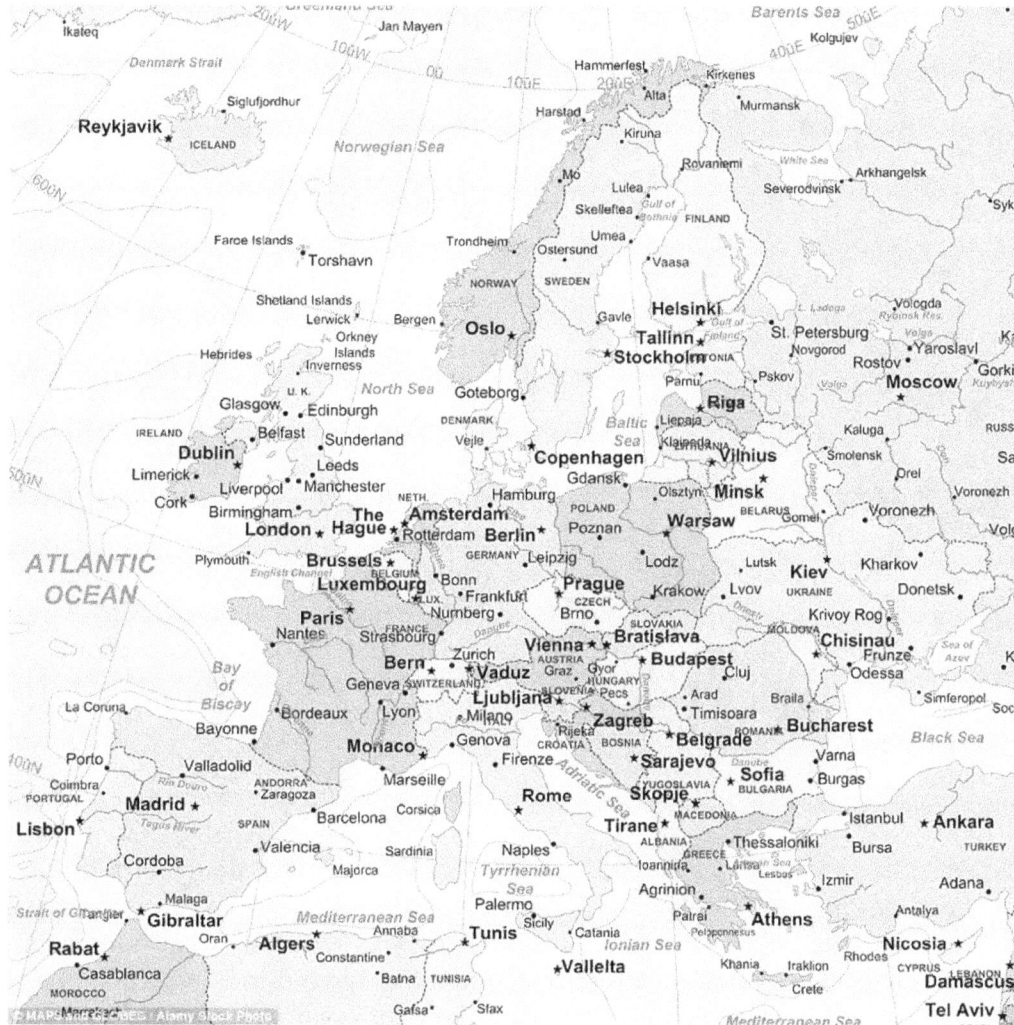

A map of Europe showing the relationship of countries with Conklin ancestors.

During the early Middle Ages people were referred to by a single given name unless they were part of the aristocracy or needed to be distinguished by place of birth (ie. William of Nottingham), distinguishing features, or occupation. So it is not uncommon that before about 1450 there were few fixed hereditary surnames, making tracing a family's past all the more difficult.

Similarly in Western Europe during the Middle Ages, there were only about twenty common names given to infants based on the New Testament. In 1545 the Catholic Church made the use of a saint's name mandatory for baptism. Only after the Reformation in the 1600s did the Protestants add to such common names as John and Mary with names from the Old Testament such as Abraham and Jacob (Halbert's Family Heritage, 1998, p. 4.10).

In this book I have repeated the spelling variations of the Conklin surname in its several forms to include Conkling, Concklin, Conkleyn, and Concklyne based on the most common usage for that individual or generation.

A view of St Peters Church in Nottingham, England where John Concklyne married Elizabeth Alsaebrook in 1625.

Nevertheless, the history of the Conklin family that we can trace are the movements of William Conkling's descendants. It begins in England during the 1500's when King Henry VIII broke with the Church of Rome and established the Church of England (Anglican Church). Some objected to parts of the newly formed religion and wanted to simplify or "purify" it. They became known as "Puritans" and faced severe laws against dissention. The first Puritans in America came to establish a separate church and by 1620 emigration from England to the American colonies began. Soon after, the Conklin's became part of the history of America.

Two of William's four sons, John and his younger brother Ananias Concklyne, sailed across the Atlantic Ocean to the Massachusetts Bay Colony of Salem in 1638. They were tradesmen from Nottingham, England and as the population near the eastern seacoast grew, as farmland became scarce, and as the threat of Indian attacks reduced, opportunities opened up elsewhere in New England. Both of the Conklin families moved to New York in the 1650's settling in East Hampton and Huntington. One of their sons was among the first four families to settle Amagansett (near East Hampton), New York in 1695 (Field, 1948, p. 33). Abraham Conklin, 6th generation descendant from William, was born in Philipsburg, New York in 1752, married in 1772, and after the Revolutionary War moved his family to Alburgh, Vermont in 1783 where they helped clear the forest and establish new farms and towns.

By 1787 the United States had incorporated 260,000 square miles of land north and west of the Ohio River known at the Northwest Territory which included the modern states of Ohio, Indiana, Illinois, Michigan, and Wisconsin. The government transferred much land into private hands and much was given to war veterans. After peace treaties were signed to remove Indian threats in 1795, enterprising Americans pushed into the frontier (Rutkow, 2012, p. 54). By 1803 the Louisiana Purchase was completed and Ohio had become a state. By 1813 two of Abraham Conklin's sons, Abraham John, and Jacob, left Vermont and settled in Ohio. Abraham John's son Josiah Conklin, 8th generation descendant from William, was born in 1838 in Marion Township, Marion County, Ohio. He married in 1864 shortly after his discharge from the Union Army, moving his family in 1870 to Kansas then by 1873 to Manistee County, Michigan, where good farmland was available at a low price and his sons could work in the burgeoning lumber industry as well.

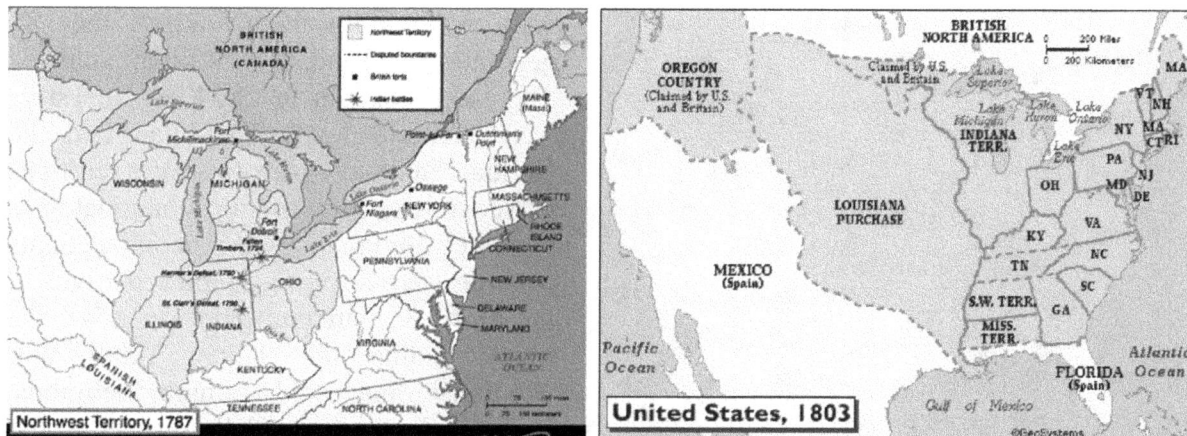

The United States incorporated the Northwest Territories in 1787 and the Louisiana Purchase in 1803, two enormous stretches of land, allowing settlers to continue their push westward from the former colonies.

But in Michigan and the other Lake States lumber production peaked in 1892 and by 1900 Frederick Weyerhaeuser and other lumber barons were finishing their 30-year assault on these forests and the lumber industry was moving west (Rutkow, 2012, p. 114). So Josiah's three sons moved west to where the jobs were. In 1903 David Elias Conklin and his family moved to California where he became a Stevedore. He soon sent word of the jobs available and brothers Eugene and Charles moved to California, then Oregon, and continued to work in the lumber industry. The youngest son, Charles W. Conklin, 9th generation descendant from William, was born in 1873 in Manistee County, Michigan. In 1908 after his mother died, he moved to Marshfield, Oregon where he worked in the lumber mills and started his family. His son, Charles F. Conklin, 10th generation descendant from William, was born in 1913 in Marshfield, Oregon. Just before World War II he moved to South Gate, California and started a business and a family, later moving them to Spokane, in Washington State.

Female Ancestors Family Movement

Although the Conklin family name came from England, the familial DNA comes from female ancestors as well as male. As the Conklins married, their spouses passed on their ancestry to Conklin descendants as well. For example John Conkelyn, the 3rd generation descendant of William, married the widow Sarah (Horton) Salmon. Her 7th great grandmother, Lady Mary Clifford, was the daughter of Sir John Clifford (1388-1422) of Appleby Castle, England and himself the descendant of Joan de Geneville (1268-1356) whose ancestors were born in Ireland and France. These ancestors in turn include David I, King of Scots (1083-1153) and Groa Thorsteinsdottir, Princess of Iceland (975-1045) *(See Appendix 1. Conklin - Marinković Pedigree Chart, p. 10).*

Also when Josiah Conklin, the 8th generation descendant of William, married Theresa Stockman in 1864 her ancestors were German Jews. They had fled the German Palatinates due to severe religious persecution. The name Palatinate is derived from the districts where the counts palatine were sovereign representatives of the Holy Roman emperors. In 1648 the treaty ending the Thirty Years War stipulated that only three religions, Catholic, Lutheran, and Reformed, would be tolerated in Germany. Religious persecution combined with harsh economic conditions motivated large numbers of families of small religious sects to immigrate from Palatine Germany to America.

Map showing the Palatine region of southwest Germany –Map by Magellan.

Theresa's 4th great grandfather, Joerg Wetzstein (1674-1742) was born in Sigmaringen, Germany but by 1732 had immigrated with his family on the ship *Samuel* to Philadelphia. Within two generations his descendants had Americanized their surname to Whetstone and became part of the "Pennsylvania Deutsch" population in several states. Theresa's great grandfather Johannes Stockman (1723-1785) tells a similar story. He was born in Siegen, Germany and in 1766 brought his family on the ship *Polly* from Amsterdam to Philadelphia to join his brothers. His son Peter served in both the Revolutionary War and the War of 1812 before becoming an early settler of Ohio (Leggett Conaway, 1883, p. 1028).

Postcard from Sigmaringen, Germany, birthplace of Joerg Wetzstein.

Josiah Conklin's son Charles William, the 9th generation descendant of William, married Caroline Lingren, a first generation American, in 1912. Her parents emigrated from Finland in the 1860's when Finland was under Russian rule and many Finns had heard about free land and a better economy in America (see Lingren Family Movement in Part II).

It was a similar story when Charles's son Charles Franklin, the 10th generation descendant of William, married first generation American Betty Marinković in 1946. Her parents were Serbian and emigrated from Croatia in the early 1900's when Croatia was under Austrian rule. Many Serbs also had heard about cheap land and a better economy in America (see Marinković Family Movement in Part III).

Famous Conklins

Probably the first noteworthy Conklins were the brothers John and Ananias Concklyne themselves. Born in Nottinghamshire, England in 1595 and 1610 respectively, they were trained in the trade of glassmaking and manufactured window glass and bottles. After arriving in Salem, Massachusetts in 1638 they built the first glass works in America (Ancestry.com Operations, Inc. Lehi, UT, USA, 2016). They were granted house lots in Salem and a ten-acre plot for a glass factory that is still known as "Glass House Field" (Rattray, p. 245). They formed a company with financial backers for their craftsmanship but things did not go well and they were forced to borrow £8 from the town of Salem in 1641. Then in 1645 they requested funds from the Governor of the colony and by 1650 they had gone out of business and moved to Long Island (Perley, 1926).

In the Revolutionary War but few families were better represented for the cause of liberty. Abraham Conklin of New York, at the age of 24 fought as a Private in Colonel Hay's Regiment, New York Continental Line (Ancestry.com Operations, Inc. Provo, UT, USA, 2011). During the war there were more than one hundred enlistments of the name "Conklin" from New York State alone, and many from New Jersey and New England. The records show that they were not all privates, but otherwise were well distributed in the various ranks up to and including that of Colonel. "Thus the Conklings have a modest claim to the distinction of being classed with true and loyal Americans" (Conkling, 1913, p. 95).

Dr. Henry Conkling was a graduate of the Sterling Medical College of Columbus, Ohio. During the Civil War he was called into service by Governor Yates of Illinois and in 1864 was sent to the South as a surgeon and to look over sanitary conditions for the soldiers as part of the 7th Illinois Cavalry Regiment. During the year he wrote a political campaign document for Abraham Lincoln's re-election campaign called *"The Inside View of the Rebellion and The American Citizens Textbook."* The Chicago Tribune and the Cincinnati Enquirer circulated thousands of them, helping the President win by a large majority. In 1870 his persistent efforts helped build the Indianapolis, Bloomington and Western Railroad from Indianapolis to Peoria (Conkling, 1913, p. 44).

No one of the family of Conklins, however, has yet attained that degree of eminence reached by U.S. Senator Roscoe Conkling (1829 – 1888). His history as lawyer, politician, senator and statesman is known to those acquainted with the political and civil history of the nation. His father, Judge Alfred Conkling, who was born on Long Island near East Hampton, was in his time a noted jurist, well known throughout the state, and a prominent figure in Congress at Washington. Reportedly there is a statue of him in Madison Square, New York.

— Roscoe Conkling —

Obeying instructions I should never dare to disregard, expressing, also, my own firm conviction, I rise in behalf of the State of New York to propose a nomination with which the country and the Republican party can grandly win.

AZ QUOTES

Quote from Roscoe Conkling, U.S. Senator from New York –from "The Conklings of America."

Senator Conkling was a politician from New York and served both as a member of the United States House of Representatives and the United States Senate. He was the leader of the Stalwart faction of the Republican Party, the first Republican senator from New York to be elected for three terms, and the last person to turn down a U.S. Supreme Court appointment after he had already been confirmed to the post by the U.S. Senate. While in the House, Representative Conkling served as body guard for Representative Thaddeus Stevens, a sharp-tongued anti-slavery representative, and fully supported the Republican Civil War effort. Conkling, who was temperate and detested tobacco, was known for being a body builder through regular exercise and boxing. Conkling was elected to the Senate in 1867 as a leading Radical, who supported the rights of African Americans during Reconstruction (Paxson. Frederic Logan, 1930).

Chapter 1. Ancestors of Josiah Conklin

This chapter presents the ancestors of Josiah Conklin beginning with William Conkling who was born in 1533. For more information about the context of the Conklin ancestors' life and times see *"The Conklings in America". www.forgottonbooks.com* (Conkling, 1913).

Generation 1

1. **WILLIAM**[1] **CONKLING** was born in 1533 in Nottinghamshire, England. He died in 1610 in Nottinghamshire, England. He married Ruth Hedges, daughter of Richard Hedges, in 1595 in Nottingham, Nottinghamshire, England. She was born in 1533 in Kent, England. She died in 1610 in Nottinghamshire, England.

Nottingham from the east, in about 1695 –painting by Jan Siberechts

William Conkling is the earliest ancestor that I have been able to trace so far. Since we know that at least two of his sons (John and Ananias) were skilled *"glassmen"* one opinion is that William Conkling may be a first or second generation English whose forbearers were skilled tradesmen in the glass business in Italy, Lorraine, or Normandy (Mann, The Family of Conklin in America, 1944, p. 49).

William Conkling and Ruth Hedges had the following children:

+2. i. JOHN[2] CONCKLYNE was born in 1595 in St Peters Parish, Nottinghamshire, England. He died on 24 Feb 1684 in Huntington, Suffolk, New York, United States (Age 89). He married Elizabeth Allsaebrook, daughter of Edward Alseabrook and Hannah Walker, on 24 Jan 1625 in Nottinghamshire, England (St. Peters Parish Church). She was born on 18 Sep 1608 in Nottingham, Nottinghamshire, England. She died on 26 Mar 1671 in Huntington, Suffolk, New York, United States.

3. ii. CORNELIUS CONKLING was born in 1603 in Nottingham, Nottinghamshire, England. He died on 21 Mar 1666 in Salem, Essex, Massachusetts, USA.

4. iii.JACOB CONKLING was born in 1607 in Nuthall, Nottinghamshire, England. He died on 25 Jun 1642 in Nuthall, Nottinghamshire, England.

+5. iv. ANANIAS CONKLIN was born in 1610 in Kings, Swineford, Stratford, England. He died on 01 Oct 1657 in East Hampton (Amagansett), Suffolk, New York, USA (Age 47). He married Mary Launder on 23 Feb 1630 in Nottinghamshire, England (St Peters Parish Church). She died in 1649.

Generation 2

2. JOHN[2] CONCKLYNE (William[1] Conkling) was born in 1595 in St Peters Parish, Nottinghamshire, England. He died on 24 Feb 1684 in Huntington, Suffolk, New York, United States (Age 84). He married Elizabeth Allsaebrook, daughter of Edward Alseabrook and Hannah Walker, on 24 Jan 1625 in Nottinghamshire, England (St. Peters Parish Church). She was born on 18 Sep 1608 in Nottingham, Nottinghamshire, England. She died on 26 Mar 1671 in Huntington, Suffolk, New York, United States.

John's younger brother Ananias Concklyne was probably the first Conklin in America, arriving in the Massachusetts Bay Colony of Salem on 25 April 1638. But records show that John Concklyne was also in Salem by 14 September 1640 and was granted land near the "glass house" for his residence (Mann, The Family of Conklin in America, 1944, p. 50). The brothers were trained in the trade of "glassmen" that manufacture window glass and bottles. After arriving in Salem, Massachusetts in 1638 they built the first glass works in America (Ancestry.com Operations, Inc. Lehi, UT, USA, 2016).

They were granted house lots in Salem and a ten-acre plot for a glass factory that is still known as "Glass House Field" (Rattray, p. 245). Ananias formed a company with financial backers for their craftsmanship in 1638 and John joined in 1640. But things did not go well and they were forced to borrow £8 from the town of Salem in 1641. Then in 1645 they requested funds from the Governor of the colony and by 1650 they had gone out of business and moved to Long Island (Perley, 1926). In 1649 John Concklyne had apparently visited the towns of Long Island, New York, and in April, 1650, the Concklyne, Scudder, and several other Salem families moved to the town of Southold on Long Island (Mann, The Family of Conklin in America, 1944, p. 51).

John Concklyne and his family settled in Southold, West Hampton and was the first of the Southold Conklin family line. His brother Ananias settled in East Hampton and became the first of the East Hampton Conklin family line. In 1660 the John Concklyne family became the first to settle in Huntington, West Hampton (Rattray, p. 245). He began buying and selling land and became the owner of several parcels including an oyster pond and a track near Southold long known as "Conklin's Neck." As he got older he deeded his home and property to his children, finally living for short periods with each of them (Mann, The Line of John Concklyne of Southold and Huntington, 1945, p. 213).

Documents and wills that survived from that period describe John as a generous and kind individual. One affidavit in 1656 said, "Mr. Frost lying upon his sick bed did by word of mouth give unto John Conckelyne Sr. all his estate wch he had: and that because the said John Conckelyne did curtiously receive him into his house when he was destitute" (Mann, The Line of John Concklyne of Southold and Huntington, 1945, p. 211). He remained an important man in Southold and Huntington and the public services linked with his name lead to the conclusion that his acquaintances had great confidence in his thoughtfulness and integrity.

John Concklyne and Elizabeth Allsaebrook had the following children:

6. i.   REBECCA[3] CONKLIN was born about 1626 in St. Peters Parish, Nottinghamshire, England. She died on 09 Apr 1670 in Huntington, Suffolk, New York, United States. She married Thomas Brush about 1650.

7. ii.   JACOB CONKLYNE was born in 1628 in St. Peters Parish, Nottinghamshire, England. He died in 1668 in Southold, Suffolk, New York, United States.

+8. iii. JOHN CONKELYN was born on 19 Sep 1630 in St. Peters Parish, Nottinghamshire, England. He died on 06 Apr 1694 in Southold, Suffolk County, New York, USA. He married Sarah Horton, daughter of Barnabas Horton and Mary Langton, on 02 Dec 1657 in Rye, Westchester, New York, United States. She was born in 1637 in Phillipsburg, Westchester, New Amsterdam, Dutch Colony of New Amsterdam, North America. She died before 1687 in Eastchester, Westchester, New York.

9. iv.   ELIZABETH CONKLIN was born Abt. 1634 in St. Peters Parish, Nottinghamshire, England. She died in 1683 in Suffolk, New York, United States

10. v.   ISAAC CONKLIN was born on 10 Jan 1634. He died on 11 Oct 1635 in Nottinghamshire, England.

11. vi.   TIMOTHY CONKLIN was born in 1640 in England. He died in 1714 in Huntington, Suffolk, New York, United States.

+5. ANANIAS[2] CONCKLYNE (William[1] Conkling) was born in 1610 in Kings, Swineford, Stratford, England. He died on 01 Oct 1657 in East Hampton (Amagansett), Suffolk, New York, USA (Age 47). He married Mary Launder on 23 Feb 1630 in Nottinghamshire, England (St. Peters Parish Church). She died in 1649.

Ananias Concklyne and Mary Launder had the following children:

12. i.   MARY[3] CONKLIN was born in 1631 in Kings, Swineford, Stratford, England.

13. ii.   JEREMIAH CONKLIN was born about 1634 in Nottingham, Nottinghamshire, England. He died on 14 Mar 1712.

14. iii. CORNELIUS CONKLIN was born about 1636 in Nottingham, Nottinghamshire,

England.
15.   iv.   BENJAMIN CONKLING was born in 1638 in Salem, Massachusetts. He died on 03 Feb 1709 (Age 71).
16.   v.   LEWIS CONKLIN was born about 1642 in Salem, Massachusetts.
17.   vi.   HESTER CONKLIN was born about 1654 in Southold, Suffolk, New York.

Ananias Concklyne House in Amagansett, New York --photo from "East Hampton History."

Generation 3

8.   JOHN[3] CONKELYN (John[2] Concklyne, William[1] Conkling) was born on 19 Sep 1630 in St. Peters Parish, Nottinghamshire, England. He died on 06 Apr 1694 in Southold, Suffolk County, New York, USA (Age 64). He married Sarah Horton, daughter of Barnabas Horton and Mary Langton, on 02 Dec 1657 in Rye, Westchester, New York, USA. She was born in 1637 in Phillipsburg, Westchester, New Amsterdam, Dutch Colony of New Amsterdam, North America. She died in 1700 in Eastchester, Westchester, New York.

By some accounts, John Conkelyn "junior" was by far more aggressive and active than his father (Mann, The Line of John Concklyne of Southold and Huntington, 1945, p. 212). He was the oldest son of John "senior" and was probably the most written about non-political person in Colonial New York. He was a landowner by 1656 and in 1657 married Sarah (Horton) Salmon, the rich young widow of William Salmon who had an estate in Hashamomack. Her parents, the Barnabas Horton family, had immigrated to America on the ship *Swallow,* and she was born on Long Island. Soon after marriage, he became engaged in a protracted legal battle in the courts of New York over the ownership of the Horse Neck lands in the Salmon estate which would have made his family and the Salmon stepchildren wealthy. It became the most completely reported lawsuit in colonial New York. Some say he only lost the suit because the challenger was a New Yorker and John was a New Englander (Mann, The Line of John Concklyne of Southold and Huntington, 1945, p. 246).

Nevertheless "Captain" Conkelyn became one of the most important men in the town of Southold. In 1683 he was the largest landowner in Southold. By 1686 his household consisted of three males, three females and five slaves. In 1690 he was a representative of Suffolk County to the Colonial Assembly and possibly received his Captain title from this work or the militia shortly before he died. John was also very active in numerous land transactions including winning a lawsuit to reclaim the brickyards once owned by the Salmon family. He also later won a suit for damages due a neighbor's "divers swine in about the commons . . . whereby his now wife in her widowhood had sustained great losse in her crop of wheat and pease." This of course led to a slander lawsuit which he also won where the same neighbor reportedly said, "that John Conckling was a neighbor not fit for an Indian to live by . . ." (Mann, The Line of John Concklyne of Southold and Huntington, 1945, p. 248).

In 1684, due to friction with other owners, Conkelyn signed away his lands in Hashamomack and in return received the famous "four score acres" that became a legend in Southold. In his lengthy 1689 will he gave his two sons John and Joseph all his lands and property, including the Negroes, in Southold to be equally divided between them, and gave his daughters his cows and household goods.

John Conkelyn's tomb is in Southold with an inscription around the border and top reading, "Here lyeth the body of Captain John Conkelyn borne in Nottinghamshire in England who departed this life the sext day of Aprill att South Hold on Longiland in the sixty fourth year of his age Anno Dom 1694."

John Conkelyn's tomb in Southold, New York.
--photo from "The Line of John Concklyne."

John Conkelyn and Sarah Horton had the following children:
18. i. JOHN[4] CONKLIN was born in 1658 in Southold, Suffolk, New York, USA. He died on 04 Mar 1705 in Southold, Suffolk, New York, USA.

+19. ii. JOSEPH CONKLIN was born in 1680 in Rye, Westchester, New York, USA. He died in Nov 1736 in Philipsburg, Westchester, New York. He married Rebecca Hyatt, daughter of John Hyatt II and Rachel Bassett, in 1706 in New York. She was born about 1680 in Sleepy Hollow, New York, USA. She died on 29 Jun 1728 in Philipsburg, Westchester, New York, USA.

20. iii. SARAH CONKLING was born in 1662 in Southold, Suffolk, New York, USA. She died on 08 Nov 1740 in Suffolk, Livingston, New York, USA. She married John Laughton on 28 Jul 1680 in Southold, Suffolk, New York, USA. He was born about 1658 in Southampton, Suffolk, New York, USA. He died before 18 Oct 1692.

21. iv. ANNA CONKLIN was born after 1668 in Southold, Suffolk, New York, USA. She died in Southold, Suffolk, New York, USA.

22. v. MARY CONKELYN was born after 1668 in Southold, Suffolk, New York, USA.

23. vi. ELIZABETH CONKELYN was born after 1668 in Southold, Suffolk, New York, USA. She died on 02 Jul 1697 in Southold, Suffolk, New York, USA.

Generation 4

19. JOSEPH⁴ CONKLIN (John³ Conkelyn, John² Concklyne, William¹ Conkling) was born in 1680 in Rye, Westchester, New York, USA (Age 56). He died in Nov 1736 in Philipsburg, Westchester, New York. He married Rebecca Hyatt, daughter of John Hyatt II and Rachel Bassett, in 1706 in New York. She was born on 21 Apr 1697 in Sleepy Hollow, New York, USA. She died on 29 Jun 1728 in Philipsburg, Westchester, New York, USA.

John³ Conkelyn's second oldest son behind John, Joseph was born in Rye and later moved to Philipsburg, both in Westchester County, New York. According to one source, Joseph Conklin was named assessor of Philipsburg in June 1716 (Mann, John Concklin of Flushing and Rye, New York, 1950, p. 142). At that time until 1779 it was an English estate called Philipsburg Manor.

To those who knew him he was called Joseph Conkling, Sr., being several years older than his cousin Joseph Conklin. Though a younger son, he inherited half of his father Capt. John Conkelyn's considerable holdings, including Negro slaves, as well as property from his maternal grandfather Barnabas Horton. Horton's will, dated 10 May 1680, bequeaths five sheep to Joseph Conkling "son of my daughter Sarah Conkling" (Mann, The Line of John Concklyne of Southold and Huntington, 1945, p. 117). In about 1706 he married Rebecca Hyatt, the first child baptized in the Old Dutch Church of Sleepy Hollow in 1697 when she was about 17 years old.

The Dutch Reformed Church of Sleepy Hollow on the Albany Post Road was built in 1685 –photo by Daniel Case.

We can only assume that Joseph led a burger's life whatever his occupation, based on what he received or could sell from his father John Conkelyn's estate. His will states: "I give unto my two sons John and Joseph Concklin during their natural lives all my whole accommodations of lands of all sorts whatsoever situate lying and being throughout ye whole bounds of ye town of Southold to be equally divided between them," . . . the negroes, stock and implements at St. Georges to be divided between sons Thomas and Joseph (Mann, The Line of John Concklyne of Southold and Huntington, 1945, pp. 116, 252).

Joseph Conklin and Rebecca Hyatt had the following children:

24. i.   MARY[5] CONKLIN was born about 1706 in Philipsburg, Westchester, New York. She died date Unknown.

+25. ii.   JOHN CONKLIN was born on 25 Apr 1707 in Philipsburg, Westchester, New York, USA. He died in 1780 in Eastchester, Westchester, New York, USA. He married (1) SARAH VANAMBURGH, daughter of Abraham VanAmburgh and Maria Lent, on 02 Apr 1726. She was born in 1705 in New York, USA. She died in 1760 in Newton, Half Moon, New York, USA. He married (2) CATRINA VANBENSCHOTEN about 1763. She was born on 30 Jun 1744 in Kingston, Ulster, New York, USA. She died in 1794 in Woodbourne, Sullivan, New York, USA.

26. iii. JOSEPH CONKLIN was born about 1709 in Philipsburg, Westchester, New York. He died date Unknown.

27. iv.   ISAAC CONKLIN was born about 1713 in Philipsburg, Westchester, New York. He died date Unknown.

28. v.   JANE CONKLIN was born about 1717 in Philipsburg, Westchester, New York. She died date Unknown.

29. vi.   JACOB CONKLIN was born about 1719 in Philipsburg, Westchester, New York. He died date Unknown in Rockland, New York.

30. vii. THOMAS CONKLIN was born on 18 Apr 1721 in Philipsburg, Westchester, New York. He died in 1790.

31. viii. GILBERT CONKLIN was born before 04 Sep 1725 in Philipsburg, Westchester, New York. He died date Unknown.

Generation 5

25. JOHN⁵ CONKLIN (Joseph⁴, John³ Conkelyn, John² Concklyne, William¹ Conkling) was born on 25 Apr 1707 in Philipsburg, Westchester, New York, USA. He died in 1780 in Eastchester, Westchester, New York, USA. He married (1) SARAH VANAMBURGH, daughter of Abraham VanAmburgh and Maria Lent, on 02 Apr 1726. She was born in 1705 in New York, USA. She died in 1760 in Newton, Half Moon, New York, USA. He married (2) CATRINA VANBENSCHOTEN about 1763. She was born on 30 Jun 1744 in Kingston, Ulster, New York, USA. She died in 1794 in Woodbourne, Sullivan, New York, USA.

Frederick Philipse I was granted a royal charter for Philipsburg Manor in 1693 which he built on the Hudson River using African slaves. The John Conklin family may have been among his Dutch and English tenant farmers.

I have found very little information on John, the oldest son of Joseph Conklin. Possibly because his given name is the same as his many other uncles, nephews, and cousins. We know both his first and second wife were of Dutch descent from the Low Lands of Holland as were many other immigrants to Dutchess and Westchester counties, New York. His son Abraham also married a Dutch girl as well. I suspect he was also a Loyalist as were many who lived near the English Philipsburg Manor estate. His son moved further north to Saratoga before the revolution, as he may have been a Loyalist too (MacKenzie). Any Conklin land and property may have been confiscated by Patriots during the Revolution which could also explain not locating a will so far.

John Conklin and Sarah VanAmburgh had the following children:

    32.   i.   HANNAH⁶ CONKLIN was born in 1737 in Southold, Suffolk, New York, USA. She died on 11 May 1815 in Waterloo, Seneca, New York, USA.

    33.   ii.   SARAH CONKLIN was born on 11 Mar 1740 in Newtown, Half Moon District, New York, British America. She died on 01 Mar 1791 in Ernestown, Ontario, Canada.

  +34. iii. ABRAHAM "ABRAM" CONKLIN was born in 1752 in Phillipsburg, Westchester, New York, British America. He died on 15 May 1853 in Chittenden County, Vermont, USA. He married Anna (Annatje) Hilliker, daughter of Jacobus James Hilliker and Elizabeth Mabie, in 1772 in New York. She was born in

1756 in Tarrytown, Westchester, New York, USA. She died on 27 Jan 1839 in Mansfield, Richland, Ohio, USA.

John Conklin and Catrina VanBenschoten had the following children:

35.   i.   CATRINA[6] CONKLIN was born on 10 Oct 1765 in Poughkeepsie, Dutchess, New York, USA. She died on 18 Apr 1850 in Greene, Chenango, New York, USA.

36.   ii.   SUSSANAH CONKLIN was born on 14 Jan 1767 in Poughkeepsie, Dutchess, New York, USA. She died in 1860 in Broome, New York, USA.

37.   iii. MARIA CONKLIN was born on 17 Jun 1768 in Poughkeepsie, Dutchess, New York, USA. She died in Sep 1850 in Williamson, Massachusetts, USA.

38.   iv.   JOHN CONKLIN was born on 09 Sep 1770 in Poughkeepsie, Dutchess, New York, USA. He died in 1850 in Milford, Lagrange, Indiana, USA.

Generation 6

34.   ABRAHAM[6] "ABRAM" CONKLIN (John[5], Joseph[4], John[3] Conkelyn, John[2] Concklyne, William[1] Conkling) was born in 1752 in Philipsburg, Westchester, New York, British America. He died on 15 May 1853 in Chittenden County, Vermont, USA. He married Anna (Annatje) Hilliker, daughter of Jacobus James Hilliker and Elizabeth Mabie, in 1772 in New York. She was born in 1756 in Tarrytown, Westchester, New York, USA. She died on 27 Jan 1839 in Mansfield, Richland, Ohio, USA.

Based on records and family notes we know that Joseph's first son Abraham Conklin was born on Philipsburg Manor. In 1772 he married Anna Hilliker who was only sixteen years old at the time. They moved north to Rondout, and were living in Saratoga, New York in 1775 (MacKenzie). After the Revolutionary War they became some of the first settlers of Grand Isle on Lake Champlain which was ceded from Canada by the British. It appears that Abraham and Anna were Loyalists, loyal to the British government, based on claims they made after the war in Montreal in March, 1788:

> "Claimant sworn - Says he was on duty in the Loghouse at Dutchman's Point, Lake Champlain, in 1783 ("Loghouse at Dutchman's Point" was the Blockhouse maintained by the British and located at Blockhouse Point, North Hero, Vt.). He is a native of America and lived in Saratoga in 1775. He joined Gen. Burgoyne's Army (British) in 1777. Before that time he never joined the Rebels (American), but was obliged to live in the woods. He served in the War in Jessup's Corps. He now lives on Caldwell's Manor (a British grant to Henry Caldwell of Quebec City, and included the present Town of Alburg) without the British lines, but considers himself a British subject. He had some stock in his Father-in-Law's farm with a yoke of oxen, 7 hogs, 15 sheep, taken by the Rebels. 148 bushels of grain cut down in the field" (Fraser, 1904, pp. 467-468).

Another claim by John Hilliker to the British government in Montreal in March, 1788 was witnessed by Abraham:

> "Witness--Abram Concklin (sic), sworn--Says that John Heliker is his Brother-in-Law.

His Father Japed (Jacob) Heliker, lost his life by rebel Indians. Japed Heliker left four sons & nine daughters the rest of the family are in New York State except Abraham and Ann who were on Caldwell's Manor (Alburgh) and both within the lines during the War" (Fraser, 1904, pp. 467-468).

The surrender of the British General John Burgoyne at Saratoga, on October 17, 1777, was a turning point in the American Revolutionary War that prevented the British from dividing New England from the rest of the colonies –painting from Dorling Kindersley LLC.

However family stories passed down to younger generations paint a different picture. The stories say the Conklins were Patriots who were forced into service by the British. Jacob Hilliker and his son were killed by the British rather than by rebel Indians. Were they Loyalists or just pretending to be? Or were they pretending to be Patriots after the War was lost by the British? We may never know. Grandson Edwin Miles Conklin wrote down what he was told and says the Conklins were living with Anna's family in 1777 (before the Battles of Saratoga) and reaping wheat in the field when Gen Burgoyne's British troops came to conscript them into the Army:

> "And their sentiments being with Washington and his army, they refused to go with the British. When Old Man Hilaker and his oldest son was shot down. Then grandfather Conklin and two of his brother-in-laws seeing the fate of the old man and one son and knowing that would be theirs also concluded to go with the British. They was taken into Canada and kept on duty and watched so close that they had no opportunity to desert to Washington's Army, as they had intended to do, Grandfather Conklin had some appointed office. My Grandfather never saw his wife from the time he left with the British Soldiers until the close of the War, some 5 years later." (Davis, 1999).

Another reason to become a Patriot, if not already one, was to attend the Grand Ball after the war and to get re-acquainted with wives, friends, and relatives according to Grandson Edwin Miles Conklin:

> "At the close of the War there was a Grand Ball given in honor of the soldiers and the victory attained on Grand Isle in Lake Champlain in the State of Vermont. My Grandfather Abram Conklin and his brother-in-laws the Hilakers as they returned from Canada took in the ball. And it had been arranged by the brothers that Anna their sister should meet them there. And unbeknown to my Grandfather, her husband, who met her and danced with her several times before he knew who she was often stating to his brother-in-laws how much she reminded him of Ann. But she had grown from a girl as she was when he last saw her to be a stately woman now. And when they told him it was Anna his wife, he could hardly believe them. Suffice to say it was a happy surprise to him and he became so attached to the place that he afterwards bought the property and lived and kept the Hotel there where they had met" (Davis, 1999).

So by about 1783 they were re-united and living on the English estate of Caldwell's Manor (now Alburgh, Vermont) where they raised anywhere from five to seven children by some accounts. Abraham took the Freeman's Oath prior to the first town meeting of Alburgh. The Grand Lists of Alburgh for 1793-1796 shows he had substantial real estate there, buying 119 acres in 1796 (Alburgh, VT, 1796, p. 93). In 1820, when he was about 68 years old, the State of Vermont granted him a ferry right from Alburgh tongue to the west shore of North Hero (Vermont, 1820, pp. 145-146). So as far as we know, he lived the rest of his life in Alburgh. His widow Anna then moving to Mansfield, Ohio to live with her children until she died in 1839.

Abraham "Abram" Conklin and Anna (Annatje) Hilliker had the following children:

+39. i. JACOB[7] CONKLIN was born on 10 Jun 1787 in St. Alburgh, Grand Isles Co., Vermont, USA. He died on 12 Mar 1875 in Westfield, Morrow, Ohio, USA (Age 87). He married Orra Payne, daughter of Ezra Payne, on 17 Sep 1818 in Liberty Twp, Delaware County, Ohio. She was born on 06 Jul 1798 in New Hartford, Litchfield, Connecticut, USA. She died on 20 Oct 1880 in Westfield, Morrow, Ohio, USA.

40. ii. JAMES CONKLIN was born before 1788 in Alburg, Grand Isle, Vermont, USA.

+41. iii. ABRAHAM JOHN "ABRAM II" CONKLIN was born in 1793 in Alburgh, Grand Isle, Vermont, USA. He died in 1870 in Ohio, USA. He married (1) MARGARET CRAWFORD in 1823 in Waldo Mills, Ohio. She was born in 1806 in New Jersey, USA. She died on 30 Aug 1841 in Marion County, Ohio. He married (2) CATHERINE ANN BOVEY on 02 Oct 1842. She was born on 08 Feb 1815 in Washington, Maryland, USA. She died on 06 Jun 1880.

42. iv. LAVINA "LOVINA" CONKLIN was born on 22 Nov 1797 in Alburgh, Grand Isle, Vermont, USA. She died on 20 Oct 1876. She married ELIHU SPEAR.

43. v. DAVID CONKLIN was born in 1803 in Alburgh Township, Grand Isle, Vermont, USA. He died in Morrow, Ohio, USA.

39. **JACOB**[7] **CONKLIN** (Abraham[6] "Abram", John[5], Joseph[4], John[3] Conckelyn, John[2] Concklyne, William[1] Conkling) was born on 10 Jun 1787 in St. Alburgh, Grand Isles Co., Vermont, USA. He died on 12 Mar 1875 in Westfield, Morrow, Ohio, USA (Age 87). He married Orra Payne, daughter of Ezra Payne, on 17 Sep 1818 in Liberty Twp, Delaware County, Ohio. She was born on 06 Jul 1798 in New Hartford, Litchfield, Connecticut, USA. She died on 20 Oct 1880 in Westfield, Morrow, Ohio, USA.

Abraham's older brother was Jacob Conklin. An accounting of his life has been provided by Jacob's youngest son, Edwin Miles Conklin, who lived on the family farm in Westfield Township, Morrow County, Ohio until his death 20 Aug 1921. He gives a handwritten account of his father's life:

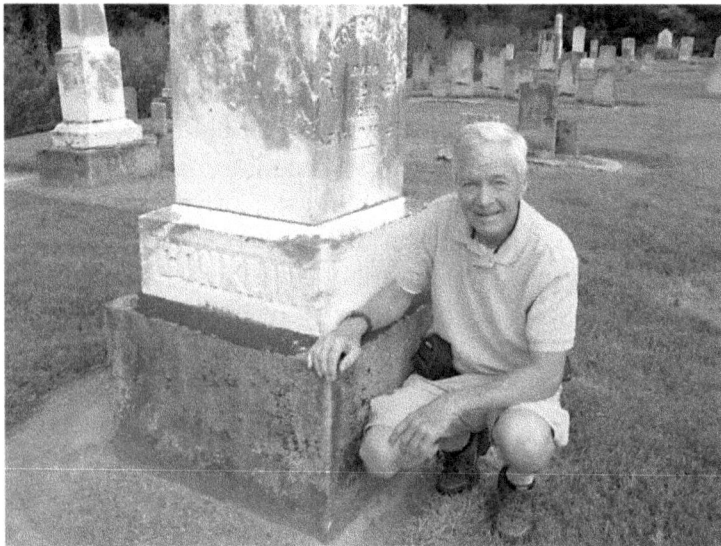

Dave Conklin at Jacob Conklin family grave in Peak Cemetery, Westfield, Morrow County, Ohio 24 Aug 2017.

"Jacob came to Ohio in 1813 staying for a short time at the Cleveland Mills as it was then called, a little Village on the Cuyahoga River since known as the City of Cleveland. His stay there however was not long. He came on to Delaware County, stopping about 5 miles south of the present city of Delaware in Liberty Township. From here he enlisted in the Light Horse Company under Captain Murry and joined (Brig) Gen (Duncan) McArthur's Brigade and served until the close of the War (of 1812) doing duty mostly in Michigan and Canada. He was discharged or mustered out of the service as it was then called at Chillicothe, Ohio and returned to Liberty Township Delaware County and lived with a man by the name of James Carpenter for a few years and married in 1818 Miss Orra Payne of the neighborhood who had come with her parents the year before from Hartford Connecticut. They moved on to this farm in Westfield Township, then in Delaware County in April 1821."

(Here Jacob Conklin cut logs and built a cabin, using blankets for doors and windows, and remained on his farm until his death. He was first a Whig and afterward a Republican; and was a member of the Methodist Church for seventy-two years) (Lewis Publishing Co., 1895, pp. 357-359).

Typical two-story log house built in the 1850's, near Easton, Ohio – photo 23 Aug 2017.

"Seven children were born unto them, one girl and six boys: Clarissa Orrilla June 8, 1820; Lyman Buel July 18, 1822; Ezra Milton August 21, 1824; William Anson March 22, 1828 - Jacob Philemon July 16, 1830 - Abram Virgil Nov. 21, 1832 and Edwin Miles September 6, 1835. Of these Lyman Buel died first Dec. 11, 1843 and was not married. Clarissa Orrilla married Elihu White Jan 1, 1839, and had three children who all died young. She also buried her husband in December 1846, a few days short of 8 years after they were married."

All the children of Jacob and Orra stayed in Ohio except William Anson Conklin who moved to Oskaloosa, Iowa and Jacob Philemon Conklin's children, who moved to Michigan (Davis, 1999).

Jacob Conklin and Orra Payne had the following children:

44. i. CLARISSA ORILLA[8] CONKLIN was born on 08 Jun 1820 in Delaware County, Ohio, USA. She died on 15 Mar 1856 in Morrow County, Ohio, USA. She married Elihu White on 01 Jan 1839. He was born about 1820. He died in Dec 1846.

45. ii. LYMAN BUEL CONKLIN was born on 19 Jul 1822. He died on 11 Dec 1843.

46. iii. EZRA MILTON CONKLIN was born on 21 Aug 1824 in Morrow County, Ohio, USA. He died on 15 Apr 1897 in Prospect, Marion County, Ohio, USA. He married (1) CLARISSA HULL, daughter of Samuel Hull and Cherrissa Wilcox, on 28 Feb 1847 in Westfield, Morrow, Ohio, USA. She was born about 1825. She died on 14 Mar 1859 in Waldo Twp., Marion Co., OH (The History of Marion County, Ohio p. 1017). He married (2) AMANDA E. WINEGARNER on 11 Dec 1859.

47. iv. WILLIAM ANSON CONKLIN was born on 22 Mar 1828 in Westfield, Morrow, Ohio, USA. He died on 11 Feb 1887 in Madison, Madison, Iowa, USA.

48. v. JACOB PHILEMON CONKLIN was born on 16 Jul 1830.

49. vi. ABRAHAM VIRGIL CONKLIN was born on 21 Nov 1832. He died on 28 Oct 1910.

50. vii. EDWIN MILES CONKLIN was born on 06 Sep 1835. He died on 30 Aug 1921.

41. **ABRAHAM JOHN**[7] **"ABRAM II" CONKLIN** (Abraham[6] "Abram", John[5], Joseph[4], John[3] Conkelyn, John[2] Concklyne, William[1] Conkling) was born in 1793 in Alburgh, Grand Isle, Vermont, USA. He died in Feb 1870 in Ohio, USA. He married (1) MARGARET CRAWFORD in 1823 in Waldo Mills, Ohio. She was born in 1806 in New Jersey, USA. She died on 30 Aug 1841 in Marion County, Ohio. He married (2) CATHERINE ANN BOVEY on 02 Oct 1842 in Marion County, Ohio. She was born on 08 Feb 1815 in Washington, Maryland, USA. She died on 06 Jun 1880.

I have not yet found any information about Abraham John Conklin's early life in Alburgh, Vermont but we know that "Abram" as he was often called, was about six years younger than his older brother Jacob and was a farmer as was his namesake father. But the War of 1812 had begun in June 1812, and continued until July 1815. By 1813 the Michigan Territory to the north was the front line of the war. At least seven land and four naval battles were fought within the territory. British forces occupied all or part of Michigan during this time.

BATTLE OF PLATTSBURG. (From an old print.)[2]

The Battle of Plattsburg from the Pictorial Field Book of the War of 1812
--Image by Benson Lossing.

Then the British burned the White House on 24 August 1814, and soon after were threatening the town of Plattsburgh, New York on the opposite shore of Lake Champlain from Alburgh, Vermont. On September 3rd, Abram enlisted as a volunteer in the Vermont Militia to fight the British, marching from North Island to Plattsburgh. (NARA, 1812, p. 10). On September 11th the Battle of Plattsburgh (also known as the Battle of Lake Champlain) began when the British attacked the town defended by New York and Vermont militias and detachments of regular troops of the United States Army, all under the command of Brigadier General Alexander Macomb. After a hard fight the British abandoned the attack, which ended the final invasion of the northern states. December of 1814 brought the war to an end with the signing of The Treaty of Ghent. This treaty defined Michigan boundaries with Canada. British controlled places were returned to Michigan leading to a westward expansion. Large scale migration occurred for the next thirty years (Michigan became a state in 1837), which included Abram and Jacob Conklin's future children and grandchildren.

Meanwhile Abram's older brother Jacob had gone to Ohio, arriving in Cleveland in 1813. But the War of 1812 had begun a year earlier in June 1812. In 1814 Jacob enlisted in the cavalry under Capt. Murray of Brigadier General Duncan McArthur's command, fighting in several skirmishes. After being mustered out of the army in Chillicothe, Ohio on September 17, 1818, Jacob worked his way down to Delaware and on to Marion, where his younger brother was now living (Leggett Conaway, 1883, p. 1017).

After being mustered out of the army, Abram, who was about 23 years old at the time, followed his brother Jacob to Ohio, working his way to Delaware and on to Marion, arriving there in 1816 where they both later married and bought farms in the Waldo Township (Leggett Conaway, 1883, p. 1030). In 1823 Abram married seventeen year old Margaret Crawford in Waldo Mills and they had eight children together before she died in 1841 at the age of 35, leaving the oldest, Mary, to help with the youngest, Josiah. In 1842 he married Catherine Bovey and they had two more children to add to their growing family.

So far I have not found any sources to document Abram and Margaret's life on the farm other than census records that show they lived near Claridon and later Cardington until their deaths.

Abraham John "Abram II" Conklin and Margaret Crawford had the following children:
- 51.   i.   HENRY[1] CONKLIN was born in 1824 in Marion, Ohio.
- 52.   ii.   MARY SHAFER CONKLIN was born on 29 Sep 1826 in Westfield, Marion County, Ohio. She died on 05 Feb 1895 in Waldo, Marion County, Ohio. She married David Hubbell Wyatt, son of Samuel David Wyatt and Lavina Brundige, on 04 Jul 1853 in Waldo, Marion County, Ohio. He was born on 21 Nov 1824 in Waldo, Marion County, Ohio. He died (while on the march in the Civil War) on 11 Oct 1864 in Murfreesboro, Rutherford, Tennessee, USA (Age 40).
- 53.   iii.   ANNA ROBINSON CONKLIN was born on 01 Jan 1828 in Ohio or Maine. She died on 12 Feb 1905 in Des Moines, Iowa, USA.
- 54.   iv.   MARIAH CONKLIN was born in 1828 in Marion, Ohio.
- 55.   v.   JACOB F. "JAKE" CONKLIN was born in 1832. He died on 12 Mar 1875 in Westfield Twp, Morrow Co., OH - Buried in Peak Cemetery, Morrow Co., OH.
- 56.   vi.   JOHN W. CONKLIN was born in 1834 in Marion, Ohio.
- 57.   vii.   WILLIAM CONKLIN was born in 1836 in Marion, Ohio.
- +58.   viii.   JOSIAH C. CONKLIN was born in Oct 1838 in Marion, Ohio. He died on 23 Sep 1902 in Marion, Marion, Ohio (suffered from typhoid fever). He married (1) THERESA M. "THURSEY, THURSA" STOCKMAN, daughter of Daniel Stockman and Elizabeth Schultz, on 15 Sep 1864 in Marion, Ohio. She was born on 09 May 1840 in Ohio. She died on 07 Jun 1908 in Bear Lake, Manistee, Michigan, USA (Age 68). He married (2) ANNA REBECCA "ANNA FAULKNER" GARVIN, daughter of Henry C. Garvin and Rebecca Jane Staley, in 1888. She was born on 05 Oct 1855 in Hagerstown, MD, US. She died on 06 Jul 1929 in Chicago, Cook, Illinois, USA (Age 72).

Abraham John "Abram II" Conklin and Catherine Ann Bovey had the following children:

59. i.   SARAH ELIZABETH[1] CONKLIN was born on 29 Dec 1843 in Cardington, Morrow, Ohio, USA. She died on 24 Jul 1919 in Springfield, Henry, Missouri, USA.
60. ii. ORRY CLERY CONKLIN was born in 1846 in Cardington, Morrow, Ohio, USA. She died on 02 May 1934.

Chapter 2. Josiah Conklin and Theresa Stockman

1. **JOSIAH C.**[8] **CONKLIN** (Abraham John[7] "Abram", Abraham[6], John[5], Joseph[4], John[3] Conkelyn, John[2] Concklyne, William[1] Conkling) was born in Oct 1838 in Marion, Ohio. He died on 23 Sep 1902 in Marion, Marion, Ohio (Age 63; contracted typhoid fever). He married (1) THERESA M. "THURSEY, THURSA" STOCKMAN, daughter of Daniel Stockman and Elizabeth Schultz, on 15 Sep 1864 in Marion, Ohio (Westfield Methodist Church). She was born on 09 May 1844 in Norton, Delaware County, Ohio. She died on 07 Jun 1908 in Bear Lake, Manistee, Michigan (Age 68; history of heart trouble). He married (2) ANNA REBECCA GARVIN, daughter of Henry C. Garvin and Rebecca Jane Staley, on 07 Jun 1888 in Marion, Ohio, USA. She was born on 05 Oct 1855 in Hagerstown, MD, US. She died on 06 Jul 1929 in Chicago, Cook, Illinois, USA (Age 72).

Josiah C. Conklin lived in Claridon, Marion, Ohio in 1850 (Listed on 1850 Census as Joshua). He lived in Waldo, Marion, Ohio in 1860 (Living with Sister Mary and Brother-in-Law David Wyatt). He was employed as a Farmer in 1861 in Marion, Marion County, Ohio. He served in the military between 15 Jun 1861 and 13 Feb 1863 in Ohio (Private, Co C, 26th Infantry Regt). He was described as Age 23; Blue Eyes, Brown Hair, 5ft 7in, in 1863 in Marion, Marion County, Ohio. He re-enlisted in the military between 14 Feb 1863 and 14 May 1864 in Ohio (Pvt, Co C, 3d US Cavalry Regt). He lived in Osawatomie, Miami, Kansas, United States on 09 Jul 1870 (farmer). He lived in Pierport, Manistee, Michigan in 1880 (Age 46; marital status: Married; Relation to Head of House: Self). He lived in Marion Ward 5, Marion, Ohio in 1900 (Age 59; Marital Status: Married; Relation to Head of House: Head). He was employed as an Oil Agent in 1901 in Marion, Ohio. He lived in Marion, Ohio in 1901 (184 Jefferson St). He was buried in Sep 1902 in Marion, Marion, Ohio (Marion Cemetery).

Josiah C. Conklin and Theresa M. Stockman had the following children:

+2. i. DAVID ELIAS[9] CONKLIN was born on 08 Mar 1866 in Ohio. He died on 30 May 1945 (Age 79) in Eureka, Humboldt, California. He married Emma Jellings on 22 Jun 1892 in Bear Lake, Manistee, Michigan. She was born in Nov 1876 in Van Buren Co., Michigan. She died on 20 Mar 1952 in Eureka, Humboldt County, California.

+3. ii. EUGENE LESTER CONKLIN was born on 15 Oct 1869 in Ohio. He died on 25 Feb 1916 (Age 46) in San Diego, California. He married Sylvia Johnson, daughter of Frank Johnson and Sarah Mathieson, on 27 Apr 1893 in Benzonia, Manistee, Michigan. She was born in Dec 1875 in Coloma, Michigan.

4. iii. DAISY CONKLIN was born about Dec 1870 in Kansas. She died in 1871 in Pierport, Manistee, Michigan.

+5. iv. CHARLES WILLIAM CONKLIN was born on 17 Sep 1873 in Manistee, Michigan. He died on 05 Feb 1957 (Age 83) in Lynwood, California. He married (1) CAROLINE "CARRIE" LINGREN, daughter of Francis Frederick "Frank" Lingren and Johanna Wilhelmina "Hannah" Dalstrom, on 27 Apr 1912 in Marshfield, Coos County, Oregon (This was Charles first marriage, Carrie's second). She was born on 10 Oct 1879 in Marshfield, Coos County, Oregon. She died on 22 Jul 1954 (Age 74) in Portland, Multnomah

County, Oregon. He married (2) MARY ANN "MINNIE" ST JOHN BUSH, daughter of William H Bush and Sarah A Brown, on 06 Jun 1934 in Vancouver, Clark, Washington (Charles third marriage and second wife). She was born in 1871 in Ontario, Canada. She died in 1947 (Age 76) in Portland, Multnomah County, Oregon.

A separate chapter is written for each of Josiah's children that lived to be adults.

In 1838 Josiah Conklin became the youngest of 8 children born to Abraham John Conklin and Margaret Crawford in Marion, Ohio. He never knew much of his mother, who died before his third birthday in 1841, and was raised by his oldest sister Mary Shafer Conklin. When his father remarried in 1842 he soon had a stepmother, Catherine Bovey, and two younger sisters. In 1853 his Sister Mary married David Hubbell Wyatt, grandson of a Revolutionary War soldier. This provided Josiah a way to get away from his stepmother and the crowded family home so he moved in with his sister and brother-in-law in Waldo, Ohio at age 15 and helped them farm their land. Unfortunately, Mary became a widow soon after her husband enlisted in the 174th Ohio Infantry Regiment in 1864 (Leggett Conaway, 1883, p. 1030).

Lithograph of the Battle of Stones River –from americasbesthistory.com.

Other than his oldest sister Mary, Josiah was closest to his next oldest brother William. When the Civil War broke out in 1861, Josiah, age 23, and William, age 25, both enlisted in the Union Army. Josiah enlisted as a Private with Company C, 26th Ohio Volunteer Infantry (OVI) Regiment. He was one of more than 300,000 men from Ohio who fought for the Union in the War; and one of nearly 800 Marion County men (25% of the male population) who enlisted in

1861 (Leggett Conaway, 1883, p. 450). According to the regimental history, the 26th OVI was ordered to the Upper Kanawha Valley, Kentucky early in July, 1861 and led the advance for General Rosecrans movement on Sewell Mountain, West Virginia. In January, 1862 the regiment was transferred to Kentucky, then marched to Tennessee to assist in the capture of Nashville. Then the regiment made a forced marched to the Battle of Shiloh in April, 1862 and was the first regiment to enter Corinth, Mississippi on May 30th. They also routed General Forest's cavalry at McMinnville, Tennessee and fought the Battle of Stones River, Tennessee in December, 1862 (Leggett Conaway, 1883, p. 461).

But apparently the forced march to Shiloh took a heavy toll on soldiers such as Josiah. For nearly three weeks his regiment's tents and supplies were left behind in the wagon train as they marched and camped in their wet clothing during continuous rain. Many came down with diarrhea, rheumatism, and other ailments (NARA, p. 150). Fellow soldier, Private Sanford Ohmstead later wrote of his friend, saying, "Josiah Conklin was very sick at Pittsburgh Landing (or Shilow) Tennessee" (NARA, p. 176). In his pension application Josiah said from that time he suffered from "diarrhea, rheumatism, piles, and catarrh (inflammation of the mucus membranes of the nose and throat)" (NARA, p. 47). Later that year, on October 20, 1862 Josiah was captured by the Confederates at Bardstown, Kentucky while he was on detached duty as a teamster for the wagon train after the Battle of Perryville. Luckily he was soon paroled only 25 miles away in Elizabethtown (NARA, p. 153).

Josiah Conklin Civil War Pension Application —from Josiah Conklin Civil War Pension file.

After heavy losses, on 13 February 1863 the 26th Ohio Volunteer Infantry Regiment was discharged, and yet the very next day Josiah and William re-enlisted for another year as privates with Co C and Co I respectively, 3d US Cavalry Regiment. Apparently the Conklin brothers' experiences in the cavalry included the Battle of Chickamauga in September, 1863 in Georgia where they lost twenty-five percent of their comrades when the Confederates assaulted Missionary Ridge (Leggett Conaway, 1883, p. 461). Josiah and William mustered out on 14 May and 31 May 1864 respectively (NARA, 1798-1914). In 1887 Josiah began receiving a Civil War pension of $2 per month, later increased to $6 in 1890 (NARA, p. 107).

For his service in the "Grand Army of the Republic" Josiah's name was etched on the wall of the Soldiers Memorial Chapel in the Marion, Ohio Cemetery.

Josiah came home from the "War of the Rebellion" in 1864 and in September married Theresa Stockman, age 20, whose family rented a farm near the Wyatt's farm in Waldo, Ohio. Her ancestors had fled Germany to Pennsylvania in the 1700's during one of the Jewish pogroms in the Palatinates. Her grandfather, Peter Stockman fought in the Revolutionary War. Josiah and Theresa settled down and evidently got back into farming, possibly by renting land from one of their relatives. By 1869 they had two sons, David, then Eugene, and by 1870 they had moved to eastern Kansas where Josiah's cousin Riley was farming near Osawatomie in Miami County. In 1870 they had a daughter Daisy, who died as an infant in 1871 (Ancestry.com Operations, Inc., Provo, UT, USA, 2012).

Apparently farming was not working out for them as Miami County District Court records filed 28 Nov 1870 show Josiah suing one Caleb Shearer over a failed contract whereby Shearer did not provide the amount of wheat seed contracted for. Three years later they had moved again, this time north to western Michigan where Josiah's brother lived. They settled near Manistee, where their third son, my grandfather, Charles William was born in 1873. Here Frederick Weyerhaeuser and other lumber barons were beginning their 30-year assault on the forests of the Lake States. The three boys grew up near the lumber mills and by the turn of the century all were working as mill hands.

1885 letter from Josiah Conklin to Bureau of Pensions
–from Civil War Pension file: Josiah Conklin p.127.

But the family was disintegrating. According to Theresa they did not live very happily together, Josiah was very abusive to her, and he did not work enough to support them. In 1885 Josiah left for good. Here's how she described it:

"I was at work at Mr. Shaw's Boarding House and Hotel at Pierport, not quite a mile from where we lived, was working by the day. When I got back to the house late in the afternoon I found that he had taken all the furniture and the bedding and also the children and went to his brother's, about 2 ½ miles. He stayed there about a week and when he found that he would have to pay for their board he brought the children back" (NARA, p. 99).

Josiah soon was living in Marion again and petitioned for a divorce citing "willful absence." Theresa was "duly served by publication" in the local newspaper and judged to be in default on October 29, 1885 for failing to answer, thus granting Josiah a divorce without her ever knowing about it. He soon met 32 year old Anna Garvin Faulkner who had a ten year old son by a previous marriage, Harry Francis Faulkner. Although Anna had been described as crazy, money hungry, and a streetwalker by various people, they married in 1888 (NARA, p. 99).

Josiah Conklin Obituary in the Marion News, 23 Sep 1902.

Josiah became an oil agent, selling oil on the streets of Marion, Ohio and joined the local post of the veterans of the Grand Army of the Republic. But his health continued to suffer from the illnesses he contracted during the Civil War. Then in April 1902 his second wife Anna left him and filed for divorce (Marion Weekly Star, 1902, p. 8). In July 1902 Josiah visited Theresa in Michigan and when she asked, he said he was married but did not bring his wife Anna along because "she was crazy." In fact, Anna had written Theresa a letter while Josiah was there saying she "did not want him to come back and that she was going to pack up her goods and earn her living like she did before" (NARA, p. 100).

> **MR. JOSIAH CONKLIN DIES THIS MORNING**
>
> Falls a Victim to Typhoid Fever. Leaves Many Relatives.
>
> Mr. Josiah Conklin died at the Marion County infirmary this morning at 7 o'clock.
>
> Mr. Conklin has been a sufferer from typhoid fever. Though sick for some time he had been an inmate of the infirmary but a week. He had money to pay his board and doctor's bill, but was unable to get any one to give him the proper care.
>
> The remains were moved this morning to the undertaking establishment of J. R. Curtis & Company.
>
> The deceased was born in this county sixty-three years ago. For many years he was engaged in selling oil about the streets of the city. He leaves three sons, who reside in Michigan, a wife and stepson in this city, a sister in Prospect and another in Cardington. He was a member of Cooper Post, No. 117, Grand Army of the Republic.
>
> The funeral will be held Wednesday afternoon at 2 o'clock. The members of the G. A. R. will meet at the office of J. R. Curtiss & Company, and will march to the church in a body just previous to the time of the ceremony.

According to U.S. Pensions Bureau Special Examiner Levi Warren, "She is said to have ruled him with a rod of iron, so to speak, often using physical force and would quite frequently give soldier a downright thrashing. Compelled soldier to give her all his pension money and earnings" (NARA, p. 23). Anna in the meantime dropped the divorce proceedings.

When Josiah did come back to Ohio, he lived for a while at the Soldiers Home in Upper Sandusky. Anna had by then spent time as a patient at the State Hospital for the Insane in Columbus. Josiah died in the Marion County Infirmary from typhoid fever from an unclean water source. He was buried in the Marion Cemetery in September 1902, leaving Anna with a widow's pension that Theresa believed was hers.

Meanwhile the two oldest boys married and started families of their own, and as the lumber business moved west after 1900, they moved west too, where there were new jobs cutting the virgin forests of the Northwest. David moved to Eureka, California and Eugene to Marshfield, Oregon. Charles, now in his twenties, stayed in Michigan and took care of his mother for another eight years until she died at age 64.

Theresa M. Stockman was born on 09 May 1844 in Norton, Delaware County, Ohio as the second child of Daniel Stockman and Elizabeth Schultz. She had six siblings, namely: Sarah Ann, Elias G, David S, Albert Henry, Francis M, and Henry L. She died on 07 Jun 1908 in

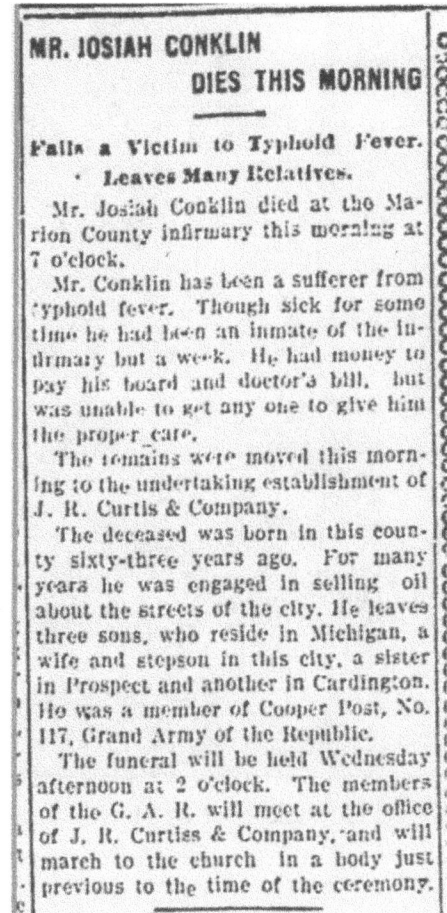

Bear Lake, Manistee, Michigan (Age 68; history of heart trouble). When she was 20, she married Josiah C. Conklin, son of Abraham John Conklin and Margaret Crawford, on 15 Sep 1864 in Marion, Ohio (Westfield Methodist Church).

Gravestone of Theresa Stockman in the Pleasanton Township Cemetery, Michigan –27 Aug 2017.

Theresa M. Stockman lived in Waldo, Marion County, Ohio in 1850 (Age 5). She lived in Waldo, Marion County, Ohio in 1860 (Age 15). She lived in Osawatomie, Miami, Kansas on 09 Jul 1870 (Age 24). She lived in Pierport, Manistee, Michigan, USA on 15 Jun 1880 (Age 33; Marital status: Married; Relation to Head of House: Wife). She lived in Bear Lake, Manistee, Michigan in 1900 (Age 57; Marital Status: "Widowed"; Relation to Head of House: Head). She lived in Lots 2-5, Blk 3, Tillson Addition, Bear Lake, Manistee, Michigan in 1908 (Marital Status: "Widowed"). She was buried on 09 Jun 1908 in Pleasanton Township Cemetery, Pleasanton, Manistee, Michigan, USA (Find a Grave #183453104). She was also known as Thursey, Thursa. She was employed as a Housekeeper in Shaw's Boarding House, Pierport. Race: (White)

Left: Theresa M Conklin signature –from Josiah Conklin Civil War Pension file.

According to Josiah's grandson Charles F. Conklin, "My dad's parents were Pennsylvania Dutch which is English, Irish, part German, and a little Scottish, real mixed up." (Conklin C. F., Charles F. Conklin Family History Audio Interview I, 1980).

ANNA REBECCA GARVIN, Josiah's second wife, was born on 05 Oct 1855 in Hagerstown, MD, US. She died on 06 Jul 1929 in Chicago, Cook, Illinois, USA (Age 72). She married (1) HARRY F. FAULKNER on 02 May 1877 in Marion, Ohio, USA. He was born in 1856 in Wisconsin. He died in Oct 1885 (Age 29) a week after divorce from railroad accident injuries. She married (2) **JOSIAH C. CONKLIN**, son of Abraham John "Abram II" Conklin and Margaret Crawford, on 07 Jun 1888 in Marion, Ohio, USA. He was born in Oct 1838 in Marion, Marion, Ohio. He died on 23 Sep 1902 in Marion, Marion, Ohio (contracted typhoid fever).

Anna Rebecca Garvin lived in Hagerstown, Washington, Maryland in 1860 (Age 4). She lived in Big Island, Marion, Ohio in 1870 (Age 13; Census Post Office: La Rue). She lived in Marion Ward 5, Marion, Ohio in 1900 (Age 43; Marital Status: Married; Relation to Head of House: Wife). She lived in the 1stWard Marion, Marion, Ohio in 1910. She lived in Marion, Ohio in 1915. She lived in Ward 1, Marion, Ohio in 1920 (Age 63; Marital Status: Widowed; Relationship: Aunt-in-law). She lived in Marion, Ohio in 1927. She was buried on 08 Jul 1929 in River Grove, Illinois (Saint Joseph Cemetery - Section RA Lot 18 Grave 19). She was also known as Anna Faulkner. She was employed working at home.

Josiah C. Conklin and Anna Rebecca Garvin had no children.

Harry F. Faulkner and Anna Rebecca Garvin had the following children:

1. HARRY FRANCIS FAULKNER was born on 08 Sep 1878 in Ohio. He died on 14 Feb 1910 in Cook, Illinois, United States (Age 31).

Chapter 3. David E. Conklin and Emma Jellings

Generation 1

1.   **DAVID ELIAS**[1] **CONKLIN** (Josiah C.[A], Abraham John[B] "Abram", Abraham[C], John[D], Joseph[E], John[F] Conkelyn, John[G] Concklyne, William[H] Conkling) was born on 08 Mar 1866 in Ohio, USA. He died on 30 May 1945 (Age 79) in Eureka, Humboldt, California, USA. He married Emma Jellings on 22 Jun 1892 in Bear Lake, Manistee, Michigan, USA. She was born in Nov 1876 in Van Buren Co., Michigan. She died on 20 Mar 1952 in Eureka, Humboldt County, California.

David Elias Conklin lived in Osawatomie, Miami, Kansas in 1870 (Age 4). He lived in Pierport, Manistee, Michigan in 1880 (Age 14; Marital Status: Single; Relation to Head of House: Son). He lived in Bear Lake, Manistee, Michigan in 1900 (Age 34; Marital Status: Married; Relation to Head of House: Head). He lived at 1576 6th St. Eureka Ward 2, Humboldt, California in 1910 (Age 40; Marital Status: Married; Relation to Head of House: Head). He lived in Eureka Ward 2, Humboldt, California in 1920 (Age 52; Marital Status: Married; Relation to Head of House: Head). He was employed as a Stevedore in 1930. He lived in Eureka, Humboldt, California in 1930 (Age 64; Marital Status: Married; Relation to Head of House: Head). He lived at 1522 2nd St. Eureka, California in 1933 (Mechanic). He lived in Eureka, Humboldt, California on 01 Apr 1940 (Age 74; Marital Status: Married; Relation to Head of House: Head). He was buried on 01 Jun 1945 in Sunset Memorial Park, 4325 Broadway, Eureka, California (next to Emma Jellings Conklin). Race: (White)

Sawmill workers in Bear Lake, Michigan pose for a postcard about 1915
–photo from Charlene Elfers McKay Collection.

David Elias Conklin was the oldest son of Josiah and Theresa Conklin. He was four years old when the family moved from Ohio to a farm in Eastern Kansas in 1870. By 1873 at the age of seven he had moved with his family from Kansas to Michigan and in 1892 at the age of 26 he married Emma Jellings. During this time he worked with his brothers, first as a mill hand in a local sawmill, then as a sawmill fireman (U.S. Federal Census, 1900). But lumber production peaked in 1892 and by 1900 Frederick Weyerhaeuser and other lumber barons were finishing their 30-year assault on the forests of the Lake States and the lumber industry was moving west (Rutkow, 2012, p. 114). So the Conklin boys moved west to where the jobs were. In 1903 David, Emma and their young son Charles Edward moved first, settling in Eureka, California where he became a Stevedore on the wharf. He soon sent word of the jobs available and Eugene, Sylvia and their two young daughters followed them to California in 1904 (where Emma attended the birth of Sylvia's third daughter) but Eugene soon moved his family on to Oregon.

Above: The Conklin brothers-Eugene (left), Charles (sitting) and David about 1892 in Manistee, Michigan –photo from Charlene Elfers McKay Collection.

David and Emma remained in Eureka for the remainder of their lives and are buried together at Sunset Park overlooking Humboldt Bay just as their house did on Second Street.

Emma Josephine Jellings lived in Bear Lake, Manistee, Michigan in 1900 (Age 27; Marital Status: Married; Relation to Head of House: Wife). She lived in Eureka Ward 2, Humboldt, California in 1910 (Age 34; Marital Status: Married; Relation to Head of House: Wife). She lived in Eureka Ward 2, Humboldt, California in 1920 (Age 35; Marital Status: Married; Relation to Head of House: Wife). She lived in Eureka, Humboldt, California in 1930 (Age 56; Marital Status: Married; Relation to Head of House: Wife). She lived in Eureka, California in 1933. She lived in Eureka, Humboldt, California in 1935. She lived in Eureka, Humboldt, California on 01 Apr 1940 (Age 65; Marital Status: Married; Relation to Head of House: Wife). She lived in Eureka, Humboldt, California on 01 Apr 1940 (Age 65; Marital Status: Married; Relation to Head of House: Wife). She was buried in March 1952 in Sunset Memorial Park, 4325 Broadway, Eureka, California (buried next to David E Conklin). Race: (White)

Emma Jellings Conklin at her home on Second Street in Eureka, California in 1951, a few months before she died —photo from Charlene Elfers McKay Collection.

David Elias Conklin and Emma Josephine Jellings had the following child:

+2.   i.   CHARLES EDWARD² CONKLIN was born on 04 May 1893 in Manistee, Manistee County, Michigan, USA. He died on 21 Jun 1952 in Yountville, Napa County, California, USA.

Generation 2

2.   **CHARLES EDWARD² CONKLIN** (David Elias¹, Josiah C.ᴬ, Abraham Johnᴮ "Abram", Abrahamᶜ, Johnᴰ, Josephᴱ, Johnᶠ Conkelyn, Johnᴳ Concklyne, Williamᴴ Conkling) was born on 04 May 1893 in Manistee, Manistee County, Michigan. He died on 21 Jun 1952 in Yountville, Napa County, California, USA. He married RUTH I. ZIMMERMAN about 1924. She died in 1932.

Charles Edward Conklin lived in Bear Lake, Manistee, Michigan in 1900 (Age 7; Marital Status: Single; Relation to Head of House: Son). He lived in Eureka Ward 2, Humboldt, California in 1910 (Age 15; Marital Status: Single; Relation to Head of House: Son). He lived in Humboldt, California between 1917 and 1918 (He served in France during World War I at Age 23). He lived in Eureka Ward 2, Humboldt, California in 1920 (Age 26; Marital Status: Single; Relation to Head of House: Son). He was employed as an Auto Mechanic in 1928. He lived in Eureka, California in 1928. He lived in Eureka, Humboldt, California in 1930 (Age 32; Marital Status: Married; Relation to Head of House: Head). He lived in Eureka, Humboldt, California in 1935 (1522 2nd St). He lived in Eureka, Humboldt, California on 01 Apr 1940 (Age 47; Marital Status: Widowed; Relation to Head of House: Son). He lived in Eureka, Humboldt County, California in 1942 (Age: 49). He was described as Brown hair, Blue eyes, two fingers missing from left hand, 5ft 10in, 163 lbs., in 1942 in Eureka, Humboldt County, California. He died in 1952 at the age of 59 and was buried in Eureka, Humboldt County, California (Sunset Memorial Park).

The Eureka newspaper carried the following obituary in June 1952 to sum up his life and times:
    "Former Eureka Resident Dead: Charles Edward Conklin, formerly of Eureka, died Saturday at Yountville, where he had lived the last two years. Conklin first came to Eureka in 1907 and had been employed as an auto mechanic before serving in France during World War I. He returned to Eureka and was employed by the Dolbeer Carson Lumber Company.

Conklin was a member of Redwood Empire Post 1872, Veterans of Foreign Wars and the American Legion at Yountville. Services will be held Thursday afternoon at 2 pm from the Chapel of the Ferns with J Eldon Anderson officiating. Interment will be in Sunset Memorial Park. Cooper Mortuary is in charge of the arrangements" (Humbolt Standard, 1952, p. 3).

In 1935 Charles Edward Conklin was living with his parents David and Emma in their house overlooking Humboldt Bay in Eureka, California at 1522 2nd Street –4 May 2016.

Charles Edward Conklin and Ruth I. Zimmerman had the following child:

+3. i. HAROLD EDWARD³ "Eddie" CONKLIN was born on 24 Aug 1925 in Eureka, Humboldt County, California, USA. He died on 26 Mar 2014 in Eureka, Humboldt County, California, USA. He married BARBARA ANN SMIGLEY. She was born on 09 Jan 1935 in Eugene Lane, Oregon. She died on 27 Dec 1978.

Generation 3

3. **HAROLD EDWARD³ "Eddie" CONKLIN** (Charles Edward², David Elias¹, Josiah C.ᴬ, Abraham Johnᴮ "Abram", Abrahamᶜ, Johnᴰ, Josephᴱ, Johnᶠ Conkelyn, Johnᴳ Concklyne, Williamᴴ Conkling) was born on 24 Aug 1925 in Eureka, Humboldt County, California, USA. He died on 26 Mar 2014 (Age 88) in Eureka, Humboldt County, California, USA. He married **BARBARA ANN SMIGLEY**. She was born on 09 Jan 1935 in Eugene Lane, Oregon. She died on 27 Dec 1978.

Harold Edward Conklin lived in Eureka, Humboldt, California in 1930 (Age 4; Marital Status: Single; Relation to Head of House: Son). He lived in Eureka, Humboldt, California in 1935.

He lived in Eureka, Humboldt, California on 01 Apr 1940 (Age 14; Marital Status: Single; Relation to Head of House: Grandson). He served in the military in April, 1944 in San Francisco, California. He lived in Eureka, Humboldt, California in 1946. He lived in Eureka, Humboldt, California in 1956. He was also known as "Conkie."

Left: Harold Edward "Eddie" Conklin with Grandpa Dave, Great Uncle Charles W., and Grandma Emma in about 1935 at the side door to Dave's home at 1522 2nd Street in Eureka, California –photo from Charlene Elfers McKay Collection.

Barbara Ann Smigley was born on 09 Jan 1935 in Eugene, Lane County, Oregon as the first child of Cleo Delano Smigley and Beatrice Naomi Cook. She died on 27 Dec 1978 in Eureka, Humboldt, California. When she was 17, she married Harold Edward Conklin, son of Charles Edward Conklin and Ruth Zimmerman on 29 Aug 1952 in Eureka, Humboldt, California. When she was 32, she married Ronald H. Fulton on 07 Dec 1967 in Humboldt, California. When she was 34, she married Howard Eugene Rhodes on 19 Sep 1969 in Reno, Washoe County, Nevada. When she was 40, she married Leonard L Brisbane on 21 Mar 1975 in Clark County, Washington.

Barbara Ann Smigley lived in Eugene, Lane, Oregon, USA on 01 Apr 1940 (Age 5; Marital Status: Single; Relation to Head of House: Stepdaughter). She lived in Eureka, Humboldt, California in 1956. She lived in Eureka, Humboldt, California in 1968. She was buried in 1978 in Eureka, Humboldt County, California (Ocean View Cemetery #108555775).

Harold Edward Conklin and Barbara Ann Smigley had the following children who did not live to adulthood:

4.   i.   GREGORY EDWARD[4] CONKLIN was born on 08 May 1956 in Eureka, Humboldt County, California, USA. He died on 08 May 1956 in Eureka, Humboldt County, California, USA.
5.   ii.   JOHN RICHARD CONKLIN was born on 11 Jun 1957 in Eureka, Humboldt County, California, USA. He died on 23 Nov 1959 in Eureka, Humboldt County, California, USA.
6.   iii.   JULIE DENISE CONKLIN was born on 19 Aug 1960 in Eureka, Humboldt County,

California, USA. She died of heart problems on 14 Apr 1961 in San Francisco, San Francisco County, California, USA.

Eddie and Barbara's third child Julie Denise Conklin was born with heart problems and only lived for 8 months –photo from Ancestry Family Trees, Ancestry.com.

baby girl that died of heart probs

Fifteen-year-old "Eddie" Conklin with Grandparents Dave and Emma Conklin about 1940. He grew up at his grandparents' home at 1522 2nd Street in Eureka, California –photo from Charlene Elfers McKay Collection.

Chapter 4. Eugene L. Conklin and Sylvia Johnson

Generation 1

1. **EUGENE LESTER**[1] **"GENE" CONKLIN** (Josiah C.[A], Abraham John[B] "Abram", Abraham[C], John[D], Joseph[E], John[F] Conkelyn, John[G] Concklyne, William[H] Conkling) was born on 15 Oct 1869 in Ohio, USA. He died on 25 Feb 1916 in San Diego, California (Bronchial Pneumonia and Typhoid Fever). He married Sylvia Johnson, daughter of Frank Johnson and Sarah Mathieson, on 27 Apr 1893 in Benzonia, Manistee, Michigan (Otis B Waters, Minister). She was born in Dec 1875 in Coloma, Michigan. She died on 30 Jun 1930 in San Diego, California.

Eugene Lester Conklin lived in Osawatomie, Miami, Kansas in 1870 (Age 8 mo). He lived in Pierport, Manistee, Michigan, USA in 1880 (Age 10; marital status: Single; Relation to Head of House: Son). He lived in Bear Lake, Michigan in Apr 1893. He lived in Arcadia, Manistee, Michigan on 15 Jun 1900 (Age 30; Marital Status: Married; Relation to Head of House: Head). He lived in 4th St. Marshfield (South Bend), Coos, Oregon in 1910 (Age 39; Marital Status: Married; Relation to Head of House: Head). He lived in South Marshfield, Coos, Oregon in 1910. He was buried on 28 Feb 1916 in San Diego, California (Greenwood Memorial Park, 4300 Imperial Ave; Acacia Place, Lot #132).

Eugene Lester Conklin was born three years after his older brother David Elias. He was the last of the family to be born in Ohio before they moved to a farm in Eastern Kansas in 1870. By 1873 at the age of three his family had moved from Kansas to Michigan where he later married Sylvia Johnson and worked with his younger brother Charles as a mill hand in the local sawmills while his older brother David was a fireman for a sawmill (U.S. Federal Census, 1900).

Eugene Conklin family in 1905. From left--Front: Eugene, baby Myrtle, Sylvia; Back: Florence May, Maude –photo from Charlene Elfers McKay Collection.

But production peaked in 1892 and by 1900 Frederick Weyerhaeuser and other lumber barons were finishing their 30-year assault on the forests of the Lake States and the lumber industry was moving west (Rutkow, 2012, p. 114). So the Conklin boys moved with them to where the jobs were. David and his wife moved first, settling in Eureka, California where he became a Stevedore on the wharf. After he sent word of the jobs available, Eugene, Sylvia and their two young daughters followed them from Michigan to California, most likely by train. By 1904 Eugene had landed a job as a lumber yard carpenter in Tuolumne, California. Here Sylvia gave birth to their third daughter Myrtle in September with brother Dave's wife Emma serving as midwife (Myrtle Conklin birth certificate affidavit).

Eugene Conklin worked as a carpenter in Tuolumne, California in 1904, possibly here at the West Side Lumber Company, now shuttered –photo 2 May 2017.

But Eugene was looking for a better job and a year later in 1905 he began working with his brother Dave on the wharf in Eureka, California (Conklin C. F., Charles F. Conklin Family History Audio Interview I, 1980). However Eugene longed to return to the lumber business that he grew up with in Michigan and within a couple of years he found a job in Marshfield, Oregon as a Millwright, probably for the Simpson Lumber Company on Coos Bay. Here Sylvia gave birth to their youngest daughter Evelyn in 1909. Eugene soon sent word to his younger brother Charles to "come live with them and that he had a job for him in the lumber mill." (Conklin C. F., Charles F. Conklin Family History Audio Interview I, 1980).

House built by Eugene Conklin in Marshfield, Oregon –photo from Charlene Elfers McKay Collection.

For the next seven years Eugene and his brother Charles worked together again, here in the sawmills of Coos Bay, Oregon. Sometime during that period Eugene lost a finger to one of the saws (McKay, 2017). We do not know whether it was this incident, his health, or the slump in the lumber industry that prompted his decision to go into a completely different occupation. So in 1915 Eugene moved his family again—this time to San Diego, California where he bought and operated a family grocery store downtown on Sixth and Market Streets where his daughters were often the clerks. Unfortunately his health was failing rapidly as he was suffering from Typhoid Fever, and a bout of bronchial pneumonia was too much to overcome. He died the next year in 1916 at the age of only 46. We assume that his wife Sylvia and daughters ran the store for a few years after his death until they grew up and married and Sylvia could find a buyer.

Eugene Conklin's grocery store at 623 W. Market St San Diego in 1915 (now CVS Pharmacy Bldg). Daughter Maude is behind the counter –photo from Charlene Elfers McKay Collection.

An undated portrait of Sylvia Johnson, possibly after she was widowed –photo from Charlene Elfers McKay Collection.

Sylvia Johnson lived in Orleans, Ionia, Michigan in 1880 (Age 2; Marital status: Single; Relation to Head of House: Daughter). She lived in Joyfield, Michigan in Apr 1893. She lived in Arcadia, Manistee, Michigan on 15 Jun 1900 (Age 24; Marital Status: Married; Relation to Head of House: Wife). She lived in South Marshfield, Coos, Oregon in 1910. She lived in South Marshfield, Coos County, Oregon in 1910 (Age 34; Marital Status: Married; Relation to Head of House: Wife). She lived in San Diego, California in 1916 (623 W Market St). She lived in San Diego, San Diego, California in 1920 (Age 45; Marital

Status: Widowed; Marital Status: Widow; Relation to Head of House: Head). She lived in San Diego, San Diego, California in 1930 (Age 35; Marital Status: Divorced; Relation to Head of House: Head). She was also known as Syloz.

Eugene Lester "Gene" Conklin and Sylvia "Syloz" Johnson had the following children:

2.   i.   FLORENCE MAY[2] CONKLIN was born in Aug 1894 in Michigan.

+3.   ii.   MAUDE M. CONKLIN was born on 07 Apr 1896 in Michigan. She died on 28 Dec 1980 in San Diego, California. She married EDWARD WRIGHT WILSON. He was born on 21 Oct 1890 in Pennington County, South Dakota. He died on 23 Dec 1984 in San Diego, California.

+4.   iii.   MYRTLE L. CONKLIN was born on 01 Sep 1904 in California. She died on 10 Apr 1995 in El Cajon, San Diego, California, United States of America. She married EDWARD ELFERS. He was born on 05 Jun 1902 in Moody, South Dakota. He died on 17 Jan 1970 in La Mesa, San Diego, California.

5.   iv.   EVELYN LOUISE CONKLIN was born on 27 Oct 1909 in Marshfield, Oregon. She died on 10 Jul 2003 (Age: 93). She married Louis A. Spink, son of Ray Louis Spink and Clara Elsie Aiken, on 12 Jan 1932 in Yuma, Arizona, USA. He was born on 24 Aug 1910 in South Dakota. He died on 22 Oct 1999 in San Diego, San Diego, California (Age 89).

Eugene Conklin's daughters in about 1952, from left: Evelyn, May, Maude, Myrtle, Maude's daughter Lois; front: Maude's granddaughter Barbara Wilson; back: Barbara's mother Mary Wilson –photo from Charlene Elfers McKay Collection.

Generation 2

3.   **MAUDE M.**^{2} **"MAUDIE" CONKLIN** (Eugene Lester^1 "Gene", Josiah C.^{A}, Abraham John^B "Abram", Abraham^C, John^D, Joseph^E, John^F Conkelyn, John^G Concklyne, William^H Conkling) was born on 07 Apr 1896 in Michigan. She died on 28 Dec 1980 in San Diego, California. She married Edward Wright Wilson, son of William Nesbit Wilson and Elizabeth Barbara Enderby, before 1921. He was born on 21 Oct 1890 in Pennington County, South Dakota. He died on 23 Dec 1984 in San Diego, San Diego, California.

Edward Wright Wilson and Maude M. "Maudie" Conklin had the following children:

6.   i.   HAROLD EUGENE^3 WILSON was born on 12 May 1921 in San Diego, San Diego, California. He died on 05 Apr 1998 in San Diego, San Diego, California. He married Mary E. Crandall, daughter of Honey C. Crandall and Opal M. Crandall, on 24 Apr 1949 in San Diego, California. She was born about 1928 in California.

7.   ii.   LOIS MAY WILSON was born on 12 Nov 1924 in San Diego, San Diego, California. She died on 24 Jul 1997 in San Diego County, California. She married John H. Wahlgren, son of Gustav A. Wahlgren and Bessie B. Wahlgren, on 15 Sep 1951 in San Diego, California. He was born on 08 Apr 1922 in San Diego, California.

Maude Conklin on a San Diego beach in about 1916
–photo from Charlene Elfers McKay Collection.

4.   **MYRTLE LUELLA**^{2} **CONKLIN** (Eugene Lester^1 "Gene", Josiah C.^{A}, Abraham John^B "Abram", Abraham^C, John^D, Joseph^E, John^F Conkelyn, John^G Concklyne, William^H Conkling) was born on 01 Sep 1904 in Tuolumne, California. She died on 10 Apr 1995 in El Cajon, San Diego, California, United States of America. She married Edward Elfers, son of Henry Elfers and Anna K. Behrens, before 1933. He was born on 05 Jun 1902 in Moody, South Dakota. He died on 17 Jan 1970 in La Mesa, San Diego, California.

Edward Elfers and Myrtle Luella Conklin in San Diego, California about 1948 –photo from Charlene Elfers McKay Collection.

Edward Elfers and Myrtle Luella Conklin had the following child:

+8.   i.   CHARLENE MAY[3] "SHERIE McKAY" ELFERS was born on 30 Oct 1933 in San Diego, California. She married Roy Curtis McKay on 11 Jul 1954 in San Diego, California. He was born on 15 Jul 1934 in Georgia.

Generation 3

8.   CHARLENE MAY[3] **"SHERIE McKAY" ELFERS** (Myrtle Luella[2] Conklin, Eugene Lester[1] "Gene" Conklin, Edward, Henry) was born on 30 Oct 1933 in San Diego, California. She married Roy Curtis McKay on 11 Jul 1954 in San Diego, California. He was born on 15 Jul 1934 in Georgia.

Roy Curtis "Curt" McKay and Charlene May "Sherie McKay" Elfers had the following children:

9.   i.   DIANE[4] McKAY was born on 09 May 1956. She married JIMMY WHEELER.

10.   ii.   SUSAN D. McKAY was born on 31 Dec 1957 in San Diego, California. She married KIRT EDWARDS.

Charlene Elfers and Roy "Curt" McKay in El Cajon, California
—17 Apr 2017.

Conklin cousins in El Cajon, California, from left: Mary Guerra (David's spouse),
Dacia Conklin (David's daughter), Charlene Elfers (Eugene Conklin's granddaughter),
David Gene Conklin (Charles W. Conklin's grandson) —17 Apr 2017.

Chapter 5. Charles W. Conklin and Caroline Lingren

Generation 1

1. **CHARLES WILLIAM**[1] **CONKLIN** (Josiah C.[A], Abraham John[B] "Abram", Abraham[C], John[D], Joseph[E], John[F] Conkelyn, John[G] Concklyne, William[H] Conkling) was born on 17 Sep 1873 in Manistee, Michigan, USA. He died on 05 Feb 1957 (Age 83) in Lynwood, California. He married (1) CAROLINE "CARRIE" LINGREN, daughter of Francis Frederick "Frank" Lingren and Johanna Wilhelmina "Hannah, Minnie" Dalstrom, on 27 Apr 1912 in Marshfield, Coos County, Oregon (This was Charles first marriage, Carrie's second). She was born on 10 Oct 1879 in Marshfield, Coos County, Oregon. She died on 22 Jul 1954 (Age 74) in Portland, Multnomah County, Oregon. He married (2) MARY ANN "MINNIE, MARY ST JOHN" BUSH, daughter of William H Bush and Sarah A Brown, on 06 Jun 1934 in Vancouver, Clark County, Washington (Charles third marriage and second wife). She was born in 1871 in Ontario, Canada. She died in 1947 in Portland, Multnomah County, Oregon.

Charles William Conklin lived in Pierport, Manistee, Michigan, USA in 1880. He was living with his mother and working as a setter in a sawmill in 1900 in Bear Lake, Manistee, Michigan. He lived in Bear Lake, Manistee, Michigan on 21 Jun 1900 (Age 26; Marital Status: Single; Relation to Head of House: Son). He lived in Bear Lake, Manistee, Michigan in 1908. He lived in Marshfield, Coos County, Oregon in 1910 (Living with brother Eugene). He was employed as a Mechanic at Northwestern Electric Co, Lincoln St., Portland (WW1 draft card) in 1917 in Portland, Multnomah County, Oregon. He lived in Portland, Multnomah County, Oregon in 1918 (187 Sherman St, Portland, OR). He was described as 5 ft 10 in, slender, blue eyes, blonde hair in 1918.

He lived in Portland, Multnomah County, Oregon in 1920 (Age 45; Marital Status: Married; Relation to Head of House: Head). He was employed as a Engineer in 1930 in Oregon, USA. He lived in Portland, Multnomah County, Oregon in 1930 (Age 55; Marital Status: Married; Relation to Head of House: Head). He lived in Portland, Multnomah, Oregon in 1935. He lived in Portland, Multnomah, Oregon on 01 Apr 1940 (Age: 66 Marital Status: Married; Relation to Head of House: Head). He was employed as an Ice Puller at LaGrande Creamery in 1941 in Portland, Multnomah, Oregon.

He lived in Portland, Oregon in 1941. He lived at 10248 Bowman Ave, South Gate, CA about 1950. He lived at 12613 Long Beach Blvd, Lynwood, California in 1957 (Lynwood Sanitarium). He was buried in Feb 1957 in Lincoln Memorial Park Cemetery, Portland, OR (Crestview, Lot 175, Space 5, next to Mary E. Conklin). His Death Cert #2397 lists causes of death as cerebral hemorrhage, anterior selotic hypertension. He was employed as an Engineer. Race: (White)

Charles William was the only one of the three Conklin boys to be born in Michigan. His older brother David was seven, and Eugene was three years old when the family moved from Kansas to Michigan before Charles was born in 1873. "They went to Bear Lake, Manistee, Michigan.

They used to take an excursion boat to the Milwaukee breweries on weekends" (Conklin C. F., Charles F. Conklin Family History Audio Interview I, 1980). But by 1888, when Charles was 15, his father Josiah had divorced Theresa and moved back to Marion, Ohio. The brothers stayed in Bear Lake Michigan with their mother, and Charles grew up working with his brothers as a mill hand in the local sawmills (U.S. Federal Census, 1900). The earliest photo we have of Charles is at age 19 with his brothers and was taken about 1892 (see Chapter 3). Production peaked in the Michigan lumber industry that year and by 1900 the lumber industry was moving west (Rutkow, 2012, p. 114). By 1904 both of his older brothers were married, had children, and had moved to California where prospects were brighter, but Charles stayed behind to look after his mother Theresa. "My two uncles moved west but my father stayed in Michigan and took care of his mother until she died (in 1908). Then he went to Coos Bay (Marshfield) where his brother Eugene had a job for him in the sawmill" (Conklin C. F., Charles F. Conklin Family History Audio Interview I, 1980).

Sawmill in Coos Bay, Oregon –photo from Charlene Elfers McKay Collection

In Coos Bay, Oregon Charles opened a new chapter in his life. Arriving in 1908 at the age of 35, he moved in with his brother Eugene's family and went to work at the sawmill which paid $3 to $12 a day depending on the job. The new C.A. Smith Lumber Company (owned by Charles Axel Smith from Minnesota) state-of-the-art mill just opened in North Bend, and employed "upwards of a thousand men" (Douthit, 1981, p. 37). He was finally making a good wage and soon met a local girl, Caroline "Carrie" Martin. She was the sixth of eight children of Finnish Immigrants Frank and Hannah Lingren who lived across Coos Bay on Kentuck Slough where other pioneer farmers had settled. She had recently divorced William Martin and had a six year-old son. In 1912 they were married and bought a house in North Bend, and in 1913 had a son, Charles Franklin, and three years later a daughter, Louise Theresa.

Caroline & Charles W. Conklin about 1913 – photo from Charlene Elfers McKay Collection.

But in about 1910 the lumber industry went into a slump due to overcapacity after rebuilding San Francisco from the 1906 earthquake. Then in 1914 war broke out in Europe, affecting international trade as well (Douthit, 1981, p. 75). So just before the U.S. declared war on Germany in 1917, Charles, Carrie and their three children moved to Portland, Oregon where he landed a job as a mechanic for the Northwestern Electric Company at $25 per week *(U.S. World War I Draft Registration Card).* But their marriage was rather turbulent and in 1925 "my parents divorced when I was 9 years old" (Conklin L. , Louise Conklin letter to Robert Livingston, Dec 1997). Four years later in 1929 when Charles was 56, he remarried Carrie, and in 1934 divorced her again and married Mary Ann "Minnie St John" Bush, a divorcee from Toronto.

Caroline and Charles at their first home in North Bend, Oregon about 1913 –photo from Louise Conklin Collection.

Caroline and Charles giving little Charles and Louise a bath near Mt Tabor, Oregon about 1919 –photo from Louise Conklin Collection.

In 1941 Charles was working as an Ice Puller at LaGrande Creamery. During World War II at age 69 he worked at the Portland Navy Yard as a rivet catcher building Liberty ships" (Conklin C. F., Charles Conklin Family History Audio Interview II, 2001). He and Minnie continued to live in Portland, Oregon until after Minnie died in 1947. But he developed health issues too and in about 1950 my father invited him to move in with us in South Gate, California where we could take care of him. I remember he always wore suspenders and always had his pipe nearby. I liked the smell of the fresh tobacco in his pouch. He enjoyed driving my sister Rita and I to Bryson Avenue grade school on weekdays. But he liked whiskey too. I will never forget my mother showing me how to steer his car over to the curb and turn the ignition key off should Grandpa keel over.

"He was a big man," my father said, "over 200 pounds. They said it took three men to pin him down, when he was young. One hand would make two of mine, yeah. When he lived with us he frequented the bar (Go Slow Joe's) that Betty's folks owned. . . Some girl went (into the restroom) and my dad with his huge damn fist was going to scare her, you know, so he hit the wall and his fist went right through the wall. Broke his hand too. When he came home he said he sprained it in the car door. . . He was always playing jokes on people" (Conklin L. C., 2002).

"He lived behind our garage and had a room of his own. He had a stroke one night; that was after (living with us) seven years. . . He couldn't talk, you know. . . I would watch him all day long and then dad would watch him all night long. . . It just got to the point that dad and I just couldn't take it. . . The ambulance came and took him to the rest home, we saw him that night, and the next morning he was dead" (Marinkovic B. , 1980).

Conklins at Berg Home in Portland, Oregon about 1947. Front: Diane & Judy Berg; Back: Louise Conklin Berg, Charles F. Conklin, Allen Berg, Caroline Conklin Wright, Charles W. Conklin –photo from Charlene Elfers McKay Collection.

Caroline Lingren lived in Marshfield, Coos County, Oregon in Jun 1880 (Marital Status: Single; Relation to Head of House: Daughter, age 8 months). She lived in North Bend, Coos County, Oregon in Jun 1900 (Marital Status: Single; Relation to Head of House: Daughter). She lived in Eugene Ward 4, Lane, Oregon in 1910 (Age 30; Marital Status: Married; Relation to Head of House: Wife). She lived in Portland, Multnomah County, Oregon in 1920 (Marital Status: Married; Relationship: Wife). She lived in Portland, Multnomah County, Oregon in 1930 (Age 50; Marital Status: Married; Relation to Head of House: Wife). She lived in Portland, Multnomah, Oregon in 1935. She lived in Portland, Multnomah, Oregon on 01 Apr 1940 (Age 59; Marital Status: Married; Relation to Head of House: Wife). She lived in Portland, Multnomah County, Oregon between 1947 and 1954 (5905 NE 17th). She was buried on 26 Jul 1954 in Portland, Multnomah County, Oregon (Rose City Cemetery, 5625 NE Fremont St). She was also known as Carrie. Her cause of death was Parkinson's disease. She was affiliated with the Lutheran religion. She was described as Brown hair, brown eyes. Race: (White).

Caroline went by the nickname "Carrie" and was the sixth of eight Lingren children, born ten years after her oldest sister, Mary Bell, who helped raise her and the youngest children with her mother "Hannah." In 1902 when she was twenty-two years old she married William Martin in Marshfield (now Coos Bay), Oregon. He worked on one of the logging company

Steam engine rail logging in the forests near Coos Bay, Oregon –photo from Charlene Elfers McKay Collection.

trains that carried logs out of the woods for rafting to the lumber mill. Carrie's first son, named William after her husband, was born in 1906. "Her husband became addicted to morphine after an operation for an accident on the logging railroad. She couldn't tolerate it anymore" (Conklin L. , Louise Conklin letter to Robert Livingston, Dec 1997). They moved to Eugene, Oregon where he tried to hold down a job as a brick mason, but they soon divorced in about 1910. To support four-year old Billy she took care of an invalid lady and did dressmaking for college students. "She was an excellent seamstress. She picked it up, as I did. But if you could look back to those days, all the many tucks she made, I'm happy I didn't have that!" (Conklin L. , Louise Conklin letter to Robert Livingston, Dec 1997).

Carrie Conklin and children at Seaside, Oregon in 1920. Front: Louise, cottage owner, Charles; Back: Billy, Carrie – photo from Louise Conklin Collection.

Carrie with her son Billy moved back to Coos Bay where her family was and in 1912 married Charles William Conklin and had two more children. They divorced, remarried, and divorced again while raising their three children. Then when she was in her 50s she married her third husband John T. Wright. But that marriage was cut short due to her illness. I barely remember the last time I saw Grandma Carrie when she was getting frail. This was in 1951 at my Aunt Louise's home in Portland, Oregon when I was almost three years old. "My mother lived with me for seven years (until she died at age 74) because she had Parkinson's disease and her husband couldn't take care of her. She was such a wonderful mom!" (Conklin L. , Louise Conklin letter to Robert Livingston, Dec 1997).

Charles William Conklin and Caroline "Carrie" Lingren had the following children:

+2.   i.   CHARLES FRANKLIN[2] "CHARLIE, CHUCK" CONKLIN was born on 17 Aug 1913 in North Bend, Coos County, Oregon. He died on 23 Mar 2005 in Scottsdale, Maricopa, Arizona.

+3.   ii.   LOUISE THERESA CONKLIN was born on 07 Feb 1916 in North Bend, Coos County, Oregon. She died on 07 Mar 2012 in Scottsdale, Maricopa, Arizona.

Generation 2

2.   **CHARLES FRANKLIN² "CHARLIE, CHUCK" CONKLIN** was born on 17 Aug 1913 in North Bend, Coos County, Oregon. He died on 23 Mar 2005 in Scottsdale, Maricopa, Arizona (Age 91, atherosclerotic stroke). He married (1) HELEN BAILEY on 21 Jun 1937 in Yuma, Arizona. She was born 16 Dec 1912 in Indiana USA. He married (2) BETTY "VUKOSAVA, ZUTA, ELIZABETH" MARINKOVIĆ, daughter of Stevan "Steve, Stevo" Marinković and Ana Marinković, on 08 Nov 1946 in 12021 Long Beach Blvd, Lynwood, Los Angeles, California (Colonial Wedding Chapel). She was born on 24 Apr 1915 in Salem Ward 3, Columbiana, Ohio (7 Prospect Street). She died on 06 Aug 1987 (Age 72) in Spokane, Washington. He married (3) PAULINE RUTH ZIMMERMAN, daughter of Paul Richard Lewis Zimmerman and Ruth Edna Smith, on 17 Jun 1989 in Spokane, Washington. She was born on 04 May 1918 in Meeteetse, Park County, Wyoming. She died on 11 Aug 2013 (Age 95).

Charles was the only son of Charles W. and Caroline Conklin, born at their home in North Bend where they lived until he was three years old. When asked for his recollections he said: "How far back do I remember?"

1913-1915:

"I remember isolated things and places but where did they happen and when? I have a vivid memory of playing with snails that had shells on their backs and this was in the Coos Bay area. Also shinnying across a log to go for milk. I think it was delivered for us to pick up. When I was about three years old we were still in North Bend, Oregon in the home where I was born. I have a vivid memory of cleaning out the wood house and wood chute. Our house was way up on the hill and the wagon would come and they would put the wood in the chute so it would slide down into the wood house. All the cooking and heating was with wood. Mother did all of our sewing. I still have a scar on my chin from falling and hitting myself on the iron leg of the Singer sewing machine while I was playing as she was sewing.

"My Uncle Henry and Aunt Ina Hohn lived at Plat B, Marshfield, Oregon, and their house sticks in my mind because they had barrels of square nails in their basement. They also had a chute, from the kitchen window to the log pigpen outside. They would scrape all the garbage and waste from the kitchen onto the chute and it would slide down to the pigs. Aunt Ina was Finnish and my mother's younger sister. Uncle Henry was German. He left Germany when they pressed him into service as one of the Kaiser's personal guards. He deserted when he was 18 years old and immigrated to the U.S. and worked as a butcher all his life. He died in the Los Angeles County Poor House in 1936. His son Larry was living in Los Angeles at the time also" (Conklin C. F., Charles Conklin Family History Audio Interview II, 2001).

1916-1918:

"In 1916 my dad, Charles W., took me to the park in North Bend to see the arrival of the first steam train to the area. It was Sunday and what a celebration! We moved to Portland in about 1917 when World War I was on. My dad took me to the Hawthorne Street Bridge to watch the launching of the wooden patrol boats. They were afraid that German submarines were coming nearby in the Pacific.

"In 1918 we were living in an apartment in downtown Portland (near the Oregon Journal newspaper building) and my dad was working in a sawmill on the Willamette River. Louise (my younger sister) and I would go down to the slag piles near the river to pick up bits of iron that we sold for pennies for the war effort. During this time I remember the sawmill next to where my dad worked burned down and we could watch it burn from where we lived. Half of the fire engines were gasoline-powered engines and half were horse-drawn steamers.

Charles F. (left) and father Charles W. Conklin about 1923—photo from Charlene Elfers McKay Collection.

"My mother registered me for school this year also and I attended for three days until they found out I was just 5 years old and they kicked me out. Then we moved to Mount Tabor in East Portland. We rented a house and what I remember most about being there was that it had five "Black Republican" cherry trees. I also remember that my grandfather Lingren came to visit and brought Louise and I each an orange and some red and white peppermints" (Conklin C. F., Charles Conklin Family History Audio Interview II, 2001).

1919-1929:

"I started school in 1919 in Mount Tabor at six years of age. After a couple of years here we moved to 78th and Stark Street in Montevilla. This is where I met my lifelong friend Darrell Ellis, whose father worked for the Oregon Journal newspaper. Darrell's mother died in childbirth so my mother semi-adopted him and his two brothers. Darrell and I loved to collect cockleburs from which we made floor mats and lots of other things. Once we made a hat for Louise and put it on her head. My mother had to cut her hair off to remove it and Darrell and I got into trouble—deep!

"The lights in our house were gas mantle lamps that were also wired for electricity. They made good light and we used the gaslights to help heat the room. Our main heat source was a big kitchen range—a wood burner. There was a big water tank on the side also. We took all of our baths on Saturday nights in the kitchen in front of the stove.

"One vivid memory is of going to the moving picture house where a lady down in front played the piano while we watched "The Birth of a Nation," the first movie I ever saw. Later we saw Pearl White in "The Perils of Pauline." This was a series that continued for several weeks.

"We were always trying to make some money, so Louise and I started selling the Sunday morning paper. I was about eight years old and Louise was six. We would get up early Sunday morning, probably five o'clock, and go to the end of the streetcar line and pick up maybe 15 papers. We had to pay two or three cents for each. Then we sold them for five or ten cents each. We hauled them in our wagon. I had Louise haul the wagon while I yelled, "Get your Sunday morning paper" and we were soon sold out. This was before we had radio.

Louise wrote in the margin about their home when she was nine years old in 1925 at 107 NE 69th Ave, 2 blocks south of Glisan St. Her mother Caroline Conklin is on the porch –photo from Louise Conklin collection.

"Our school was just a block away and we took our own lunches and ate in the basement by the wood furnace. We could buy milk for two cents in tiny bottles. We always walked to school in the rain and my feet were always wet because my shoes had a hole in the bottom. I would put cardboard in my shoes but it did not keep the water out. I would get to school and it was still soaking in. It didn't bother me too much. I just thought it was the way things were. I remember when my dad would come home after a week's work and would have one $20 gold piece about as big as a quarter, and one $5 gold piece about as big as a dime –that was his payday. He was working at the laundry now, as a "steam engineer" on the boilers. There was an accident at the laundry one day and dad was scalded and I remember that he was in the hospital for about a month.

"The next I remember we were in Gresham, Oregon. I was probably in the sixth grade. I loved the school and was there until I graduated from eighth grade. I couldn't go to high school because we could not afford to buy the books so I missed the first year. I had lots of odd jobs: a paper route and sold the Oregon Journal (I had 30 customers), but for the final baseball edition I had 13 customers. I earned enough money that year to buy a $30 bicycle. I had a bicycle before that. I can't remember exactly how old I was, maybe nine or ten. It was a 30-inch bicycle, much too big for me, and I had to learn to ride it between the bars. That one cost only $6 but I was happy to have the transportation!

"My mother was first married to a man named William Martin. They had one child, William Samuel Martin who was my (seven year older) half-brother. His father William was critically injured in a logging accident and was in extreme pain from his injuries and became addicted to morphine and his addiction finally killed him. After he died my mother married my father Charles. My half-brother Bill was a guiding influence in my life" (Conklin C. F., Personal History Notes, 1996).

1930-1935:
"Later my mother and father divorced and I lived with my brother Bill. Sometime in this space of years I went to Benson Polytechnic School for my education. It was a wonderful education. It gave me skills that I still use today. Unfortunately, soon the Great Depression hit its peak. I had a job for $13 a week in a grocery store and my family: Louise and my mother, had no other means of support other than my job."

"I soon met the guy that sold apples to the store and got a job in Yakima with my friends Darrell Ellis and Vick Ferreras. We thinned out the new apples on the trees, and later picked apples, pears, and peaches. I was happy to find out that there was some place in the world that it didn't rain constantly. We had a 1929 Chevy truck that Scottie's Aunt bought for us. I remember celebrating my 21st birthday with Darrell and Vick at Bumping Lake near Yakima. We shot a cottontail rabbit and ate it for lunch that day" (Conklin C. F., Personal History Notes, 1996).

1936-1945:

LA Shipyard Port Identification Card
–from Charles F. Conklin Collection.

"After the picking season was over I went back to Portland and then in 1936 was working in Marshfield when my cousin Larry Hohn, who was working for GM in Flint, Michigan said that General Motors was transferring him to South Gate, California to start up a new automobile factory. He said he could get us a job there so we hopped a freight train and went with him to California. I started as an inspector for General Motors when the plant opened on October 16,

1936, and then became a welder. I also studied welding in the evenings at school."

"When General Motors laid me off on January 26, 1942 and closed to go into tank production for World War II, I got a job welding Navy ships at the Los Angeles Shipyards in Long Beach, California. It was fascinating building destroyers from the bottom up for Bethlehem Steel. They said they could go as fast as 70 knots. By that time I had a house and a new car. I also worked building forty-thousand ton Navy repair ships, sea-plane tenders, and hospital ships until August, 1945, becoming a foreman in charge of a hundred men. "For the first two years I never had a day off. . . I was drafted twice but the shipyard got me released. The day Japan surrendered I quit and started my mattress manufacturing business in South Gate with my father-in-law Wiley Bailey" (Conklin C. F., Charles Conklin Family History Audio Interview II, 2001).

1946-1966:
Charlie was married to Helen Bailey during the war, but after she ran off with a soldier, he divorced her in 1945. His father-in-law at that time, Wiley Bailey, knew the mattress business from Jackson, Mississippi and partnered with Charles to buy and set up machines for making mattresses after the war. As soon as Japan surrendered in 1945, Charles quit his job at the Navy

Local Resident— Local industry

Charles F. Conklin, owner and operator of the Atlantic Mattress Co., has been a resident of South Gate for 17 years.

ATLANTIC MATTRESS

The Atlantic Mattress Co. was started in South Gate in 1945 and moved to the present factory location at 5236 Tweedy in September 1947.

The complete plant is equipped to build any size or shape of mattress from "the ground up." Every operation through springing, filling, tape-edge sewing to automatic button tufting is completed on the premises.

Most of the 15 employes, each an expert in his own line, have been with the firm since its formation and reside in the Southeast.

In August 1953 a mattress sterilizer was added to the renovating plant.

The company, which has branches in North Hollywood, Fresno, Oakland, San Francisco, Redwood, San Jose and San Leandro opened its newest retail outlet at 3625 Tweedy, South Gate, November 1953.

Left: Atlantic Mattress Company story in the South Gate Press in 1962.

Yard and they started the Atlantic Mattress Company in South Gate where Charles had been living since working for General Motors. He soon met Betty Marinković Deutsch at a bar in Newport Beach, who was also a recent divorcee, and they were married in 1946. Soon I was born and I remember our family living in an apartment above the mattress factory that dad built. Betty soon had Rita and was pregnant with Joan when we moved to a larger house on Bowman Avenue. Yet Betty still helped out at the retail store as well as sometimes at the factory sewing mattress ticking. The business grew, celebrating its 17th year in 1962. But by 1966 I

was graduating from high school, grandma Ana had passed away, and the mattress workers unionized, driving Charles and Betty out of California. In June of that year we sold all our property and loaded all our belongings and business machines onto two railcars and moved to

Spokane, Washington, where my dad used to pick apples. My dad liked the new name I suggested for the business and Northwest Bedding Company opened its doors on July 4, 1966.

1967-2005:
Dad retired in 1979 shortly after my sister Joanie died in a plane crash, selling his half of the business to his partner Robert Evanson. Mom and dad bought a winter house in Scottsdale, Arizona and became snowbirds. In 1987 my mom passed away at the age of 72 from acute pancreatitis aggravated by diabetes, high blood pressure, and cigarette smoking.

In June 1989 I had the honor of being Best Man at my dad's wedding to Pauline "Polly" (Zimmerman) Abell, also a widow herself with two grown children of her own: Richard and Charmin. She was a great cook, took care of him, and became his best friend. She made him eat well and they took long walks together every day. She was just what he needed after losing Betty and I am sure that is why he lived as long as he did, despite having 2 strokes. Charlie passed away sixteen years later at age 91 at his winter residence in Scottsdale, Arizona. Polly lived another eight years, passing away at age 95 in Spokane, Washington.

Josie offers comfort, even from beyond

Charles and Pauline Conklin met, fell in love and got married late in life. She's now 82 and he's 87, and, for both of them, this is a second marriage.

With grown kids, the only real merging of families that had to be negotiated was that his much loved 12-year-old dog, Josie, had to find her place in their new lives together.

Charles loved his Josie, a mature sheltie-German shepherd mix. Pauline was quite clear that she and Josie could live together and share this good man but, in her words, "I was sure that she was his dog, and I was not going to become attached to her." Wrong.

It took only about a week for Josie to pull her blanket around to Pauline's side of the bed. It seems that Josie was not willing to choose between an old friend and a new one; in her opinion, loving two people was the way

KENNETH WHITE
Arizona Humane Society

to go. The feeling became mutual.

The Conklins' permanent home is in Spokane, Wash., but they travel each winter to Arizona so that they can remember what the sun looks like. Josie would accompany them on the leisurely drive, comfortable to wait for them in the motel room while they went to dinner, as long as their belongings were where she could smell them.

After seven years of marriage, Jose had reached 19. Gradually, she grew weak. Finally, the time came to put her to sleep. As last summer approached, Josie's cremated remains were with Charles

and Pauline for one last drive home to Washington.

The last drive included a side-trip to Pauline's original home state of Wyoming, a chance for her and her husband to see the beautiful Big Horn Mountain Range. They stopped at one of the scenic viewing spots along the road to appreciate the majesty, so different from the natural beauty of both the Pacific Northwest and the desert Southwest.

Lost for a moment in the view, they barely noticed as another car of tourists drove up and parked beside them. Out popped a young family with three children and a dog.

"Look at that dog," Pauline urgently whispered to her husband, "look at that dog."

The dog was the image of their own, dear Josie. Instinctively and instantly, Charles dropped to one knee. Instinctively and instantly, this strange yet familiar little pup walked up to him

and placed her muzzle into his open hands.

Through their tears, Charles and Pauline explained to the young family why their dog, Sadie, had caused such a strong, visceral reaction. In turn, they learned that Sadie was usually quite shy of strangers, and that her eager approach and obvious trust of Charles was extraordinary.

Pauline looks at it like this: "Perhaps Sadie, with a dog's sensitive nature, knew that my husband was grieving for his dog. But we will always feel that Josie's spirit was there, that she had sent us a message that everything was alright. That she was happy and well."

Josie's ashes are entombed in the Conklins' back yard. Her memory lives forever in their hearts.

Kenneth White is president of the Arizona Humane Society. Contact him in care of the AHS, 9226 N. 13th Ave., Phoenix, AZ 85021.

ARIZONA REPUBLIC 3 MAR 2001

Charlie loved animals as related in this poignant story about his last dog Josie in the Phoenix Arizona Republic –3 Mar 2001.

Charlie never forgot his childhood wearing shoes with holes in them and dropping out of school to support his family during the depression and I will never forget his favorite phrase, "It makes you wonder what the poor folks are doing tonight."

Charles Franklin "Charlie, Chuck" Conklin and Betty "*Vukosava, Zuta*, Elizabeth" Marinković had the following children:

+4. i. DAVID GENE[3] "DAVE" CONKLIN was born on 03 Nov 1948 in Lynwood, California (St Francis Hospital). He married MARY LAVONNE GUERRA on 22 Nov 1969 in Moscow, Latah, Idaho, USA. She was born on 15 Jun 1949 in Boise, Ada, Idaho.

5. ii. RITA MARIE CONKLIN was born on 23 Aug 1950 in Lynwood, California (St Francis Hospital). She married (1) JAMES MACDONALD in Spokane, Washington. She married (2) RODNEY N REEVE in Seattle, King, Washington (Episcopal Church in The Highlands).

+6. iii. JOAN LOUISE "JONI" CONKLIN was born on 16 Feb 1952 in Lynwood, California. She died on 04 Aug 1979 in Idaho (died in plane crash in Salmon River, Idaho). She married (1) MICHAEL SCIACCOTTI. She married (2) ROBERT FULTON.

+7. iv. LORIE ANN "LORI" CONKLIN was born on 14 Apr 1955 in Lynwood, California (St Francis Hospital). She married JAMES GRAY about 1975. He was born about 1955 in Spokane, Washington.

3. **LOUISE THERESA CONKLIN** was born on 07 Feb 1916 in North Bend, Coos County, Oregon. She died on 07 Mar 2012 (Age 96) in Scottsdale, Maricopa, Arizona. She married (1) ALLEN GARRETT BERG, son of Emanuel Berg and Elsie, on 18 Sep 1938 in Vancouver, Clark, Washington. He was born on 27 Aug 1909 in North Bend, Coos County, Oregon. He died on 12 Dec 1987 in Portland, Multnomah County, Oregon. She married (2) LOUIS NELSON "BUD" BOSS SR. on 03 Sep 1989 in Seaside, Clatsop, Oregon. He was born on 19 Jan 1912 in Mount Rainier, MD. He died on 19 Jul 2004 in Scottsdale, Maricopa, Arizona.

Aunt Louise poses with "Uncle Jack" at her home in Scottsdale, AZ in January, 2011. At age 95 Louise said she owed her longevity to taking a "nip" of whiskey every day.

Louise was Caroline's third and Charles' second child and only daughter. She was also born in North Bend (Coos Bay). But Louise did not remember much about North Bend like her brothers did, as the family moved to Portland when she was only a year old in 1917. They lived downtown, then in Mt. Tabor before moving to Montevilla.

In Montevilla, Louise helped her brother Charles sell papers on the weekends. "Sunday Oregonian Journal Paper! I can still remember hollering that. I guess I must have been eight or nine years old" (Conklin L. , Louise Conklin Family History Audio Interview, 2002). Louise was so cute that everyone would buy a paper according to Charlie. After high school and before she was married, Louise worked as a wool spinner for the Oregon Worsted Company for five years. In 1938 she married Al Berg who worked for a paper company. Three years later they had their first child Diane in 1941, followed by Judy in 1943. From 1947 to 1954 Louise's mother Caroline, who had Parkinson's disease, moved in with them so Louise could take care of her while raising the children. After Caroline died in 1954 she began working for department stores, retiring from Nordstrom after fifteen years. After Al passed away in 1987, Louise met Louis "Bud" Boss whom she married in 1989. They too became snowbirds, between Seaside, Oregon in the summer and Scottsdale, Arizona in the winter where Louise bought a condo next to her daughter Judy. When Bud passed away in 2004 she became a full-time resident of Arizona until she died in 2012 at the age of 96.

Louise (left) & mother Caroline at her father Charles' house in Portland in 1936 –photo from Louise Conklin Collection.

I remember the many fun times our families had together during our visits to Oregon. In the summer we would all go to Cannon Beach where cars were allowed to drive on the beach. That is where I learned how to use a skim board in the surf. Dad would buy fresh Dungeness crab and we would build a fire on the beach in front of our cottage every night. Every morning Louise would moan from her bed, "kaaa-fee, kaaa-fee" as if she would die if she did not get a cup of coffee soon. One time we all went to the Sandy River in Dodge Park for the smelt run. I was so excited to hear my dad recall that day, "You could see them coming, thousands of them. Your net would be brimming. You could hardly drag it, you had to pull it in, you couldn't lift it" (Conklin L. C., 2002). Louise was also an excellent self-taught swimmer and she taught us how to swim there in the Sandy River. I'll never forget those days.

Allen Garrett Berg and Louise Theresa Conklin had the following children:

+8. i.   DIANE CAROLINE[3] BERG was born on 31 Oct 1941 in Portland, Multnomah County, Oregon. She married STEVE COLVIN.

+9. ii. JUDY ANN BERG was born on 20 May 1943 in Portland, Multnomah County, Oregon. She married (1) DONALD JOHNSON. She married (2) TED ARMACK on 05 Oct 1973 in Las Vegas, Nevada.

Louise Conklin and Al Berg about 1938 –photo from Louise Conklin Collection.

From left: Louise Conklin Berg, Diane Berg, Judy Berg about 1952 –photo from Louise Conklin Collection.

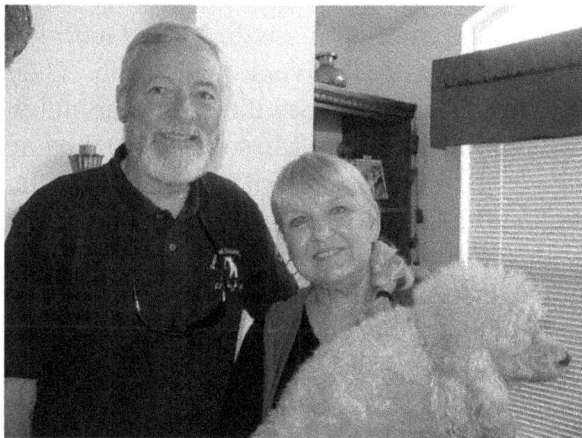

Dave Conklin and cousin Diane Berg Colvin and her dog Selly in Arizona on 13 Feb 2016.

Mary and Dave Conklin with their dog Mai Tai and cousin Judy Berg Armack (right) in Arizona on 23 Dec 2013.

4. **DAVID GENE**[3] **"DAVE" CONKLIN** (Charles Franklin[2] "Charlie, Chuck", Charles William[1], Josiah C.[A], Abraham John[B] "Abram", Abraham[C], John[D], Joseph[E], John[F] Conkelyn, John[G] Concklyne, William[H] Conkling) was born on 03 Nov 1948 in Lynwood, California (St Francis Hospital). He married Mary Lavonne Guerra on 22 Nov 1969 in Moscow, Latah, Idaho, USA. She was born on 15 Jun 1949 in Boise, Ada, Idaho, USA. Dave graduated in May 1966 in South Gate, Los Angeles, California, USA (High School Diploma). He served in the military from Jun 1969 to Oct 2008 in the Army Reserve and National Guard. He received a BS (Forestry) degree in 1970 from the University of Idaho. He received a MS (Natural Resources) degree in 1972 from the University of Montana. Public Service: from 1972 to 2000 in Montana (State Park Ranger). He received an MBA degree in 1998 from the University of Montana. He was described as Gray hair, blue eyes, left-handed, 5ft 8in, 145 lbs. (from HI driver lic) in 2006 in Honolulu, Hawaii, USA. He was known as Dave. He was also known by the title of Lieutenant Colonel. He was affiliated with the Serbian Orthodox religion.

David Gene Conklin was named after his great uncles David E. Conklin, and Eugene L. Conklin. Dave was born in Lynwood and raised in South Gate, California. Upon graduation from High School in 1966, his family moved to Spokane, Washington where his father moved his Atlantic Mattress Company and started Northwest Bedding. Dave graduated from the University of Idaho in 1970 with a BS in Forestry, and the University of Montana in 1972 with an MS in Natural Resources and later an MBA.

Portrait of Dave Conklin at Army ROTC commissioning ceremony in Missoula, Montana, June 1971.

He met and married his wife Mary Guerra in 1969 while at the University of Idaho. Their daughter Dacia was born the next year and in 1970 they moved to Missoula, Montana to attend the University of Montana. After graduation, in 1973, they moved into a log cabin outside of Helena, Montana and Dave started his 27-year career with the Montana Department of Fish, Wildlife and Parks while Mary worked for the Montana Legislative Council. While working as a Park Ranger they moved to Miles City where their son Christopher was born in 1982. They returned to Helena in 1983 where Dave became Chief of Park Operations and built a new log house. In 1990 they moved to Kalispell where Dave was a Regional Park Manager.

While serving in the Montana National Guard's 163d Armored Cavalry Regiment, he volunteered for military service in the European Command in 1997 and served in the Republic of Bulgaria for two years (Conklin D. , Two Years Among the Bulgars, 1999). Dave retired from the State of Montana in 1999 at age 50 and began consulting and writing travel books, (Conklin D. , Montana History Weekends: Fifty-two Adventures in History, 2002), until volunteering for military service in Operation Iraqi Freedom in 2003.

Dacia, Dave and Mary Conklin pose for an old-fashioned photo in Helena, Montana, May 1977.

Even though his draft card lottery number was 349 he joined the Reserve Officer Training Command in 1969 during college and was commissioned an officer in the US Army Reserve Corps of Engineers in 1971. He continued to serve for 37 years, retiring as a Lieutenant Colonel in 2008. Along the way he learned Spanish, German, Bulgarian, and Arabic languages and made many friends while serving as an exchange officer with the German Army, on a Military Liaison Team in Bulgaria, and with the 350th Civil Affairs Command in Baghdad during Operation Iraqi Freedom (Conklin D. , Letters from Baghdad, 2005). His military decorations include the Bronze Star, Defense Meritorious Service Medal, four Army Commendation Medals, and the Iraq Campaign Medal among many others.

After returning from the Iraq war in 2004 Dave was recruited by Tapestry Solutions, a logistics information technology company and spent the next 10 years as a military contractor training Soldiers, Marines and security contractors in Iraq, Japan, Korea, Thailand, Philippines, Australia, and the U.S., moving with Mary to Hawaii for 7 years and to Camp Pendleton, California for 2 years before retiring for a third time at age 65. Dave and Mary then bought a winter home and moved to Sun City, AZ where he has been active in hiking, travel, and other clubs. In 2017 at age 68 he was diagnosed with Parkinson's disease and suffered a heart attack while hiking which required two stents.

Although he was raised in metropolitan Los Angeles, family camping trips in the Sierras led Dave to become an avid outdoorsman, horseman, gardener, sportsman, living history buff, surfer, skier and, from 1973 to 1990, a sled dog racer. The family home in Montana always included a couple of horses, a team of Siberian Huskies, and a dozen chickens or rabbits as well as a large garden full of raspberries and strawberries.

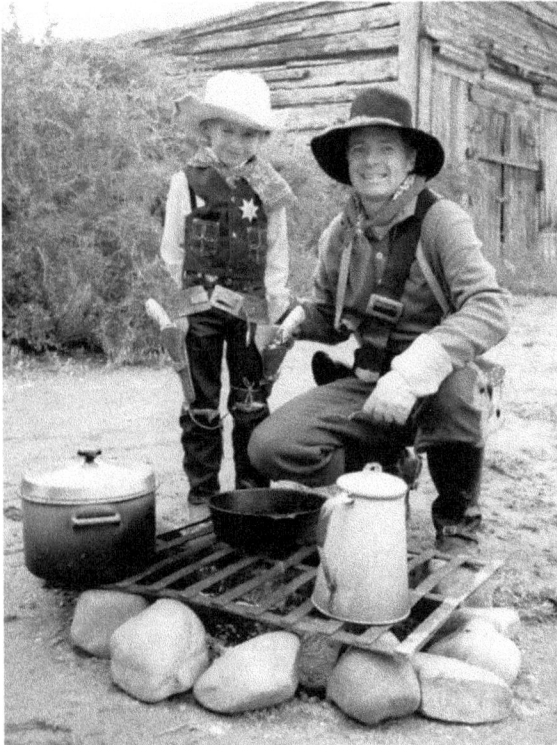

Chris and Dave Conklin cooking salt pork
For a living history demonstration at
Bannack State Park Montana, July 1987.

Mary (Guerra) and Dave Conklin at Dave's
50ᵗʰ High School Reunion, South Gate, CA
22 Oct. 2016.

David Gene "Dave" Conklin and Mary Lavonne Guerra had the following children:

+10.   i.   DACIA MARIE⁴ CONKLIN was born on 06 Feb 1970 in Moscow, Latah, Idaho.

+11.   ii. CHRISTOPHER ANDREW⁴ CONKLIN was born on 29 Apr 1982 in Miles City, Montana.

5.   **RITA MARIE³ CONKLIN** was born on 23 Aug 1950 in Lynwood, Los Angeles, California, USA (St Francis Hospital).   She married (1) JAMES MACDONALD in Spokane, Spokane, Washington, USA.   She married (2) RODNEY N REEVE in Seattle, King, Washington, USA (Episcopal Church in The Highlands).

KNXT TO FILM ACTION

S.G. Girl Picked for Capitol Trip

A South Gate sixth grade student is one of 12 from the entire Los Angeles School District who has been selected to tour the nation's capitol the first week in April. It was announced today by Robert D. Wood, vice-president of CBS Television Division and general manager of KNXT.

The South Gate pupil chosen is Rita Conklin, 11, the daughter of Mr. and Mrs. Charles Conklin, 10248 Bowman Ave. A sports enthusiast and a hobbyist, Rita collects stamps and pennies, and enjoys swimming and tennis. Her father is president of Spring Craft, Inc., in South Gate.

She attends the Bryson Avenue School where she sing in the chorus and participates in many student activities. She is also a member of the Camp Fire Girls. Other members of her fam-

ily include an older brother David, 13, and two younger sisters, Joanne, 10, and Lori, 6.

The 12 students were chosen to make the trip because of their understanding of democracy, experience in student government, maturity and a bent for leadership, according to Wood. They also represent a balance of races, faiths, and economic groups. Robert Content, a teacher at the 133rd St. Elementary School in Gardena, is preparing the

6th graders for the trip and will act as their guide in Washington, D.C.

In Washington, KNXT film crews will capture the action and reaction of the students to questions posed by Content at various points of interest, including the Tomb of the Unknown Soldier, Library of Congress, Supreme Court, Lincoln Memorial, Capitol Building, White House and Smithsonian. Meetings also will be scheduled with members of the government.

RITA CONKLIN

Let's talk One to One.

Finally, one banker who knows you by name, not by number.

When Rita was in the 6th grade she was one of 12 chosen for a CBS sponsored field trip to Washington D.C. where she met Vice President Lyndon Johnson. Several news articles were written by the local newspapers about her trip (Daily Signal, 1962). After Rita graduated from high school she went to college in Bellingham, WA where she met and married Jim MacDonald. She went through two marriages and divorces. She started working as a teller for Rainier Bank in Seattle and was featured in a 1982 ad (above) by the Bank. Later she became a mortgage banker and worked for many years in Seattle and Spokane.

6.   JOAN LOUISE[3] "JOANIE" CONKLIN was born on 16 Feb 1952 in Lynwood, Los Angeles, California, USA. She died on 04 Aug 1979 in Idaho. She married (1) MICHAEL SCIACCOTTI. She married (2) ROBERT FULTON.

One story my mom told about Joanie was when she learned to iron at the age of 8. It seems Joanie had a favorite dress that mom made her for school and would not change to go out and play. So mom said "OK then every time I have to wash it you will have to iron it." So sure enough she began to iron all her own clothes, and soon Rita learned to iron also (Marinkovic B. , 1980).

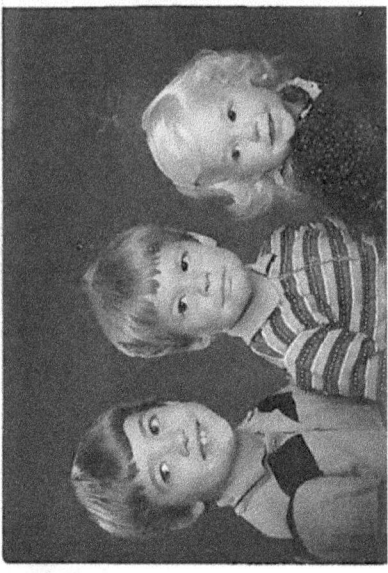

Left: The last Christmas card Joan Conklin sent in 1978 included a photo of all her children. From left: Joshua-8, Seth-4, and Anna-2.

Joanie had a son Joshua with Michael Sciaccotti, later divorcing and marrying Dr. Robert Fulton, M.D. whom she met while studying to become a nurse, and having a son Seth and daughter Anna with Bob. Joanie died while on a river floating vacation at age 27 in a small plane crash near Lowman, Idaho when the pilot became trapped in the Salmon River Canyon (Idahonian, 1979).

Pilot Tried to Flee Canyon, Then Crashed

LOWMAN, Idaho (AP) — The pilot of a light airplane that crashed Saturday, resulting in the deaths of six persons, apparently was trying to climb out of a dead-end canyon when the crash occurred, a Federal Aviation Administration investigator said.

Veteran pilot Max Sandborn, Boise, and five passengers were fatally injured in the crash. All but Sandborn died at the scene, just short of the Indian Creek landing strip in the Idaho Primitive Area. Sanborn died Sunday in a Salt Lake City hospital of burns.

The single-engine Cessna 210 was on a charter flight from Boise to Indian Creek, where the passengers were to launch a float trip down the Middle Fork of the Salmon River.

Killed in the crash were Patricia Sue Bell, 37. Lewiston, Idaho; Joan Louise Fulton. 30, Spokane, Wash.; Jacolyn Junker, 36. Vancouver; Guy Cook, 18, Garden City and Carl Torrey, 23, Steamboat Springs. Colo.

"The plane was largely intact," said Russell Fishback, Federal Aviation Administration investigator.

The plane burned when it hit the ground, he said. "He hit some trees for about 50 yards, then hit the ground. His path of descent was very shallow," Fishback said.

Other airplanes were ferrying other members of the party to the float trip. Officials said Sandborn radioed another airplane in the party to check whether his landing gear was down and fixed in place.

The other pilot confirmed that the landing gear was properly in place.

Investigators said as that radio exchange was completed, Sandborn flew into a dead-end canyon, with walls about 2.000 feet higher than surrounding canyons.

The plane apparently crashed as he was trying to climb above the canyon walls. Investigators said the airplane's propeller blade angle was set for low speed. high power — the setting used in climbing.

Our father Charles commissioned portraits of all his children including Rita (left) and Joan Conklin (right), in 1970.

Michael Sciaccotti and Joan Louise "Joanie" Conklin had the following child:

+12. i. JOSHUA⁴ SCIACCOTTI was born on 21 May 1970 in Spokane, Washington.

Robert Fulton and Joan Louise "Joanie" Conklin had the following children:

+13. i. SETH R[4] FULTON was born on 7 February 1974 in Spokane, Washington.

+14. ii. ANNA FULTON was born on 6 September 1976 in Spokane, Washington.

7. **LORIE ANN[3] "LORI" CONKLIN** (Charles Franklin[2] "Charlie, Chuck", Charles William[1], Josiah C.[A], Abraham John[B] "Abram II", Abraham[C] "Abram", John[D], Joseph[E], John[F] Conkelyn, John[G] Concklyne, William[H] Conkling) was born on 14 Apr 1955 in Lynwood, California (St Francis Hospital). She married James Gray about 1975. He was born about 1955 in Spokane, Washington.

Lori has been a top producing loan officer in the mortgage industry since 2003 and was a member of the President's Club. Her previous background as a custom homebuilder included being President of the local homebuilder's association. When Lori was still in high school and my sister Joanie and I brought our young kids, Joshua and Dacia, over during the holidays, she would tell them stories. One story was about the "Toilet Monster" that would suck little kids down the toilet and into the sewer where he kept them as slaves. It was several months after that story before we could get the kids to go to the bathroom by themselves!

Hawaii vacation in 1984. From left: "Jimmy" Gray with sons Mitchell & Justin, Betty & Charles Conklin, Lorie (Conklin) Gray with son Ryan –from Charles Conklin Collection.

James "Jimmy" Gray and Lorie Ann "Lori" Conklin had the following children:

+15. i. RYAN[4] GRAY was born on 13 Jan 1978 in Spokane, Spokane County, Washington, USA. He married Katie Anne Musacco.

+16. ii JUSTIN GRAY was born in 1980 in Spokane, Spokane County, Washington, USA. He married Tarah Coffey on 28 Jun 2003 in Spokane, Spokane County, Washington, USA.

17. iii. MITCHELL GRAY was born on 25 Oct 1983 in Spokane, Spokane County,

Washington, USA.

David, Lorie, Rita, and Joan Conklin pose
for this portrait taken in California in 1955.

Rita, David, and Lorie Conklin in June 1989

8.   **DIANE CAROLINE³ BERG** (Louise Theresa² Conklin, Charles William¹ Conklin, Allen Garrett, Emanuel) was born on 31 Oct 1941 in Portland, Multnomah County, Oregon. She married **STEVE COLVIN**.

Steve Colvin and Diane Caroline Berg had the following children:

+18.   i.   CORY⁴ COLVIN was born on 24 Jun 1965 in Spokane, Washington. He married Lisa Hundeby in Spokane, Washington.

+19.   ii.   MARLY COLVIN was born on 15 Feb 1967 in Spokane, Washington. She married Allen Krause about 1988.

9.   **JUDY ANN³ BERG** (Louise Theresa² Conklin, Charles William¹ Conklin, Allen Garrett, Emanuel) was born on 20 May 1943 in Portland, Multnomah County, Oregon. She married (1) DONALD JOHNSON. She married (2) TED ARMACK on 05 Oct 1973 in Las Vegas, Nevada.

Donald Johnson and Judy Ann Berg had the following children:
+20.   i.   CHRISTY⁴ JOHNSON was born on 24 Oct 1963 in Portland, Multnomah, Oregon. She married Ladd Howell about 1989 in Scottsdale, Maricopa, Arizona.

+21.   ii.   STEPHANIE JOHNSON was born on 30 May 1967 in Portland, Multnomah, Oregon. She married Shawn Stevenson about 1996 in Scottsdale, Maricopa, Arizona.

Judy (Berg) Armack celebrates Christmas in Phoenix, Arizona with her Daughters Stephanie Johnson (left) and Christy (Johnson) Howell (right) on 25 Dec 2013.

Generation 4

10. **DACIA MARIE**[4] **CONKLIN** (David Gene[3] "Dave", Charles Franklin[2] "Charlie, Chuck", Charles William[1], Josiah C.[A], Abraham John[B] "Abram II", Abraham[C] "Abram", John[D], Joseph[E], John[F] Conkelyn, John[G] Concklyne, William[H] Conkling) was born on 06 Feb 1970 in Moscow, Latah, Idaho, USA (Gritman Memorial Hospital). She had a child with (1) TROY MYRON KUNZ on 21 Jul 1994 in Mesa, Maricopa, Arizona, USA (Partner-split in 1998). He was born on 12 May 1968 in Sandy, Utah. She married (2) RANDAL ENGLISH on 16 Mar 2000 in Bullhead City, Mohave, Arizona, USA. He was born on 26 Jan 1970 in Helena, MT.

Troy Myron Kunz and Dacia Marie Conklin had the following child:

22.   i.   JUSTIN TROY[5] KUNZ was born on 21 Jul 1994 in Mesa, Maricopa, Arizona, USA (Mesa Lutheran Hospital).

11.   **CHRISTOPHER ANDREW**[4] **CONKLIN** (David Gene[3] "Dave", Charles Franklin[2] "Charlie, Chuck", Charles William[1], Josiah C.[A], Abraham John[B] "Abram II", Abraham[C] "Abram", John[D], Joseph[E], John[F] Conkelyn, John[G] Concklyne, William[H] Conkling) was born on 29 Apr 1982 in Miles City, Custer, Montana, USA (Holy Rosary Hospital). He had a child with (1) BRITTANY SMITH on 29 Apr 2004 in Kalispell, Flathead, Montana (Partner-split in 2006). She was born in Kalispell, Flathead, Montana (Adopted daughter). He met his current partner (2) JESSICA SWANSON about 2007 in Kalispell, Flathead, Montana (Partner). She was born on 13 Apr 1984 in St Paul, Hennepin, Minnesota, USA.

Christopher Andrew Conklin and Brittany Smith had the following child:

23.   i.   ISABELLE IONA[5] CONKLIN was born on 29 Apr 2004 in Kalispell, Montana, USA.

Dacia and Chris Conklin at the Launer Ranch   Chris working as an Arborist in July 2014.
in the Sweetgrass Hills Montana, July 2015.

Dacia's son Justin Kunz, age   Chris' daughter Isabelle Conklin, age 10,
17, --Sep 2011.   in 2014.

12.   **JOSHUA CORY[4] SCIACCOTTI** (Joan Louise "Joanie" Conklin, Charles Franklin[2] "Charlie, Chuck", Charles William[1], Josiah C.[A], Abraham John[B] "Abram II", Abraham[C] "Abram", John[D], Joseph[E], John[F] Conkelyn, John[G] Concklyne, William[H] Conkling, Michael) was born on 21 May 1970 in Spokane, Washington. He died on 20 Dec 2017 in Spokane, Washington (organ failure). He married Sandra Noguera in Portland, Multnomah County, Oregon on 24 Jun 2004.

Joshua Cory Sciaccotti and Sandra Noguera had the following child:
    24.   i.   ISABELLA[5] "BELLA" SCIACCOTTI.

Sandra, Isabella and Joshua Sciaccotti in 2017.

Anna Fulton and Arian Gibson with baby Audrey in 2009.

13. **SETH R**[4] **FULTON** (Joan Louise[3] "Joanie" Conklin, Charles Franklin[2] "Charlie, Chuck" Conklin, Charles William[1] Conklin, Robert J) was born on 07 Feb 1974. He married Brooke Fulton in 2011 in Bora Bora.

Seth R. Fulton and Brooke Fulton had the following children:
    25.   i.   YURI[5] FULTON was born in 2013.
    26.   ii. GEORGEANNA FULTON was born in Mar 2016.

14. **ANNA LOUISE**[4] **FULTON** (Joan Louise[3] "Joanie" Conklin, Charles Franklin[2] "Charlie, Chuck" Conklin, Charles William[1] Conklin, Robert) was born on 06 Sep 1974 in Spokane, Spokane County, Washington, USA. She married Arian Gibson on 08 Jul 2005.

Arian Gibson and Anna Louise Fulton had the following children:
    27.   i.   AUDREY[5] GIBSON was born in 2008.
    28.   ii. ALEX GIBSON was born in 2010.

15. **RYAN**[4] **GRAY** (Lorie Ann[3] "Lori" Conklin, Charles Franklin[2] "Charlie, Chuck" Conklin, Charles William[1] Conklin, James) was born on 13 Jan 1978 in Spokane, Spokane County, Washington, USA. He married KATIE ANNE MUSACCO.

Ryan Gray and Katie Anne Musacco had the following children:
    29.   i.   HAYDEN[5] GRAY was born on 24 Apr 2008 in California.
    30.   ii. CHARLIE GRAY was born on 15 Mar 2010 in California.

16. **JUSTIN**[4] **GRAY** (Lorie Ann[3] "Lori" Conklin, Charles Franklin[2] "Charlie, Chuck" Conklin,

Charles William[1] Conklin, James) was born on 06 Jan 1980 in Spokane, Spokane County, Washington, USA. He married Tarah Coffey on 28 Jun 2003 in Spokane, Spokane County, Washington, USA.

Justin Gray and Tarah Coffey had the following children:
  31. i. JUDAH[5] GRAY was born on 27 Oct 2005 in Spokane, Spokane, Washington, USA.
  32. ii. ASHER GRAY was born on 30 Apr 2007 in Spokane, Spokane, Washington, USA.
  33. iii. LEVI GRAY was born on 15 Oct 2010 in Spokane, Spokane, Washington, USA.

18. **CORY[4] COLVIN** (Diane Caroline[3] Berg, Louise Theresa[2] Conklin, Charles William[1] Conklin, Steve) was born on 24 Jun 1965 in Spokane, Washington. He married Lisa Hundeby in Spokane, Washington.

Cory Colvin and Lisa Hundeby had the following children:
  34. i. SYDNEY COLVIN was born on 05 Oct 1990 in Spokane, Washington.
  35. ii. STEPHEN COLVIN was born on 15 Dec 1992 in Spokane, Washington.
  36. iii. SOMMER COLVIN was born on 06 Aug 1994 in Spokane, Washington.

19. **MARLY[5] COLVIN** (Diane Caroline[3] Berg, Louise Theresa[2] Conklin, Charles William[1] Conklin, Cory[4], Steve) was born on 15 Feb 1967 in Spokane, Washington. She married Allen Krause about 1988.

Allen Krause and Marly Colvin had the following child:
  37. i. KELBY[6] KRAUSE was born on 11 Jan 1989.

20. **CHRISTY[4] JOHNSON** (Judy Ann[3] Berg, Louise Theresa[2] Conklin, Charles William[1] Conklin, Donald) was born on 24 Oct 1963 in Portland, Multnomah, Oregon. She married Ladd Howell about 1989 in Scottsdale, Maricopa, Arizona.

Ladd Howell and Christy Johnson had the following children:
  38. i. AUSTIN[5] HOWELL was born on 08 Sep 1990 in Scottsdale, Maricopa, Arizona.
  39. ii. PAIGE PILAR HOWELL was born on 23 Jun 1995 in Scottsdale, Maricopa, Arizona.

21. **STEPHANIE[4] JOHNSON** (Judy Ann[3] Berg, Louise Theresa[2] Conklin, Charles William[1] Conklin, Donald) was born on 30 May 1967 in Portland, Multnomah, Oregon. She married Shawn Stevenson about 1996 in Scottsdale, Maricopa, Arizona.

Shawn Stevenson and Stephanie Johnson had the following child:
  40. i. QUYNTON[5] STEVENSON was born on 08 Feb 1997.

Part II. The Descendants of Francis Lingren

Introduction to Part II

My purpose in compiling Part II is to promote an appreciation of the Lingren family as part of the Conklin family history and an appreciation of both those born into the family and those married into the family as my grandfather did. I have centered this part of the book on my paternal great grandparents on my paternal grandmother's side, Francis Frederick Lingren and Johanna Wilhelmina Lingren. Although I never met my maternal great grandparents, I am thankful that I knew their daughter, my paternal Grandmother Caroline Lingren who was still alive when I was a child.

When we look at our parents and grandparents we often catch glimpses of ourselves, and it's not just from shared DNA. The people who raise us shape us, almost invisibly, through the values they convey, their convictions, and especially through their actions. The Lingren grandparents also passed down to us a strong work ethic, moral values, self-discipline, concern for neighbors, the importance of hospitality, and the importance of family and love.

I have included brief information about each person's education, occupation, military and public service when that information was available. I would hope that "Frank" and "Hanna" would be pleased to know that many in the family seek to honor their parents, their communities, and their heritage.

The findings presented here are based solely on my research, primarily over the past three years. The discovery of additional sources or interpretations may affect the conclusions.

The Format

The National Genealogical Society Quarterly (NGSQ) generation numbering system format is also used in Part II of this book in order of descent from the oldest paternal ancestor (Frank Lingren, 1832) to the sixth generation (Isabelle Conklin, 2004). I only show the direct lineage for each of the ancestors of Frank. I list all of the children for each ancestor, but only the ancestors of Frank are listed in the next generation. Details of ancestors' lives are mentioned when available. I included all the descendants of Frank Lingren that I found. Even with this family history going back only six generations, it has still been a challenge. Other than family interviews, I have had to rely solely on documents and records available to me in America in the English language. There are probably records of the ancestors of Francis Frederick Lingren and Johanna Wilhelmina Lingren in Finland, but those records are in the Finnish language and I have not been able to do research in Finland as yet.

Although this part the book is written in English using the Latin alphabet, our Finnish ancestors' names and locations were originally written in the Finnish alphabet first used by the Bishop of Turku in 1548 to translate the Bible. Even so, the Russians banned books written in Finnish during their 19th century occupation. Also many Finns living on the west coast of Finland (known as the "Swedish Finns") spoke Swedish and had Swedish as well as Finnish names for their villages as Sweden occupied Finland from 1155 to 1807. It is understandable that many immigrants adopted English names or at least English pronunciation and spelling of their names soon after they arrived in America.

For the purposes of this book I use the Finnish rather than Swedish spelling of family names and locations (i.e Raahe vs. Brahestad). Though the spoken word will not always be phonetic in the English pronunciation, the written word will recognizable by both English and Finnish speakers. If it is a Finnish word but not a family name, it will be italicized to indicate it should be pronounced as such (i.e. *Terve*) or "Hello."

Practically all the information about Frank's ancestors was obtained from published sources describing Finland, northern Europe, and their ethnic history due to the lack of both written and oral sources from family ancestors themselves.

Chapter 1 focuses on the lives of Francis Frederick Lingren and Johanna Wilhelmina Dalstrom, the parents of Caroline Lingren, my grandmother. The chapter also lists their immediate descendants. The life of Caroline Lingren is discussed in more detail in Chapter 5, Part I as she married into the Conklin family.

Each descendant is assigned a number. Also, for both ancestors and descendants, a small number appears after their first name, or after their middle name if they have a middle name. This number indicates what generation of descendant this person is relative to "Frank" Lingren and "Hannah" Dalstrom listed at the beginning of the chapter. For example, in Generation 4 the 4 after Jean Cleo Livingston signifies that she is the 4th generation descending from Frank Lingren at the beginning of the Chapter as person number 1.

Frank Lingren in Generation 1 is followed by 1 indicating that he is the 1st generation that I have any information on. If we someday find Frank's father, he would become the 1st generation, and so on.

For descendants that married a person that already had children, I have included these children and their families in the book. Although they are not descendants by blood line, they are part of the Lingren family through marriage. Similarly, adopted children are included when their information was provided.

As a reminder, this book was developed with the "Family Tree Maker" computer application. The chapter on the descendants of Frank Lingren and Hannah Dalstrom was developed from a separate "Descendant" genealogy report file built with "Family Tree Maker." Each generation has a number for each descendant of the primary person starting with a "2." When there is a plus sign in front of the number, it indicates that the descendant also had children and will be listed again under the next generation up to generation 4.

This methodology is used to keep all of the descendants of each of Frank's children in one chapter. If we had just used one file for all the descendants, the family members would appear mixed throughout this section of the book, because the report file lists all descendants by generation. You can also use the index to find the name and page with information for that individual.

Lingren Family Movement

Francis Frederick Lingren, my father's maternal Grandfather, was born in Raahe on the Swedish-speaking west coast of Finland. Finns from this part of Finland, which had been under Swedish rule for 500 years, were known as the "Swedish-Finns" (Douthit, 1981, p. 62). We do not know whether he was born on the coast or on one of the islands off the coast of Finland. However he grew up here when Finland was under Russian rule and the coastal Finns were building and sailing ships around Cape Horn and into the Pacific Ocean for the Russian Tsar.

What is now the republic of Finland was ruled by Sweden for 700 years, and then ruled by Russia for 100 years until 1917.

So at age 14 he hired on as a cabin boy, sailing around the world twice, on ships commissioned by the Tsar. On one of these voyages he may have been to California and Oregon. One account translated from Finnish says, "Frank Lingren, a sailor from Raahe, came first to New York in about 1860, and subsequently moved to California, prospecting for gold. He is the owner of real estate in the city (Marshfield, Oregon) (Ilmoen, 1919).

Census reports indicate that in 1856 at age 24, both Frank and his younger brother Charles (age 20), immigrated to America (U.S. Federal Census, 1900). We do not know whether Frank traveled from New York to California to Oregon by wagon or boat, but ten years later in 1866 he was living in Empire City, Oregon (Douthit, 1981, p. 57). By 1867 the U.S. had purchased Alaska from the Russians, and they and the Finns under their hire were moving out of Alaska into thriving U.S. coastal towns. This was also the time of "The Great Exodus" out of Scandinavian countries in search of a better life in the new world where they had heard great tales of prosperity, and promises of almost free land under the 1862 U.S. Homestead Act.

Frank's spouse, Johanna Wilhelmina Dalstrom (also spelled Dahlstrom) was a Laplander whose family was from the northern-most region of Finland which is mostly north of the Arctic Circle. As such she may have been a member of the indigenous people known as the Sami, who can trace their heritage back more than 8,000 years. They have their own language, traditions, and customs and lead a nomadic life herding reindeer across the permafrost of the Arctic tundra.

Left: The nomadic reindeer herding Sami have inhabited Lapland for thousands of years. These girls are in traditional costume, 1898 – Nordiska Museet.

Famous Lingrens

Finland's famous Lingrens (also spelled Lindgren) are mostly associated with Finnish culture which has existed for only a little over a century. Prior to Sweden ceding Finland to Russia in 1809, and Finnish independence from Russia in 1917, arts were influenced by the invading powers of Sweden and Russia and artists studied and worked in Stockholm or Saint Petersburg. The contemporary Lindgrens mentioned below brought Finnish culture to the forefront. I do not have evidence of lineage, only the family name to suggest that these Lindgrens may be related to the same ancestors. Armas Lindgren (1874-1929) and his partners defined Finnish architecture with the Art Nouveau architectural style known as *Jugend* style. With them he designed Helsinki's National Museum, National Theatre, and the Hvittrask, their stone and log workplace in the forest. One of the most widely read Swedish writers is Astrid Lindgren who wrote many free-spirited children's stories including *Pippi Longstocking* and *Emil of Lonneberga*.

Chapter 1. Francis Lingren and Johanna Dalstrom

Generation 1

1.   **FRANCIS FREDERICK**[1] **"FRANK" LINGREN** (Unknown[4] Lindgren) was born on 07 Jan 1832 in Raahe, Oulun Laani, Finland (aka Brahestad in Swedish). He died on 14 Jun 1922 (Age 90) in Monterey, California, USA. He married **JOHANNA WILHELMINA**[1] **"HANNAH, MINNIE" DALSTROM**, daughter of Gustav Dahlstrom and Ulrica Wilhelmina Wiberg, in 1868 in Finland. She was born on 06 Jul 1846 in Finland. She died on 16 Jul 1921 (Age 75) in Coquille, Coos County, Oregon.

Francis Frederick Lingren left Finland and arrived in New York, New York, USA (Arrived with younger brother Charles) in 1856 (Age 24). He lived in Empire, Coos County, Oregon in 1866 (Dodge, 1898, p. 57). He lived in Marshfield, Coos County, Oregon in 1880 (Age 44; Marital status: Married; Relation to Head of House: Self). He lived in Marshfield, Coos County, Oregon in 1890 (Marital Status: Married; Relation to Head of House: Self). He lived in North Marshfield, Coos County, Oregon in 1900 (Marital Status: Married; Relation to Head of House: Head). He lived in South Marshfield, Coos County, Oregon in 1910 (Marital Status: Married; Relation to Head of House: Head). He lived in Marshfield, Coos County, Oregon in 1920 (Age 88; Marital Status: Married; Relation to Head of House: Head). He was also known as Frank. He was affiliated with the Lutheran religion.

Map --Finland lies between and was ruled for many years by Sweden and then Russia.

Not much has been found about Frank Lingren's family or early life in Finland before he immigrated to America. According to research by his daughter Mary Bell's descendants (Livingston, Dec 1997), Frank, as his friends called him, was born in Raahe, on the northern west coast of Finland in 1832. Finns from this Swedish-speaking west coast of Finland, which had been under Swedish rule for 500 years, were known as the "Swedish-Finns" (Douthit, 1981, p. 62). The surname Lingren (also spelled Lindgren) means "branch of a lime tree" from Swedish *lind* "lime tree" and *gren* "branch. His middle name *Fredrik* is derived from ancient Germanic words "*fridu*" shelter, protector, peace and "*rich*" which means powerful, mighty.

Much of what I know about the Lingrens comes from the daughter of Wilhelmina Lingren, my Aunt Alice Mauzey, who took care of Frank during his last year. According to Alice, Frank, like many Finns, had blue eyes and was of Tatar origin. While attending school in Finland, Frank got into trouble when he slapped a girl, so in 1846 at age 14 he ran off to sea. Apparently he spent the next ten years as a cabin boy, sailing around the world twice. He probably served on ships commissioned by the Tsar as Finland was under Russian rule during most of the 19th century. One account translated from Finnish says, "Frank Lingren, a sailor from Raahe, came first to New York in about 1860, and subsequently moved to California, prospecting for gold. He is the owner of real estate in the city" (Marshfield, Ore.) (Ilmoen, 1919).

"Frank" Lingren (left) and "Hannah" Dalstrom
–undated photos from Robert Livingston Collection.

Census reports indicate that in 1856 at age 24, Frank and his younger brother Charles, age 20, immigrated to America (U.S. Federal Census, 1900). We do not know whether Frank traveled from New York to California to Oregon by wagon or boat, but ten years later in 1866 Frank was already living in Empire City, Oregon (Dodge, 1898, p. 57). According to Frank's great grandson Fred, (grandson of Mary Bell Lingren) he worked in Empire City for four years, then in 1868 at age 36 he returned to Finland to find a wife and bring her back.

Frank's new fiancé, Johanna Wilhelmina "Hanna" Dalstrom, was a "very pretty" Laplander Finn with brown hair and brown eyes. She came from a large family and by 1864 at age 18 was working at a wooden match factory in Finland making the equivalent of 5 cents per day. We do not know how they met, but every spring in Finland each community had a communal wash day where they would heat rocks and put them in a large tub of water with their winter clothes to clean. They may have been introduced there after their families arranged the marriage. They were married in Finland and had their honeymoon on the boat trip to America, arriving in New York in 1868 (Mauzey, 1981).

One year later, in August, 1869 the first of their 8 children, Mary Bell Lingren, was born in Empire City, Oregon. During this time Frank was most likely a sawmill worker at the Simpson Lumber Company mill founded north of Marshfield in 1856 (Douthit, 1981, p. 32) and a launch boat pilot in Coos Bay. By 1870 Frank and Hannah had saved enough money to buy a small farm on Kentuck Slough (Conklin C. F., Charles F. Conklin Family History Audio Interview I, 1980) north and across the bay from Marshfield where other Swedish-speaking Finns were living including the Andrew Sandine family (Douthit, 1981, p. 62). One of the main reasons the Lingrens moved to Kentuck Slough was to supplement Frank's income with what they could raise on the farm.

According to granddaughter Louise Conklin, "Grandpa cut down trees and built their log cabin. They had a big garden. My mom (Caroline) said her back got rounded from carrying and planting potatoes. They had to cross the slough in a rowboat to get supplies from Marshfield. Their cabin burnt down once and Grandpa had to build another one. He was a hard worker! (Conklin L. , Louise Conklin letter to Robert Livingston, Dec 1997).

Coos Bay, Oregon postcard, 1914 –photo from Robert Livingston Collection.

Here they raised 7 more children over the next 30 years before moving into Marshfield (now Coos Bay) in about 1900. The Lingrens and their Finnish neighbors were the largest emigrant group in Coos Bay until the 1940's and built the one-room schoolhouse in Kentuck Slough, the Lutheran Church, and fraternal halls including the Runeberg Hall, the fraternal

Suomi Lodge for men, and the Martha Lodge for women (Douthit, 1981, pp. 63-65).

JOHANNA WILHELMINA[1] **"HANNAH, MINNIE" DALSTROM** was born on 06 Jul 1846 in Finland. She died on 16 Jul 1921 in Coquille, Coos County, Oregon. She married Francis Frederick Lingren in 1868 in Finland. Unfortunately nothing has been found so far about Johanna's family or early life in Finland before she emigrated. The name Johanna is the female version of Johannes. Names used in other countries which have same origin are for example Jane, Jenny, Joan, Juanita, Giovanna and Jeannette. Johanna's nameday is July 21st. Vilhelmina is the sister name of the ancient German name Vilhelm which roughly translates to "strong willed helmed man." Names in other cultures with same origin include Willa, Vilma, Helmine, and Minette. Vilhelmina's nameday is May 26th.

Hanna & Frank Lingren at their home on 405 8th Street South in Marshfield, Oregon about 1910 –photo from Charles F. Conklin Collection.

Hanna arrived in Oregon in 1868 (Age 22). She lived in Empire, Coos County, Oregon on 07 Aug 1869 (Birth of daughter Mary Bell). She lived in Marshfield, Coos County, Oregon in 1880 (Age 34; Marital status: Married; Relation to Head of House: Wife). She lived in North Marshfield, Coos County, Oregon in 1900 (Marital Status: Married; Relation to Head of House: Wife). She lived in South Marshfield, Coos County, Oregon in 1910 (Marital Status: Married; Relation to Head of House: Wife). She lived in Marshfield, Coos County, Oregon in 1920 (Age 74; Marital Status: Married; Relation to Head of House: Wife). She was buried on 18 Jul 1921 in Coos Bay, Coos County, Oregon, USA (Sunset Memorial Park, Pioneer 2, Block 50, Lot 5). She was affiliated with the Lutheran religion. She was described as Laplander; brown hair, brown eyes.

Frank and Hanna Lingren continued to live in Marshfield, Oregon after they retired. Frank was remembered by his granddaughter Louise Conklin as a kind and generous man. She said, "I'll never forget the time Grandpa brought us the biggest oranges I had ever seen. He lived in Monterey, California with Aunt Minnie (Wilhelmina Lingren) at that time (Conklin L. , Louise Conklin letter to Robert Livingston, Dec 1997). Hannah died at age 75 in 1921 and was buried in Sunset Memorial Park. Her obituary in the local paper was a simple one, "Mrs. Frank Lingren, pioneer resident, died at her home in this city (Marshfield) last week. The funeral occurred Monday" (Marshfield Sun, 1921). Soon after she died Frank moved in with his granddaughter Alice and daughter Wilhelmina in Monterey, California until he died a year later in 1922 after a full and adventurous life at age 90. He was laid to rest with his dear wife Hannah in Coos Bay, Oregon.

Above: Johanna Dalstrom grave marker and inscription at Sunset Cemetery Coos Bay, Oregon: "In memory of Gohanna Wilhelmina, wife of F. Lingren born 1846, died Jul 16, 1921. Gone but not forgotten." –photo 6 May 2016.

Francis Frederick "Frank" Lingren and Johanna Wilhelmina "Hannah, Minnie" Dalstrom had the following children:

+2.   i.   MARY BELL[2] LINGREN was born on 07 Aug 1869 in Empire City, Coos County, Oregon. She died on 26 Apr 1902 in Marshfield, Coos County, Oregon (liver abcess). She married George Likins Wheeler, son of William Samuel Wheeler and Hannah Rodgers Wolf, on 22 Jun 1888 in Marshfield, Coos County, Oregon. He was born on 01 Aug 1864 in Nevada, USA. He died on 23 Dec 1938 in Scotia, Humboldt, California, USA.

+3.   ii.   INA MAY LINGREN was born in 1871 in Marshfield, Coos County, Oregon. She married Henry Hohn on 11 Aug 1894 in Marshfield, Coos County, Oregon.

4.   iii.   FRANCIS FREDERICK "FRED" LINGREN JR. was born in 1873 in Marshfield, Coos County, Oregon

5.   iv.   ELIZABETH LINGREN was born in 1874 in Marshfield, Coos County, Oregon.

+6.   v.   WILHELMINA "MINNIE" LINGREN was born on 17 Nov 1877 in Marshfield, Coos County, Oregon. She died on 17 Jan 1966 in Monterey, California (Age: 89). She married John Edgar Mauzey, son of Levi Wilcoxen Mauzey and Lydia

Katherine McKern, on 08 Jun 1901 in Coos County, OR. He was born on 12 Jan 1879 in Marshfield, Coos County, Oregon. He died on 01 Feb 1952 in Monterey, California (Age 73).

+7.   vi.   CAROLINE "CARRIE" LINGREN was born on 10 Oct 1879 in Marshfield, Coos County, Oregon. She died on 22 Jul 1954 in Portland, Multnomah County, Oregon (suffered from Parkinson's). She married (1) WILLIAM D. MARTIN on 23 Dec 1902 in Marshfield, Coos County, Oregon (This was Carrie's first of 4 marriages to 3 men.). He was born in California. She married (2) CHARLES WILLIAM CONKLIN, son of Josiah C. Conklin and Theresa M. "Thursey, Thursa" Stockman, on 27 Apr 1912 in Marshfield, Coos County, Oregon (This was Charles first marriage, Carrie's second). He was born on 17 Sep 1873 in Manistee, Michigan, USA. He died on 05 Feb 1957 in Lynwood, California (Age 83; suffered a stroke). She married (3) JOHN T WRIGHT, son of Thomas Wright and Martha Young, before 1940 in Portland, Multnomah, Oregon (This was Carrie's third husband & 4th marriage). He was born on 11 Dec 1879 in Illinois. He died on 18 Nov 1957 in Vancouver, Clark, Washington (Age 77).

+8.   vii.   KATHERINA "KATIE" LINGREN was born on 12 Oct 1882 in Marshfield, Coos County, Oregon. She died on 25 Aug 1955 in Coos, Oregon, United States. She married Frank Edward Terry on 02 Jul 1904 in Coos County, Oregon. He was born about 1881 in Oregon.

9.   viii.   WILLIAM H LINGREN was born in June 1883 in Marshfield, Coos County, Oregon. He died in 1932 (He went to fight forest fires and was never heard from again- Caroline Lingren

Generation 2

2. **MARY BELL[2] LINGREN** (Francis Frederick[1] "Frank", Unknown[4] Lindgren) was born on 07 Aug 1869 in Empire City, Coos County, Oregon. She died on 26 Apr 1902 in Marshfield, Coos County, Oregon (liver abscess). She married George Likins Wheeler, son of William Samuel Wheeler and Hannah Rodgers Wolf, on 22 Jun 1888 in Marshfield, Coos County, Oregon. He was born on 01 Aug 1864 in Nevada, USA. He died on 23 Dec 1938 in Scotia, Humboldt, California, USA.

George Likins Wheeler and Mary Bell Lingren had the following children:

10.   i.   ANNIE E[3] WHEELER was born in Apr 1889 in Coos County, Oregon. She died in 1923 in Porland, , Oregon, USA.

11.   ii.   HARRIET MCNEIL "HATTIE" WHEELER was born on 31 Dec 1893 in Coos County, Oregon. She died on 22 Sep 1958 in Rio Dell, Humboldt, California, USA. She married Lester Elwin Saling on 17 May 1913 in Coos County, Oregon.

12.   iii.   HANNAH MARIE "MARIE" WHEELER was born in Sep 1896 in Coos County, Oregon. She died in 1960 in Oakland, Alameda, California, USA. She married Cleo Dean Berry on 18 Jun 1920 in Eureka, Humboldt, California. He was born on 09 Nov 1894 in Sebastopol, Sonoma, California, USA. He died on 26 Dec 1982 in Santa Cruz, Santa Cruz, California, USA.

+13.   iv.   MINNIE EDDEVA "EDDEVA" WHEELER was born on 25 Aug 1899 in Marshfield, Coos County, Oregon. She died on 26 Jun 1961 in Rio Dell, Humboldt, California, USA. She married Roy Livingston on 10 Nov 1917 in Eureka, Humboldt, California. He was born on 14 Nov 1894 in Eureka, Humboldt, California. He died on 16 Oct 1982 in Fortuna, Humboldt, California, USA.

Mary Bell Lingren (above left) was the oldest of the Lingren children and married George Wheeler (above right) in 1888 in Marshfield, Oregon –undated photos from Robert Livingston collection.

3.   **INA MAY**[2] **LINGREN** (Francis Frederick[1] "Frank", Unknown[4] Lindgren) was born in 1871 in Marshfield, Coos County, Oregon. She married Henry Hohn on 11 Aug 1894 in Marshfield, Coos County, Oregon.

Henry Hohn and Ina May Lingren had the following children:

14.   i.   LAWRENCE[3] "LARRY" HOHN was born on 27 Mar 1910 in Marshfield, Oregon. He died on 23 Dec 1999 (Age 89). He married Signe Pherson on 05 Oct 1929 in Kitsap, Washington, USA.

15.   ii.   FRIEDA HOHN.

16.   iii.   OLGA HOHN.

17.   iv.   WALLACE HOHN.

6.   **WILHELMINA**[2] **"MINNIE" LINGREN** (Francis Frederick[1] "Frank", Unknown[4] Lindgren) was born on 17 Nov 1877 in Marshfield, Coos County, Oregon. She died on 17 Jan 1966 in Monterey, California (Age: 89). She married John Edgar Mauzey, son of Levi Wilcoxen Mauzey and Lydia Katherine McKern, on 08 Jun 1901 in Coos County, OR. He was born on 12 Jan 1879 in Marshfield, Coos County, Oregon. He died on 01 Feb 1952 in Monterey, California (Age 73).

John Edgar Mauzey and Wilhelmina "Minnie" Lingren had the following children:

18.   i.   EDGAR L.[3] MAUZEY was born on 01 Apr 1902 in Oregon. He died on 29 Nov 1973 (Age 71) in Monterey, California.

19.   ii.   FRANCIS LEE MAUZEY was born on 02 May 1903 in Oregon. He died on 25 Jul 1906 in Marshfield (Coos Bay), Coos, OR.

20.   iii.   FENTON M.. MAUZEY was born on 17 Feb 1905 in Oregon. He died on 21 Jul 1906 in Marshfield (Coos Bay), Coos, OR.

21.   iv.   ALICE KATHRYN MAUZEY was born on 20 Jan 1908 in Oregon (Twin sister of Dale). She died on 25 Mar 1995 in Monterey, Monterey, California, USA (Age 87). She married (1) WILLIAM F KIRKMAN about 1928 in California. He was born about 1908 in South Carolina. She married (2) ROBERT LEE MELDER, son of Lonnie Melder and Ammie D Melder, before 1954 in Monterey, Monterey, California, USA. He was born on 23 Jun 1914 in Louisiana. He died on 12 Mar 1982 in Monterey, California (Age 67).

22.   v.   DALE COLLING MAUZEY was born on 20 Jan 1908 in Oregon (Twin brother of Alice). He died on 05 Sep 1990 in Monterey, CA.

23.   vi.   HOWARD MAUZEY was born on 23 May 1913 in Marshfield, Oregon. He died on 22 May 2000 in Santa Clara, CA.

7.   **CAROLINE**[2] **"CARRIE" LINGREN** (Francis Frederick[1] "Frank", Unknown[4] Lindgren) was born on 10 Oct 1879 in Marshfield, Coos County, Oregon. She died on 22 Jul 1954 in Portland, Multnomah County, Oregon (suffered from Parkinson's). She married (1) WILLIAM D. MARTIN on 23 Dec 1902 in Marshfield, Coos County, Oregon (This was Carrie's first of 4 marriages to 3 men.). He was born in California. She married (2) CHARLES WILLIAM CONKLIN, son of Josiah C. Conklin and Theresa M. "Thursey, Thursa" Stockman, on 27 Apr 1912 in Marshfield, Coos County, Oregon (This was Charles first marriage, Carrie's second). He was born on 17 Sep 1873 in Manistee, Michigan, USA. He died on 05 Feb 1957 in Lynwood, California (Age 83; suffered a stroke). She married (3) JOHN T WRIGHT, son of Thomas Wright and Martha Young, before 1940 in Portland, Multnomah, Oregon (This was Carrie's third husband & 4th marriage).

He was born on 11 Dec 1879 in Illinois. He died on 18 Nov 1957 in Vancouver, Clark, Washington (Age 77).

William D. Martin and Caroline "Carrie" Lingren had the following child:

+24.   i.   WILLIAM SAMUEL³ "BILL" MARTIN was born on 24 Feb 1906 in Marshfield, Coos County, Oregon. He died on 30 Jul 1974 in Portland, Multnomah County, Oregon. He married Alma Olsen about 1925 in Portland, Multnomah County, Oregon.

Charles William Conklin and Caroline "Carrie" Lingren had the following children:

+25.   i.   CHARLES FRANKLIN³ "CHARLIE, CHUCK" CONKLIN was born on 17 Aug 1913 in North Bend, Coos County, Oregon. He died on 23 Mar 2005 in Scottsdale, Maricopa, Arizona (Age 91, atherosclerotic stroke). He married (1) HELEN BAILEY on 21 Jun 1937 in Yuma, Arizona. She was born 16 Dec 1912 in Indiana USA. He married (2) BETTY "VUKOSAVA, ZUTA, ELIZABETH" MARINKOVIĆ, daughter of Stevan "Steve, Stevo" Marinković and Ana Marinković, on 08 Nov 1946 in 12021 Long Beach Blvd, Lynwood, Los Angeles, California (Colonial Wedding Chapel). She was born on 24 Apr 1915 in Salem Ward 3, Columbiana, Ohio (7 Prospect Street). She died on 06 Aug 1987 (Age 72) in Spokane, Washington. He married (3) PAULINE RUTH ZIMMERMAN, daughter of Paul Richard Lewis Zimmerman and Ruth Edna Smith, on 17 Jun 1989 in Spokane, Washington. She was born on 04 May 1918 in Meeteetse, Park County, Wyoming. She died on 11 Aug 2013 (Age 95).

+26.   ii.   LOUISE THERESA CONKLIN was born on 07 Feb 1916 in North Bend, Coos County, Oregon. She died on 07 Mar 2012 in Scottsdale, Maricopa, Arizona. She married (1) ALLEN GARRETT BERG, son of Emanuel Berg and Elsie Nelson, on 18 Sep 1938 in Vancouver, Clark, Washington. He was born on 27 Aug 1909 in Marshfield, Coos County, Oregon. He died on 12 Dec 1987 in Portland, Multnomah County, Oregon. She married (2) LOUIS NELSON "BUD" BOSS SR. on 03 Sep 1989 in Seaside, Clatsop, Oregon. He was born on 19 Jan 1912 in Mount Rainier, MD. He died on 19 Jul 2004 in Scottsdale, Maricopa, Arizona.

8.   KATHERINA² "KATIE" LINGREN (Francis Frederick¹ "Frank", Unknown⁴ Lindgren) was born on 12 Oct 1882 in Marshfield, Coos County, Oregon. She died on 25 Aug 1955 in Coos, Oregon, USA. She married Frank Edward Terry on 02 Jul 1904 in Coos County, Oregon. He was born about 1881 in Oregon.

Frank Edward Terry and Katherina "Katie" Lingren had the following children:

27.   i.   KATHLEEN I.³ TERRY was born about 1906 in Oregon. She died on 04 Jul 1966 in Lane, Oregon, United States.

28.　ii.　CLAIR EDWARD TERRY was born about 1916 in Oregon. He died on 11 Sep 2002.

Generation 3

13.　**MINNIE EDDEVA³ "EDDEVA" WHEELER** (Mary Bell² Lingren, Francis Frederick¹ "Frank" Lingren, George Likins, William Samuel) was born on 25 Aug 1899 in Marshfield, Coos County, Oregon. She died on 26 Jun 1961 in Rio Dell, Humboldt, California, USA. She married Roy Livingston on 10 Nov 1917 in Eureka, Humboldt, California. He was born on 14 Nov 1894 in Eureka, Humboldt, California. He died on 16 Oct 1982 in Fortuna, Humboldt, California, USA.

Right: Minnie Eddeva Wheeler and Hannah Marie Wheeler (on right) posed for this photo in about 1909 –photo from Robert Livingston collection.

Roy Livingston and Minnie Eddeva Wheeler had the following children:

29.　i.　DALE LEROY⁴ LIVINGSTON was born on 19 Oct 1920 in Eureka, Humboldt County, California. He died on 14 Dec 1994 in Fortuna, Humboldt, California, USA.

+30.　ii.　JEAN CLEO LIVINGSTON was born on 31 Jan 1922 in Eureka, Humboldt County, California. He died on 21 Mar 1967 in Eureka, Humboldt County, California. He married Delphine Frances Meister on 28 Feb 1947 in Eureka, Humboldt County, California. She was born on 24 Sep 1924 in Ferndale, Humboldt, California, USA.

21.　**ALICE KATHRYN³ MAUZEY** (Wilhelmina³ "Minnie" Lingren, Francis frederick¹ "Frank" Lingren, John Edgar, Levi Wilcoxen) was born on 20 Jan 1908 in Oregon (Twin sister of Dale). She died on 25 Mar 1995 in Monterey, Monterey, California, USA (Age 87). She married (1) WILLIAM F KIRKMAN about 1928 in California. He was born about 1908 in South Carolina. She married (2) ROBERT LEE MELDER, son of Lonnie Melder and Ammie D Melder, before 1954 in Monterey, Monterey, California, USA. He was born on 23 Jun 1914 in Louisiana. He died on 12 Mar 1982 in Monterey, California (Age 67).

William F. Kirkman and Alice Kathryn Mauzey had the following children:

31. i. DUANE EDGAR*4* KIRKMAN was born on 12 Feb 1929 in Monterey, California. He died on 15 Nov 1993 in Monterey, California (Age 64).

32. ii. DALE KENNETH KIRKMAN was born on 27 Mar 1930 in Monterey, California. He died on 17 Aug 2001 in Cave Junction, Josephine, Oregon, USA (Age 71).

33. iii. WARD ALAN KIRKMAN was born on 21 Jul 1931 in Monterey, California. He died on 26 Jan 1987 (Age 55).

Robert Lee Melder and Alice Kathryn Mauzey had the following child:

34. i. ROBERT*4* MELDER JR.

24. **WILLIAM SAMUEL*3* "BILL" MARTIN** (Caroline*2* "Carrie" Lingren, Francis Frederick*1* "Frank" Lingren, William D.) was born on 24 Feb 1906 in Marshfield, Coos County, Oregon. He died on 30 Jul 1974 in Portland, Multnomah County, Oregon. He married Alma Olsen about 1925 in Portland, Multnomah County, Oregon.

William Samuel "Bill" Martin and Alma Olsen had the following children:

35. i. VIRGIL*4* MARTIN was born in Portland, Multnomah County, Oregon.

36. ii. BILLY MARTIN was born in Portland, Multnomah County, Oregon.

25. **CHARLES FRANKLIN*3* "CHARLIE, CHUCK" CONKLIN** (Caroline*2* "Carrie" Lingren, Francis Frederick*1* "Frank" Lingren, Charles William, Josiah C., Abraham John "Abram II", Abraham "Abram", John, Joseph, John Conkelyn, John Concklyne, William Conkling) was born on 17 Aug 1913 in North Bend, Coos County, Oregon. He died on 23 Mar 2005 in Scottsdale, Maricopa, Arizona (Age 91) (atherosclerotic stroke). He married (1) HELEN BAILEY, daughter of Wiley Bailey, on 21 Jun 1937 in Yuma, Arizona, USA. She was born on 16 Dec 1912 in Indiana, United States of America. She died on 07 Apr 2008 in Marion, Linn County, Iowa, United States of America. He married (2) BETTY "VUKOSAVA, ZUTA, ELIZABETH" MARINKOVIĆ, daughter of Stevan "Steve, Stevo" Marinković and Ana "Anna, Annie" Marinković, on 08 Nov 1946 in 12021 Long Beach Blvd, Lynwood, Los Angeles, California, USA (Colonial Wedding Chapel). She was born on 24 Apr 1915 in Salem Ward 3, Columbiana, Ohio (7 (now 417) Prospect St). She died on 06 Aug 1987 in Spokane, Washington (Acute pancreatitis). He married (3) PAULINE RUTH ZIMMERMAN, daughter of Paul Richard Lewis Zimmerman and Ruth Edna Smith, on 17 Jun 1989 in Spokane, Washington, USA. She was born on 04 May 1918 in Meeteetse, Park County, Wyoming, USA. She died on 11 Aug 2013 in Spokane, Spokane County, Washington, USA (Age 95).

Charles Franklin "Charlie, Chuck" Conklin and Betty "Vukosava, Zuta, Elizabeth" Marinković had the following children:

+37. i. DAVID GENE*3* "DAVE" CONKLIN was born on 03 Nov 1948 in Lynwood, California (St Francis Hospital). He married Mary Lavonne Guerra on 22 Nov 1969 in

Moscow, Latah, Idaho, USA. She was born on 15 Jun 1949 in Boise, Ada, Idaho.

38.   ii.   RITA MARIE CONKLIN was born on 23 Aug 1950 in Lynwood, California (St She married (2) RODNEY N REEVE in Seattle, King, Washington (Episcopal Church in The Highlands).

+39.   iii.   JOAN LOUISE "JONI" CONKLIN was born on 16 Feb 1952 in Lynwood, California. She died on 04 Aug 1979 in Idaho (died in plane crash in Salmon River, Idaho). She married (1) MICHAEL SCIACCOTTI. She married (2) ROBERT FULTON.

+40.   iv.   LORIE ANN "LORI" CONKLIN was born on 14 Apr 1955 in Lynwood, California (St Francis Hospital). She married James Gray about 1975. He was born about 1955 in Spokane, Washington.

26. **LOUISE THERESA[3] CONKLIN** (Caroline[2] "Carrie" Lingren, Francis Frederick[1] "Frank" Lingren, Charles William, Josiah C., Abraham John "Abram II", Abraham "Abram", John, Joseph, John Conkelyn, John Concklyne, William Conkling) was born on 07 Feb 1916 in North Bend, Coos County, Oregon. She died on 07 Mar 2012 in Scottsdale, Maricopa, Arizona. She married (1) ALLEN GARRETT BERG, son of Emanuel Berg and Elsie Nelson, on 18 Sep 1938 in Vancouver, Clark, Washington. He was born on 27 Aug 1909 in Marshfield, Coos County, Oregon. He died on 12 Dec 1987 in Portland, Multnomah County, Oregon. She married (2) LOUIS NELSON "BUD" BOSS SR. on 03 Sep 1989 in Seaside, Clatsop, Oregon. He was born on 19 Jan 1912 in Mount Rainier, MD. He died on 19 Jul 2004 in Scottsdale, Maricopa, Arizona.

Allen Garrett Berg and Louise Theresa Conklin had the following children:

+41.   i.   DIANE CAROLINE[3] BERG was born on 31 Oct 1941 in Portland, Multnomah County, Oregon. She married STEVE COLVIN.

+42.   ii.   JUDY ANN BERG was born on 20 May 1943 in Portland, Multnomah County, Oregon. She married (1) DONALD JOHNSON. She married (2) TED ARMACK on 05 Oct 1973 in Las Vegas, Nevada.

Generation 4

30. **JEAN CLEO[4] LIVINGSTON** (Minnie Eddeva[3] "Eddeva" Wheeler, Mary Bell[2] Lingren, Francis Frederick[1] "Frank" Lingren, Roy) was born on 31 Jan 1922 in Eureka, Humboldt County, California. He died on 21 Mar 1967 in Eureka, Humboldt County, California. He married Delphine Frances Meister on 28 Feb 1947 in Eureka, Humboldt County, California. She was born on 24 Sep 1924 in Ferndale, Humboldt, California, USA.

Jean Cleo Livingston and Delphine Frances Meister had the following children:

43.   i.   ROBERT ROY[5] LIVINGSTON was born on 11 Jul 1954. He died about 2010 in

Placerville, El Dorado, California, USA.

44.   ii.   MARY FRANCES LIVINGSTON was born on 22 Mar 1959 in Eureka, Humboldt County, California. She married Craig Carbrey in 1996 in Petaluma, Sonoma, California, USA. He was born on 11 Jul 1948 in Colusa, California, USA.

Dave Conklin and Mary (Livingston) Carbrey (2nd cousins 1x removed) meet for the first time at her house near Sacramento, 3 May 2017.

37.   DAVID GENE[3] "DAVE" CONKLIN was born on 03 Nov 1948 in Lynwood, California (St Francis Hospital). He married Mary Lavonne Guerra on 22 Nov 1969 in Moscow, Latah, Idaho, USA. She was born on 15 Jun 1949 in Boise, Ada, Idaho.

38.   RITA MARIE CONKLIN was born on 23 Aug 1950 in Lynwood, California (St Francis Hospital). She married (1) JAMES MACDONALD in Spokane, Washington. She married (2) RODNEY N REEVE in Seattle, King, Washington (Episcopal Church in The Highlands).

39.   JOAN LOUISE "JONI" CONKLIN was born on 16 Feb 1952 in Lynwood, California. She died on 04 Aug 1979 in Idaho (died in plane crash in Salmon River, Idaho). She married (1) MICHAEL SCIACCOTTI. She married (2) ROBERT FULTON.

40.   LORIE ANN "LORI" CONKLIN was born on 14 Apr 1955 in Lynwood, California (St Francis Hospital). She married James Gray about 1975. He was born about 1955 in Spokane, Washington.

41.   DIANE CAROLINE[4] BERG (Louise Theresa[3] Conklin, Caroline[2] "Carrie" Lingren, Francis Frederick[1] "Frank" Lingren, Allen Garrett, Emanuel) was born on 31 Oct 1941 in Portland, Multnomah County, Oregon. She married STEVE COLVIN

42.   JUDY ANN[4] BERG (Louise Theresa[3] Conklin, Caroline[2] "Carrie" Lingren, Francis Frederick[1] "Frank" Lingren, Allen Garrett, Emanuel) was born on 20 May 1943 in Portland, Multnomah County, Oregon. She married (1) DONALD JOHNSON. She married (2) TED ARMACK on 05 Oct 1973 in Las Vegas, Nevada.

Generation 5

For Generation 5 see "Generation 4" in Part I, Chapter 5 Charles William Conklin and Caroline Lingren, beginning on page 71.

Part III. The Descendants of Stevan Marinković

Steve marenkovré

With information on his ancestors
to the 1860s in Croatia

Introduction to Part III

My purpose in compiling Part III is to promote an appreciation of the Marinković family as part of the Conklin family history and an appreciation of both those born into the family and those married into the family as my grandmother did. I have centered this part of the book on my maternal grandparents, Stevan Marinković and Ana Marinković. Although I never met my maternal great grandparents, I am thankful that I knew their daughter, my maternal Grandmother Ana Marinković who was still alive when I was a child.

Again, remember that when we look at our parents and grandparents we often catch glimpses of ourselves, and it's not just from shared DNA. The people who raise us shape us, almost invisibly, through the values they convey, their convictions, and especially through their actions. I have included brief information about each person's education, occupation, military and public service when that information was available. I would hope that Stevan and Ana would be pleased to know that many in the family seek to honor their parents, their communities, and their heritage.

The findings presented here are based solely on my research, primarily over the past three years. The discovery of additional sources or interpretations may affect the conclusions.

The Format

The National Genealogical Society Quarterly (NGSQ) generation numbering system format is also used in Part III of this book in order of descent from the oldest paternal ancestor (Josif Marinković, 1850s) to the sixth generation (Isabelle Conklin, 2004). I only show the direct lineage for each of the ancestors of Stevan. I list all of the children for each ancestor, but only the ancestors of Stevan are listed in the next generation. Details of ancestors' lives are mentioned when available. I included all the descendants of Josif Marinković that I found. Even with this book only going back six generations, it has still been a challenge as there are more than 40 descendants of Stevan and Ana Marinković and the number continues to increase.

For the most part this book is written in English using the Latin alphabet, however our Serbian ancestors' names and locations were originally written in Serbian which uses the Cyrillic alphabet used by the Serbian Orthodox Church beginning in the sixth century. Families in Croatia that converted to the Catholic Church after the invasion of Charlemagne in the ninth century, began using the Latin alphabet. So modern Serbo-Croatian is written in either alphabet depending upon the country. This therefore affects the English spelling and pronunciation.

For example, when you change the Serbian Cyrillic spelling of our family name МАРНHKOBNh to the Croatian Latin spelling, it becomes **Marinković**. However, if you spell it phonetically in English it becomes **Marinkovich** with the **ch** representing the sound of the Cyrillic letter **h**. So it depends if you want to spell it closer to how it looks in Cyrillic, or closer to how it sounds In Cyrillic. That is why it is difficult to understand and to translate family history research from Serbo-Croatian to English. Also, poor spelling and not hearing the name spoken correctly by immigration, census, and other government officials (ie. Betty Marinković's birth certificate: "Wubasanna Moronkovitz") can make the name of a person or location almost incomprehensible. It is not hard to see why many family members adopted English names, or at least English pronunciation and spelling of their names, soon after they began attending school in America.

For the purposes of this book I use the Serbo-Croatian Latin spelling of family names and locations (i.e *Ana Marinković* vs. Anna Marinkovích). Though the spoken word will not always be phonetic in the English pronunciation, the written word will recognizable by both English and Croatian speakers. If it is a Serbo-Croatian word but not a family name, it will be italicized to indicate it should be pronounced as such (i.e. *Slavonija*).

Chapter 1 is about the Marinković ancestors. Practically all the information about Stevan's ancestors was obtained from published sources describing the Balkan region and its ethnic history due to the lack of both written and oral sources from family ancestors themselves.

Chapter 2 is about the lives of Stevan Marinković and Ana Marinković, the focus of this part of the book.

The remaining chapters list the descendants of Stevan and Ana Marinković with a separate chapter for each of Stevan and Ana Marinković's 10 children that lived to be adults, beginning with the oldest, Mileva (Chapter 3) to the youngest, Dantsa (Chapter 8).

Each descendant is assigned a number. Also, for both ancestors and descendants, a small number appears after their first name, or after their middle name if they have a middle name. This number indicates what generation of descendant this person is relative to the person listed at the beginning of the chapter. For example, Stevan Marinković is person number 2 listed in Chapter 1. The 6 after Isabelle signifies that she is the 6th generation descending from Josif Marinković who is listed at the beginning of Chapter 1 as person number 1.

Each of Stevan's ancestors' names appears in parentheses after their name. First, his father Josif Marinković is followed by 1 indicating that Josif Marinković is the 1st generation that I have any information on. If we someday find Stevan's grandfather, he would become the 1st generation, and so on.

For descendants that married a person that already had children, I have included these children and their families in the book. Although they are not descendants by blood line, they are part of the Marinković family through marriage. Similarly, adopted children are included when their information was provided.

As a reminder, this book was developed with the "Family Tree Maker" computer application. Each of the chapters of the descendants of Stevan and Ana Marinković was developed from a separate "Descendant" genealogy report file built with "Family Tree Maker." Each generation has a number for each descendant of the primary person starting with a "2." When there is a plus sign in front of the number, it indicates that the descendant also had children and will be listed again under the next generation farther along in the book.

This methodology is used to keep all of the descendants of each of Stevan's children in one chapter. If we had just used one file for all the descendants, the family members would appear mixed through the entire book, because the report file lists all descendants by generation. You can also use the index to find the name and page with information for that individual.

Marinković Family Movement

Much of the Serbian population in former Yugoslavia was forced to migrate from one area to the other throughout the centuries. During the Middle Ages and especially during Ottoman occupation (1371-1878), and later during Austro-Hungarian and Habsburg rule (1878-1918), Serbian people were constantly migrating. During the middle ages they were resettled on large areas which were depopulated as Croatian nobles and their peasants left fearing the Turks. The Ottoman Turks colonized Croatian lands by forcing Serbian peasants from the Old Serbia around Kosovo to move north, farm the land, pay taxes, and defend their interests (Kinross, 1977, p. 47).

The region of Slavonia became a Slavic state in the 7th century. It was once in the Roman Imperial provinces of Illyricum and Pannonia.

As the border between Austria and the Ottoman Empire shifted back and forth these settlements in Croatia were used as a border shield. Later Austrians did the same by offering Serbian people privileges. Other Serbian people migrated to Croatian lands in an attempt to flee from the Turkish tax collectors. After some time Turkish expansion to the West forced them to flee further to the West and North. One of the routes was Northern Macedonia to Old Serbia to Bosnia, then to the Dalmatian hinterland and the Croatian part of the Pannonian Plain (Slavonia).

Since the Serbian people often moved from one area to another, tracing families is very difficult. The family name Marinković means "son of Marinko" (Professor Milica Grkovic, Serbian Academy of Sciences and Arts in Belgrade). The name can be found all over former Yugoslavia so not all persons with the Marinković surname are related. Today, Marinković families can be found in all three ethnographic regions of Croatia: the Adriatic Coast, Dalmatian Hinterland, and Pannonian Plain.

Right: Damage from the Croat-Serb war of 1991-1996 is still evident on the Serbian Orthodox Church in Pakrac, 25 Aug 2016.

One way to determine which Marinković family we may be related to is by the family patron saint. Patron Saints are extremely important in the Eastern Orthodox faith and it is extremely rare that a family would change the saint. Sons continue to celebrate the patron saint of their fathers and paternal grandfathers. On the day (*Slava*) of the family patron saint there is a celebration at home and friends and family visit to celebrate. Special food is served and special bread decorated with Christian symbols is blessed by the priest (a cross is made with a knife and wine is poured on it). Since there were many Eastern Orthodox churches in the area of Slavonia dedicated to Saint Sava (January 27), and our family celebrated *Slava* Day near the end of January at Saint Sava Serbian Church in Los Angeles, Saint Sava may be our patron saint, but I am still trying to confirm this. Other patron saint days celebrated in January include Saint Stefan (January 9), just after Orthodox Christmas, and Saint John (January 20).

Another way is to find Marinković relatives in the Croatian villages (Kricke, Pakrac) where grandparents Stevan and Ana Marinković say they were born. To this end my sister Rita and I traveled to Croatia in August 2016 and contracted with Snezana Bulatovic of Serbian Heritage Tours in Belgrade to research these locations and be our guide and interpreter to these villages.

We found that there are not one but three Kricke villages in Croatia, two of which are within 15 kilometers of the larger town of Pakrac:

1. Kricke (Sibenik) lies east of Sibenik in Dalmatian hinterland. It could have been one of the migratory stations of the other Kricke inhabitants. All three villages were mostly inhabited by Orthodox Serbs and during migrations Serbian people would often give the names of their ancestor's villages (from where they started migrations or villages where they stayed for a longer time) to their new villages. The two other villages are in *Slavonija*.

2. Kricke (Novska), is near the town Novska, about 15 kilometers southwest of Pakrac. According to the 2011 Census there were only 23 inhabitants. In 1900 the population numbered 633 inhabitants and after that it was in constant decline. The inhabitants are using the cemetery in the village of Rajic today and went to the Church of Holy Archangels Gabriel and Michael in Rajic in the past. Later a new church dedicated to the Transformation of Our Lord was built in 1815. However, during the Second World War the church and complete archive with all registry books were burned down by Ustashe from the nearby Concentration Camp in *Jasenovac*. Today there is new church in Rajic.

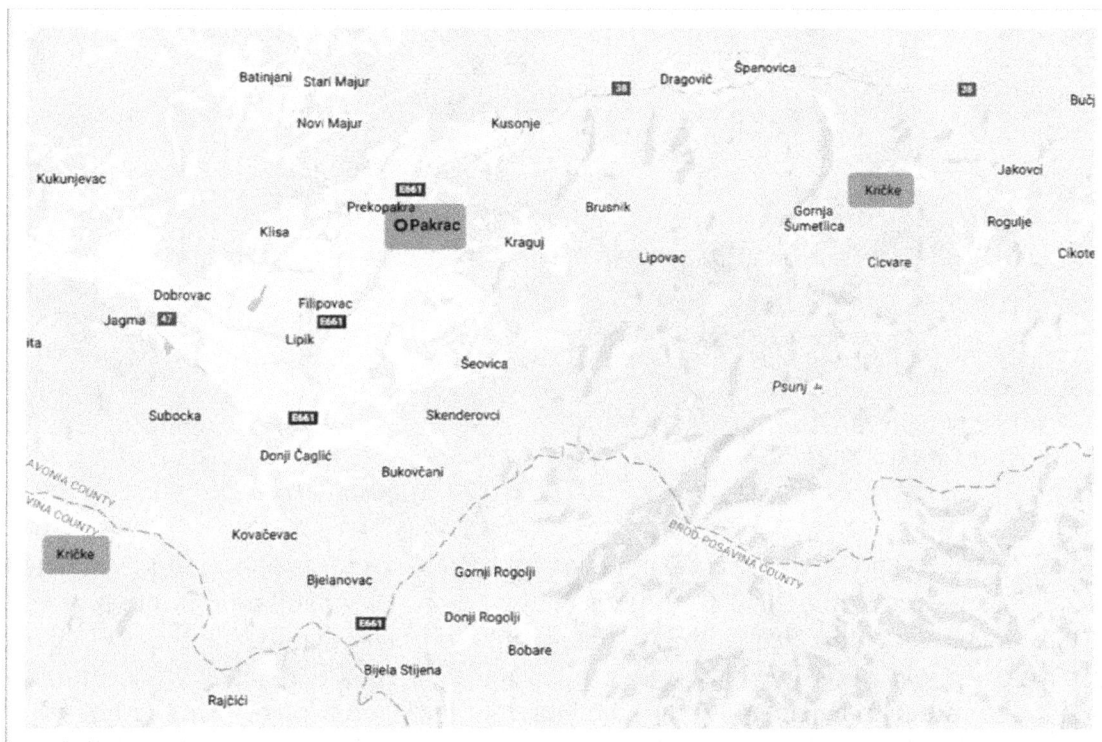

Map showing relationship of Kricke (Novska), on the left, to Kricke (Pakrac), on the right.

We found one church book with only two entries with the Marinković surname. These people could be relatives but also might not be. So we went to Kricke (Novska), took photos of the village, and spoke to Mr. Savo Marinković, Kricke #64, Novska 44330, Croatia who confirmed that Marinković families lived in both Krickes, two different villages at least 30 kilometers apart. Savo is 51 years old and does not know about his ancestors and his parents are dead but he says his family has lived in the village for more than 300 years. Savo also found out from an 80 year old lady in the village that Marinković families lived in both villages and as they were not related there were cases of marriages between them. That indicates that they probably came from different areas, or at least one branch came later, but definitely they did not come from the same area. Among Serbian Orthodox people it is very important not to marry relatives. They must be at least 4 generations apart, although usually it is far more. Inevitably living among Catholic population such marriages with relatives are common and it must have influenced Orthodox people up to a certain extent. (An Ancestry DNA test revealed a 71 percent probability that Savo Marinković is our 4th cousin-see Appendix 2).

David & Rita Conklin with Savo Marinković(center) and his Uncle Dushko Popović (right) in Kricke (Novska), Croatia. 24 August 2016.

3. Kricke (Pakrac) (known as Kričke Zabrdske from 1910-1981) is about 15 kilometers East of Pakrac. According to the 2011 Census there were only 19 inhabitants. In the period from 1900-1910 there were more than 250-280 inhabitants. It is clear that the number of inhabitants was growing and was a possible reason for emigration. Orthodox Serbs here were baptized and married in the church in Bucje known as the Church of the Ascension of Our Lord. It was built on the road between towns of Pakrac and Pozega in 1762 on the same place where there was a former Orthodox Church dedicated to Saint Nicholas. During the Second World War the church was destroyed by the Ustashe on the day of Saint Sava (January 27, 1942). The Parish Home was also destroyed and Birth, Marriage and Death Records are missing.

We traveled to the Kricke (Pakrac), took photos of the village, and inquired about Marinković families. We met a middle-aged man who was born there who said there were no Marinkovićs in the village that he knew of. Both villages have very few inhabitants as they suffered not only during the Second World War when many farmers were assassinated in concentration camps, but also in the Croat-Serb War of 1991-1996. Many inhabitants fled to other parts of former Yugoslavia.

We also traveled to the town of Pakrac, stayed overnight, visited the museum, Orthodox Church and Orthodox cemetery and took photos. In the cemetery we found only one Nicola Marinković gravestone (1894-1971) and could not read the older, taller gravestones from around 1900 when family members were still there. In fact I photographed a notice on one grave that says if the family does not maintain a grave for ten years, it will be removed for another burial on top of it. Since some if not all of the Marinković family had emigrated, it would almost be assured that any remaining graves would have been removed or molested by now. Similarly, I found that both Kricke's had cemeteries but they were not kept up and not accessible due to possible minefields left from the Croat-Serb war of 1991-1996.

Picture postcard "Greetings from Pakrac" dated 16 Mar 1899 –in the Hotel Pakrac.

In conclusion, during the Second World War, the Croatian Ustashe destroyed many Serbian Orthodox churches, and very few registry books from Orthodox churches survived the war. Also, many Serbian Orthodox people were assassinated either in their homes or were sent to concentration camps like the one in *Jasenovac* south of Pakrac. After the war the socialists did not care much about churches, but authorities collected registry books and sent them to the archives. Later some of the books were returned to churches and some books were later stolen from the churches.

Many people, including my ancestors, emigrated at the end of 19th century and beginning of the 20th century. For those that remained during the First World War the Austro-Hungarian Army was very hostile to Serbians. They recruited soldiers regardless of religion or nationality and many Serbians refused to fight against Serbia and left the Austro-Hungarian Army to join the Serbian Army. After the War during Agrarian Reform many Serbians from poor areas were given land in *Slavonija* (which was taken from Austro-Hungarian landlords).

During the Second World War many Serbians were either forced to convert to Catholicism or assassinated. After the War many left the countryside and moved to the cities. It was a time of intense industrialization and factory workers were in demand. Recently during the Croat-Serb war of 1991-1996, Serbians and their villages and churches in Croatia were again targeted. All of that contributed to the severe depopulation of Serbian villages in Croatia including Pakrac and Kricke.

Savo Marinković home, garden and corral in Kricke (Novska), Croatia. His ancestors have lived in the village for over 300 years, 24 August 2016.

Chapter 1. Ancestors of Stevan Marinković

This chapter presents the ancestors of Stevan and Ana Marinković beginning with Josif Marinković who was born in the 1860's. For more information about the context of these ancestors' life and times see *The Balkans: Nationalism, War and the Great Powers 1804-1999* (Glenny, 1999).

Generation 1

1. Josif[1] "Joe" Marinković was born about 1860 in Austria-Hungary (Slavonia). He married Stoja Babić about 1884 in Austria-Hungary (Slavonia). She was born about 1860 in Austria-Hungary (Slavonia).

Josif Marinković is the earliest ancestor that we can trace at this time. We only have his nickname on Stevan Marinković's death certificate and can only guess the date of his birth and death. We do not know who his parents were or where he was born but know that he and his wife Stoya Babić (also from Stevan Marinković's death certificate) were living in Kricke in 1885 when Stevan and his twin brother Mato were born. There were probably several more children but we do not know.

Possibly they came to the Pakrac area in 1876 after Serbia's disastrous war with the Turks, or in fear of the Serbo-Bulgarian war of 1885 (Glenny, 1999, p. 175), but probably hundreds of years earlier as other Marinković families had done. Perhaps they came from Bosnia where Turkish land laws retained by the Austro-Hungarian Empire (1878-1908) allowed 6,000 Muslim landowners to keep more than 100,000 Serb peasants under feudal conditions (Gerolymatos, 2002, p. 38). At that time, Slavonia was part of the Austro-Hungarian Empire and both Croats and Serbs were living and farming the area (see Introduction).

Left: Wood barn and fence with grape arbor and plum tree in Kricke (Pakrac), 25 Aug 2016.

These Serb peasants lived in small villages like Kricke; in primitive dwellings of brick, stone, timber and mud. Here in the forested hills above the Pannonian plain they relied on raising sheep, goats, pigs and chickens, and farming small plots of corn, beans, squash, grapes, plums and flax to maintain their meager existence as they continue to do today (Glenny, 1999, p. 293).

Other Marinković families did indeed live in Kricke. Records show that Ilija Marinković, a farmer, son of Petar and Pava Marinković, was born in 1879 in Kricke and lived in Lipik (a nearby village). At the age of 25, on February 1, 1904 he married Savida Marinković, a widow. She was the daughter of Stevo and Anica Martić, born in 1876 in Jagma (one of the villages in the area). Both Ilija and Savida were born and married around the same time as Stevo and Ana Marinković (Bulatovic, Feb 2016).

Also Jovan Marinković, a vegetable farmer born in Prnjavor, Bosnia, who was married and lived in Pakrac, died in a nearby hospital from marasmus universalis (a form of severe malnutrition) at the age of 66 on May 21, 1894. He was buried in Pakrac on May 23, 1894. At the time, many people from both Macedonia and Bulgaria were immigrating to the area. Bulgarians were known for growing vegetables and Macedonians for baking. Jovan Marinković, probably came to Pakrac from Prnjavor in search of work. So, there is a possibility that some Marinković families came with him or were his descendants (Bulatovic, Feb 2016).

We can only assume that for Josif Marinković and his wife Stoja Babić, there were probably very few opportunities to rise above the level of mere subsistance. They were probably illiterate, took on additional odd jobs to supplement their income, and hoped to have many children that could help on the farm.

Josif "Joe" Marinković and Stoja "Stojanka" Babić had the following children:

+2. i. STEVAN[2] "STEVE, STEVO" MARINKOVIĆ was born on 18 Oct 1885 in Kricke, Pozesko-Slavonska, Croatia. He died on 23 Jul 1936 in Los Angeles, California, USA (Buried in St Sava Serbian Cemetery, Los Angeles, CA). He married Ana Marinković, daughter of (Unknown) Marinković and Stojca Mattić, about 1905 in Croatia. She was born on 14 May 1883 in Pakrac, Pozesko-Slavonska, Croatia. She died on 29 May 1965 in Lynwood, Los Angeles, California, USA (Buried in St Sava Serbian Cemetery, Los Angeles, CA).

3. ii. MATO "MATKO, PANTO?" MARINKOVIĆ was born on 18 Oct 1885 in Kricke, Pozesko-Slavonska, Croatia (Twin brother of Stevan). He died on 17 Oct 1920 in Mahoning, Lawrence, Pennsylvania, USA (Reportedly killed in a train or lightning accident).

Generation 2

3. MATO[2] "MATKO, PANTO?" MARINKOVIĆ (JOSIF[1] "JOE" MARINKOVIĆ) was born on 18 Oct 1885 in Kricke, Pozesko-Slavonska, Croatia (Twin brother of Stevan as the second child of Josif Marinković and Stoja Babić). He had one sibling, namely Stevan. He died on 17 Oct 1920 in Mahoning, Lawrence, Pennsylvania, USA (Reportedly killed in a train or lightning accident).

Mato Marinković lived in Zagreb, Croatia in 1905. He arrived in America in 1906 (Age 21). He departed from Liverpool, England on 14 Mar 1906 (Ship S.S. Cedric). He arrived in New

York on 24 Mar 1906 (Reportedly arrived before brother Steve and sponsored him). He lived in Pittsburgh Ward 16, Allegheny, Pennsylvania, USA in 1910 (Age 25; Marital Status: Married; Relation to Head of House: Boarder). He was later employed by the Erie Steel Mills and was an Iron Mill Worker on 30 Jun 1912 in Lackawanna, Erie, New York, USA. He lived at 479 Thomas Ave, Lackawanna, New York on 30 Jun 1912. He was also known as Matko, Panto? Race: (White).

Mato may be Matko, the Serbian diminutive of Matej or Matija, meaning "gift of Jehova." According to my Aunt Dorothy, Mato immigrated to America so he would not get drafted into the Austro-Hungarian Army. She also said that Ana liked him more than her future husband Steve. Passenger lists show that Mato emigrated on the S.S. Cedric from Liverpool to New York in March 1906, and worked as a laborer in Fairmont, West Virginia. Within a year he was in Pittsburgh probably working in the Steel Mills where Steve joined him when he emigrated in 1907. Border crossing documents for Steve show Mato living in Lackawanna, New York in June, when brother Steve visited. Aunt Dorothy said he was killed either in a train or lightning accident in Pennsylvania sometime during the First World War. We do not know if he was ever married or where he is buried at this time.

Stevo Marinković Border Crossing from Canada to U.S. June, 1912.

Chapter 2. Stevan Marinković and Ana Marinković

1. **STEVAN**[2] **"STEVE, STEVO" MARINKOVIĆ** (Josif[1] "Joe") was born on 18 Oct 1885 in Kricke, Pozesko-Slavonska, Croatia. He died on 23 Jul 1936 (Age 50) in Los Angeles, California, USA heart disease aggravated by pneumonia). He married ANA MARINKOVIĆ, daughter of (Unknown) Marinković and Stojca Mattić, about 1905 in Croatia. She was born on 14 May 1883 in Pakrac, Pozesko-Slavonska, Croatia. She died on 29 May 1965 (Age 82) in Lynwood, Los Angeles, California, USA (Buried in St Sava Serbian Cemetery, Los Angeles, CA).

Stevan "Steve, Stevo" Marinković and Ana "Anna, Annie" Marinković had the following children:

2. i. (BOY)[3] MARINKOVIĆ was born about 1906 in Slavonia (Born when Ana was living with Steve's parents). He died about 1912 in Slavonia.

+3. ii. MILEVA "MILLIE, MILDRED" MARINKOVIĆ was born on 24 Jul 1913 in Salem Ward 3, Columbiana, Ohio, USA (133 Mill Street). She died on 14 Feb 1978 in Anaheim, Orange, California, USA (Buried in St Sava Serbian Cemetery, Los Angeles, CA). She married Arthur Jensen on 08 Nov 1935 in Los Angeles, California, USA.

+4. iii. BETTY "VUKOSAVA, ZUTA, ELIZABETH" MARINKOVIĆ was born on 24 Apr 1915 in Salem Ward 3, Columbiana, Ohio, USA (7 Prospect Sreet). She died on 06 Aug 1987 in Spokane, Spokane, Washington, USA. She married (1) WILLIAM DEUTSCH on 04 Jan 1935 in Santa Ana Canyon, Orange, California, USA. He was born in 1912 in Connecticut, USA. She married (2) CHARLES FRANKLIN "CHARLIE, CHUCK" CONKLIN, son of Charles William Conklin and Caroline "Carrie" Lingren, on 08 Nov 1946 in 12021 Long Beach Blvd, Lynwood, Los Angeles, California (Colonial Wedding Chapel). He was born on 17 Aug 1913 in Marshfield, Coos, Oregon. He died on 23 Mar 2005 in Scottsdale, Maricopa, Arizona.

5. iv. MARY MARINKOVITZ was born on 08 Jun 1916 in Salem Ward 3, Columbiana, Ohio, USA. She died on 28 Mar 1918 in Salem Ward 3, Columbiana, Ohio, USA.

6. v. ANDY MARINKOVIĆ was born about Aug 1917 in Salem Ward 3, Columbiana, Ohio, USA. He died on 20 Apr 1918 in Salem Ward 3, Columbiana, Ohio, USA.

7. vi. MARY MARINKOVITCH was born about Aug 1917 in Salem Ward 3, Columbiana, Ohio, USA. She died on 20 Apr 1918 in Salem Ward 3, Columbiana, Ohio, USA.

8. vii. MARY MARINKOVIĆ was born on 06 Nov 1918 in Salem Ward 3, Columbiana, Ohio, USA. She died on 17 Nov 1964 in Los Angeles, California, USA (Buried in St Sava Serbian Cemetery, Los Angeles, CA). She married GEORGE WIRTZ.

+9. viii. BOGDAN MARINKOVIĆ-ROBERT CROSS "BILL, WILLIAM" MARKOVIC was born on 10 Jul 1920 in Salem Ward 3, Columbiana, Ohio, USA. He died on 10 Apr

1995 in Lynwood, Los Angeles, California, USA (Buried in Rose Hills Memorial Park, Whittier, California). He married Florba May Grazier on 03 May 1946 in Lynwood, Los Angeles, California, USA (Lutheran Church). She was born on 10 Apr 1922 in Akron, Summit, Ohio, USA. She died on 11 Apr 1992 in Aurora (Marionville), Missouri (Crafton-Cantrell Funeral Home).

+10.   ix.   JOY "ZORKA, JOY RUBE" MARINKOVIĆ was born on 13 May 1922 in New Castle, Lawrence, Pennsylvania, USA. She died on 10 Mar 1973 in Ferndale, Whatcom, Washington, USA (Niche in Greenacres Memorial Park). She married (1) EDWARD "SWAMPY" DAVES on 12 Jun 1944 in Los Angeles, California, USA. He was born in 1922. She married (2) SIDNEY MAURICE ASHER, son of Louis L. Asher and Bessie Pantoskey, about 1945 in Fresno, Fresno, California, USA. He was born on 25 Dec 1897 in Lithuania. He died on 16 Jul 1966 in Fresno, Fresno, California, USA (Age: 68). She married (3) THEODORE T. FURBER on 16 Nov 1966 in Fresno, Fresno, California, USA. He was born about 1921. He died on 09 Apr 1977 in Bellingham, Whatcom, Washington, USA.

+11.   x.   DOROTHY "DOTTIE, DANTSA, DANITSA" MARINKOVIĆ was born on 13 Jun in New Castle, Lawrence, Pennsylvania, USA. She died on 16 Oct 2005 in Fresno, California. She married Ervin Schmale in about 1942 (Ervin "Smiley" Schmale

A separate chapter is written for each of Stevan and Ana's children that lived to be adults.

Thursday June 13, 2013 my wife Mary, daughter Dacia and I went to the Serbian Cemetery at the old St. Sava Church on Eastern Ave & 3rd Street in Los Angeles (Boyle Heights), California to see the Marinković family graves. We located Stevan Marinković's gravestone on the east side in the 3rd Row from Humphreys Avenue. As a child I used to come here with my family every year on Orthodox Easter to celebrate (*na zadushnitsa*) at the church with my cousins, aunts, uncles and Grandma Ana and to visit my grandfather's grave, who died 12 years before I was born.

Inscription:

FATHER
HERE RESTS
STEVAN MARINKOVIĆ
BORN OCT 1885 IN VILLAGE
KRICKE, SLAVONIJA
DIED JULY 23, 1936
GRAVESTONE ERECTED BY
HIS WIFE ANA AND CHILDREN
REST IN PEACE

The difference this time is that I had learned the Cyrillic during my Army tour in Bulgaria and could finally read his epitaph and discover the village he came from.

We soon met the Mexican caretaker Pedro Gabbarro "vich" (so he told us) from nearby East Los Angeles and gave him some money to restore and polish the tombstone so we could read it better and make it last longer. This is how I discovered where my grandfather was born.

Nothing has been found about his family or early life in Croatia before he immigrated to America. Since he was born in Kricke, we know he was the son of a farmer as most likely was his father. They called him "Stevo" which is the Serbian diminutive for Stevan, and later "Steve" in America. We know that he was already 20 years old and married to Ana with a child when his brother Mato immigrated to America in March 1906 about the time of the "Pig War" between Austria and Serbia (Lyon, 2015, p. 44). According to his daughter Betty, Stevan and Ana were living with Stevan's parents at that time. After hearing from his brother in America, in May 1907 Stevan also immigrated to America (possibly anticipating Austria's annexation of Bosnia in 1908) leaving his family behind for five more years (Marinkovic B. , 1980).

Right: Undated photo of Stevan Marinković –from Don Jensen collection.

Stevan Marinković lived in Kricke, Slavonia in 1906 (then part of Austria). He departed from Liverpool, England on 08 May 1907 (SS Adriatic). He was described as light complexion, black hair, black eyes, 5ft 6in tall when he arrived in New York, New York on 18 May 1907 (Age 24). He was employed by Carey Alley as an Iron Mill Worker in 1910 in Pittsburgh, Allegheny, Pennsylvania, USA. He lived in Pittsburgh, Allegheny, Pennsylvania, USA in 1910 (Age 25; Marital Status: Single; Relation to Head of House: Boarder). He lived at 84 Strand Street, Hamilton, Ontario, Canada in June 1912 (Laborer). He was described as medium complexion, brown hair, brown eyes, 5ft 7in tall on 30 Jun 1912 in Niagara Falls, New York. He arrived in Niagara Falls, New York, USA on 30 Jun 1912. He lived in Salem Ward 3, Columbiana, Ohio, USA on 24 Jul 1913 133 (now 451) Mill Street. He lived in Salem Ward 3, Columbiana, Ohio, USA in 1917 at 67 (now 470 E) Perry Street. He was described as Medium height, stout build, black hair, and brown eyes in 1917 in Salem Ward 3, Columbiana, Ohio, USA. He was employed by a Pool Room he operated at 108 Broadway Ave on 12 Sep 1918 in Salem Ward 3, Columbiana, Ohio, USA. He lived in Salem Ward 3, Columbiana, Ohio, USA in 1920 at 22 (now 154) Broadway Ave. He lived in New Castle, Lawrence, Pennsylvania, USA on 13 May 1922 (Joy & Dorothy born in New Castle). He lived in South Gate, Los Angeles, California, USA in 1930 (Age 43; Marital Status: Married; Relation to Head of House: Head). He lived in 10414 San Antonio Ave, South Gate, Los Angeles, California, USA on 09 Jan 1930.

1890s photo of Serbian children in Pakrac --photo from Hotel Pakrac.

Stevan Marinković photo on his gravestone in the Serbian Cemetery in Los Angeles CA.

He was employed by Whiting-Meade Enamel Worker in 1934 in Vernon, Los Angeles, California, USA. He was buried on 25 Jul 1936 in Los Angeles, California, USA (St Sava Serbian Cemetery). He was also known as Steve, Stevo. His cause of death was Heart Disease and Bronchopneumonia. He was affiliated with the Serbian Orthodox religion. Race: (Serbian).

When Stevan arrived in America he went to Pittsburgh where his brother was working and first shows up on the 1910 Census. Between 1910 and 1912 he was apparently working as a laborer in Ontario, Canada. By this time he had sent for Ana, and she met him in New York after she arrived in June 1912. According to his daughter Betty, "My father went to America and sent for my mother. He was in New York when she arrived and they moved to Ohio (Marinkovic B. , 1980). From 1913-1920 they lived in Salem, Ohio and continued building a family, having seven more children in Ohio and two in Pennsylvania of which six survived.

Right: Steve Marinković's 1918 World War I draft registration card.

He ran a Pool Room on 108 Broadway according to his 1917 Draft Registration; and according to his children he was a drinker, a gambler, and was so mean to Ana that she requested her grave be at the opposite end of the cemetery from his when she died many years later.

Sometime in 1920, perhaps due to his drinking or gambling, the family moved to a farm outside of New Castle, Pennsylvania where two more daughters were born. Steve might have known someone who got him a job here from his earlier stay in Pittsburgh. According to his daughter Betty, "I was five or six years old when we moved to New Castle, and then we had to go to the farm (Marinkovic B. , 1980).

By the beginning of the Great Depression in October 1929 the family had left Pennsylvania and moved to California by train according to Millie's daughter Susan Jensen (Jensen S. , 2015). Most likely Steve was invited by an earlier co-worker who had moved there. "My mother Ana said I lost a bootie at the Chicago train station during the trip," (Marinkovic D. , 2002).

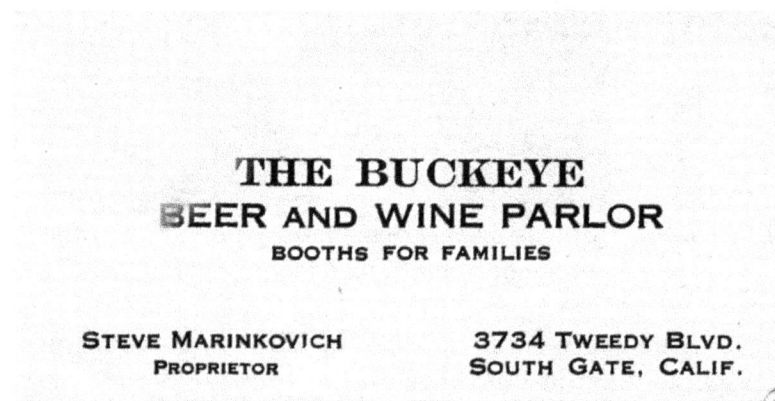

Left: Steve   Marinković's business card from the Buckeye Café.

THE BUCKEYE
BEER AND WINE PARLOR
BOOTHS FOR FAMILIES

STEVE MARINKOVICH
PROPRIETOR

3734 TWEEDY BLVD.
SOUTH GATE, CALIF.

According to granddaughter Susan Jensen, Steve started another Pool Room in South Gate. "My father (Art Jensen) bought the Buckeye Cafe (later renamed Arts Dine & Dance, then Go Slow Joes) in South Gate on San Gabriel and Tweedy Blvd. after Steve died." (Jensen S. , 2015). To make ends meet, or possibly to pay off gambling debts, Steve also became a bathtub enameller at Whiting-Meade in nearby Vernon, California. "He didn't use a mask and got it all down his lungs." (Marinkovic B. , 1980). The primary cause of his death in 1936 was a heart attack but it was aggravated by bronchopneumonia. He left behind a widow, a son, and five daughters who grew to adulthood.

Ana Marinković was born on 14 May 1883 in Pakrac, Pozesko-Slavonska, Croatia as the first child of (Unknown) Marinković and Stojca Mattić. She had at least three siblings, namely: Sister1, Sister2, and Brother1. She died on 29 May 1965 in Lynwood, Los Angeles, California, USA (head trauma from fall). When she was 21, she married Stevan Marinković, son of Josif Marinković and Stoja Babić, about 1905 in Croatia.
Ana Marinković lived in Kricke, Slavonia in 1912 (then part of Hungary). She departed from Trieste, Italy on 25 May 1912. She arrived in New York, New York, USA on 09 Jun 1912 (Age 28, ship name Kaiser Franz Josef I).

Left: The Kaiser Franz Josef was the largest passenger ship of its kind in Austria-Hungary in 1912. More than 200,000 immigrants departed from Trieste during the first decade of the 20th century, including Ana Marinković.

She lived in 133 (now 451) Mill St Salem, Columbiana, Ohio, USA on 24 Jul 1913. She lived in 7 (now 417) Prospect St, Salem, Columbiana, Ohio, USA on 24 Apr 1915. She lived in 67 (now 470 E) Perry St Salem, Columbiana, Ohio, USA on 08 Jun 1916. She lived in 67 Perry St Salem, Columbiana, Ohio, USA on 06 Nov 1918. She lived in 22 (now 154) Broadway St, Salem Ward 3, Columbiana, Ohio, USA in 1920 (Age: 37; Marital Status: Married; Relation to Head of House: Wife). She lived in 22 Broadway St Salem, Columbiana, Ohio, USA on 10 Jul 1920. She lived in New Castle, Lawrence, Pennsylvania, USA on 13 May 1922. She lived in South Gate, Los Angeles, California, USA in 1930 (Age: 46; Marital Status: Married; Relation to Head of House: Wife). She lived at 10414 San Antonio Ave, South Gate, Los Angeles, California, USA on 9 Jan 1930. She lived in 10414 San Antonio Ave, South Gate, Los Angeles, California, USA on 1 Apr 1940 (Age 56; Marital Status: Widowed; Relation to Head of House: Head). She was described as medium complexion, grey hair, blue eyes, stocky, 4ft 11in tall about 1960 in Lynwood, Los Angeles, California, USA. She lived at 10908 Lewis Rd, Lynwood, Los Angeles, California, USA in May 1965. Her funeral took place on 2 Jun 1965 in Lynwood, Los Angeles, California, USA (Carter-Liewer Funeral Home). She was buried on 02 Jun 1965 in Los Angeles, California, USA (Buried in St Sava Serbian Cemetery, Los Angeles, CA). She was also known as Anna, and Annie. Her cause of death was cerebral contusions & subdural hemorrhage (cranial trauma from fall). She was affiliated with the Serbian Orthodox religion. Race: (Serbian).

Left: Ana Marinković, widow of Stevan Marinković, Los Angeles, May 1940.

Unfortunately nothing has been found about Ana's family or early life in Croatia before she immigrated to America. She said she was from Pakrac near Zagreb. She was probably the offspring of a peasant farmer, possibly from Kricke where several Marinković families lived as well, but we do not know. She must have had some formal schooling in Croatia because she told me she was left-handed like me, but was hit on her left hand with a stick if she did not write right-handed. She said she had two sisters and a brother (Jensen S. , 2015), and was two years older than her husband Stevan Marinković when they married. As was the custom, they moved in with Stevan's parents in Kricke after they were married, and she soon had a little boy (Marinkovic B. , 1980). She wove a *kilim* (blanket, see photo) for him which she brought to America after he died. It was later given to her daughter Betty for her son David, then to Betty's daughter Joan for her daughter Anna, and was destroyed in a house fire in 1982.

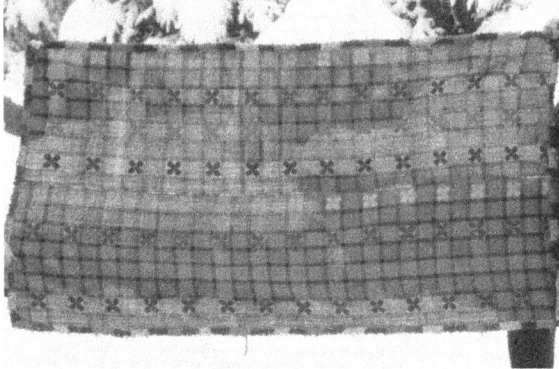

Left: The 40 by 72in Kilim Ana wove for her first child in Kricke, Croatia about 1906.

Right: Kilim in the Ethnographic Museum in Zagreb, Croatia, 21 Aug 2016.

We do not know the name of Ana's first son, but she was probably working in the fields, washing clothes, and milking goats up until she gave birth. Custom did not permit her to make any sign that she was in labor (Gerolymatos, 2002, p. 39). As was the custom, she was most likely assisted in birth at home or in the field by her mother-in-law. Within a year "Stevan went to America and sent for her. She didn't want to come, but she couldn't stand living with her mother-in-law either. When her boy died with diarrhea at the age of 5, she finally decided to join Stevan in America" (Marinkovic B. , 1980). Ana's daughter Dorothy said Ana didn't know why he died, he just "*dobi, bola, stani uva*" (good, (then) sick, (then)up and died) (Marinkovic D. , 2002). So in 1912, just as the First Balkan War broke out, Ana set sail for America. Her husband Stevan met her in New York after she arrived and they soon moved to Ohio (Marinkovic B. , 1980).

The family lived in Salem, Ohio for about eight years, then moved to New Castle, Pennsylvania for another eight years before moving to Southern California in about 1929 where Stevan and Ana raised their son and five daughters. Ana still corresponded with her sisters and brother back in Croatia during this time. They had survived the First World War, but then came the Second. After the German occupation of Yugoslavia in 1941 Croatian Fascists, known as the Ustashe, established an independent state of Croatia and began to exterminate Eastern Orthodox Serbs, turning Croatia into a slaughterhouse. Between 1941 and 1944 they rounded up and killed 750,000 Serbs in Yugoslavia (Gerolymatos, 2002, p. 242). According to her granddaughter Susan Jensen, "My family and I lived with Ana in South Gate from about 1938 to 1948. During the Second World War she got this letter and sat down and started crying. It said the Croatians turned her relatives in to the Nazis who shot them all: her two sisters, her niece, and brother. The only relatives she had left were the children (Kata and Ljubomir) of the daughter of one of her sisters that was killed. She was able to visit them in Zagreb in 1961." (Jensen S. , 2015).

Woman using a handmade loom, Zagreb Ethnographic Museum, 19 Aug 2016.

Ana Marinković (center) with niece Kata and nephew Ljubomir in Zagreb 1961.

I remember visiting Ana's house in South Gate, California many times during the 1950s where she watched us grandkids while our parents worked. It seemed to me that Ana always smelled like garlic, and she barked out orders to us in Serbian that we ignored at our own peril, as she only spoke broken English. One of her favorite phrases was, *"Ja sam proua Serbska"* (I am a proud Serbian). She turned her backyard into a garden of cabbage, melons, Concord grapes on overhead arbors, and pole beans growing up sticks for support, just as the gardens I saw in Kricke in 2016. She also had chickens and I remember seeing a turkey once. I also remember watching her make by hand large wide noodles for *pileca supa* (chicken soup) that all of us grandkids consumed with delight. Two other Serbian dishes we loved were *povitica* (poor man's bread, a kind of flatbread), and *sarma* (stuffed cabbage rolls). In December 1979 I wrote down the recipes for them as I watched my mother Betty make them like her mother did.

One of my mother Betty's favorite stories about Ana was when my mom brought her classmates over every day after school for peanut butter and jelly sandwiches. This would require Ana to walk to the nearby market and buy a jar of peanut butter almost every day. Finally one day the grocer asked her, "Lady what do you do with all this peanut butter? Are you using it to paper your walls?" Betty said that day was the last time she ever had a peanut butter and jelly sandwich.

Another story involves the aftermath of the March 1933 Long Beach Earthquake (Magnitude 6.4). Powerlines were down, and gas and water pipes were broken, but their house was still standing. Now Steve and Ana were worried about aftershocks and a possible tsunami. Soon daughter Millie heard a man yelling "water, water" and told her parents there was a tidal wave coming. So Ana packed up their 1929 Touring Buick, grabbed the children, and Steve drove them toward the mountains to avoid the tsunami. On Tweedy Boulevard they passed a policeman who asked where they were going in such a hurry, and when they told him he began laughing. Ana asked what was so funny and he said, "There's no tidal wave. The man yelling "water" came from the city to distribute drinking water from his tanker truck." Ana died in 1965 at the age of 82 after hitting her head from a fall in her house. We buried her at the other end of the Serbian Cemetery from her husband Steve, as she requested. In 1966 my dad sold his business and house in South Gate and we moved to Spokane, Washington.

Chapter 3. Mileva Marinković and Arthur Jensen

Generation 1

1. **MILEVA**[1] **"MILLIE, MILDRED" MARINKOVIĆ** was born on 24 Jul 1913 in 133 Mill Street, Salem Ward 3, Columbiana, Ohio, USA as the second child of Stevan Marinković and Ana Marinković. She had nine siblings, namely: (Boy), Betty, Mary, Andy, Mary, Mary, Bogdan, Joy, and Dorothy. She died on 14 Feb 1978 (Age 64) in Anaheim, Orange, California, USA. She married Einar Arthur Jensen, son of John William Jensen and Christine Ruth Finkelsen, on 08 Nov 1935 in Los Angeles, California, USA.

Mileva Marinković lived in Salem Ward 3, Columbiana, Ohio, USA in 1920 (Age 6; Marital Status: Single; Relation to Head of House: Daughter). She lived in New Castle, Pennsylvania in 1922, and in South Gate, Los Angeles, California in 1930 (Age 16; Marital Status: Single; Relation to Head of House: Daughter). She was described as light complexion, brown hair, brown eyes, 5ft 6in tall on 08 Nov 1935 in Los Angeles, California, USA. She lived in 10414 San Antonio Ave, South Gate, Los Angeles, California, USA in 1940 (Mother's house). She lived in Pioneer Blvd, Norwalk, California, USA in 1953 (Pioneer Paint & Hardware). She lived in Paramount Blvd, Downey, California, USA in 1961 (Jensens Paint & Hardware). She was buried in Feb 1978 in Los Angeles, California, USA (St Sava Serbian Cemetery). She was also known as Millie, Mildred. Race: (Serbian).

Millie was the first child of the Marinković family to be born in America. Maybe that is why I always remember her as a "take charge" kind of person. She had to be to help her mother Ana with a growing family. She was the first to attend school in America and the first to Americanize her name to "Mildred" or "Millie" while in grade school. As the story goes, when 8-year-old Millie and her 6-year-old sister *Vukosava* (my mother) attended grade school in the 1920s in Pennsylvania, the teacher could not pronounce her sister's name and began calling her "Sister." So Millie gave her the name of "Elizabeth" which soon became "Betty" for the rest of her life (Marinkovic B. , 1980). In 1929 the family moved by train from Pennsylvania to California.

Millie, daughter Susan, and Art Jensen in 1941—photo from Don Jensen collection.

Einar Arthur Jensen was born on 08 Oct 1912 in Minneapolis, Hennepin, Minnesota, USA as the second child of John William Jensen and Christine Ruth Finkelsen. He had five siblings: Irene, Juell, John, Lillian, and Henry. He died on 08 Sep 1990 in San Diego (Age 77). When he was 23, he married Mileva Marinković, daughter of Stevan Marinković and Ana Marinković, on 08 Nov 1935 in Los Angeles, California, USA.

Einar Arthur Jensen lived in Minneapolis Ward 12, Hennepin, Minnesota, USA in 1920 (Age 7; Marital Status: Single; Relation to Head of House: Son). He was described as light complexion, blond hair, blue eyes, 5ft 10in tall in 1935 in Los Angeles, California, USA. He lived in Norwalk, California, USA in 1953. He lived in Paramount Blvd, Downey, California, USA in 1961 (Jensens Paint & Hardware). He was buried in Sep 1990 in Rose Hills Memorial Park, Whittier, Los Angeles, California. He was also known as Art. Race: (White).

Art's father John William "JW" was a stonemason in Minneapolis (worked on the West Hotel) when Arthur was born. When he was 15 years old the family moved to Colfax, Wisconsin and bought a 212-acre farm. After a few years of working for his dad, Art had had enough of farm work and moved out, finding his way to Minnesota, Texas, and eventually California. Art met Millie and her four sisters while working at a fruit cannery in Southern California. Art and Millie spent time bowling and at Millie's father Steve's bar and poolroom on Tweedy Boulevard (Jensen E. A., 1985). They were married in 1935 and only a few months later Millie's father Steve died. They agreed to buy Steves' bar from his widow Ana and keep it open. In 1938 they moved in with Ana where they lived for the next ten years. Soon they changed the name of the bar to "Art's Dine & Dance." When they sold it, the bar was renamed "Go Slow Joe's Tavern," then it later became a Save-On drug store. In 1949 Art and Millie

moved to Desert Hot Springs with their young children and built a four-unit motel on a lot they bought for $200 (Jensen D. , Susan Jensen Eulogy, Oct 2017). Then in the early 1950's they moved to Norwalk and got into the hardware business, first building Pioneer Paint & Hardware, then Jensen's Paint & Hardware in Downey, where they eventually retired.

Left: Art Jensen at Steve's bar in South Gate, California in about 1938 –photo from Don Jensen collection.

Einar Arthur Jensen and Mileva Marinković had the following children:

+ 2. i. Susan Marian[2] Jensen was born on 14 Aug 1938 in Lynwood, Los Angeles, CA.
+ 3. ii. Donald Jensen was born on 27 Jul 1942 in Lynwood, Los Angeles, California.
  4. iii. Robert Arthur Jensen was born on 19 Aug 1948 in Lynwood, Los Angeles, California.

Generation 2

2. **SUSAN MARIAN**[2] **JENSEN** (Mileva[1] Marinković) was born on 14 Aug 1938 in Lynwood, Los Angeles, California, USA as the first child of Arthur Jensen and Mileva Marinković. She died on 25 Sep 2017 in Beaumont, San Bernadino, California. She had two siblings, namely: Donald Roy, and Robert Arthur. She married (1) Oscar Raymond "Ray" Walston in 1955 in Huntington Park, Los Angeles, California, USA (Baptist Church). She married (2) Thomas Scherwerts.

Susan Marian Jensen lived in 10414 San Antonio Ave, South Gate, Los Angeles, California, USA in 1940. She lived in 333 Calvert Park, Beaumont, Calif in 2015. She lived in 5260 W. Palmer Drive Banning, CA in 2016. She was also known as Marian Mildred Jensen and Susie Scherwerts. Her birth certificate shows her first name as Marian, but she said her father never liked that name so they changed it to Susan and her middle name to Marian. Nevertheless, when she was in trouble, her mother Millie would call out "Susan Jane Jensen, get over here!" adding "Jane" to make it rhyme for some reason (Jensen S. , 2015). Also, since I had two cousins named Susie and she was the oldest, as kids we referred to her as "big Susie," and called the younger one "little Susie."

Don and Susie Jensen (right) pose for a portrait in 1944 –photo from Don Jensen collection.

According to her brother Don, Susie began her "working career" at age 11 by helping her mom with the "cleaning chores" at the family-owned Motel in Desert Hot Springs. Susie attended grade school in Palm Springs, and it was only later she learned that her "girlfriends" were the children of Mafia gangsters from Chicago! She couldn't figure out why those men were always around them when they were playing.

In the early fifties the whole family participated in the building of what was to become "Pioneer Paint & Hardware" in Norwalk. Susie became Employee #1, followed shortly by Don at age 11. Susie went to middle-school and then Excelsior High School in Norwalk, where they later filmed the movie Grease. It was here she met her two life-long friends, Darleen and Fern. Don remembered them all listening to the latest "craze" called "Rock and Roll" on the Hunter Handcock Show. He also remembered that Mom made Susie drive him to Junior High School. Susie would drop him off at least one block away from school so that she wouldn't be spotted doing this duty! In High School, Susie was captain of the Flag Twirling Team that performed all over Southern California. The team performed at many events, including the Pomona State Fair.

After many secretarial and office manager positions during her early working career, Susie went to work for the State of California, with her final position serving as a tax consultant. She held seminars dealing with businesses big and small where she often answered at least 50 detailed questions on business taxation issues in California. She worked as a State Auditor for California for 15 years.

Later Susie was President of the local homeowner's association at two sub-divisions where she lived. She loved to tell the stories of all her people problems. Being the organizer she was, Susie was also President of her local Chapter of the California Federation of Republican Women. She really loved this job and the people she worked with. She also enjoyed the cruises she took with her daughter Ginger and brother Don. As Don recalled, "Susie and I took another cruise together in the Caribbean. In Costa Rica, I signed us up for a "Zip-Line" Tour through the jungle canopy. Susie thought it was going to be a bus tour! Being the good sport that she was, she joined me in climbing the tallest tree in the forest that led to the starting platform. I can still hear her screams as she disappeared into the jungle!" (Jensen D. , Susan Jensen Eulogy, Oct 2017).

Oscar Raymond Walston and Susan Marian Jensen had the following children:

+5.   i.   Ginger[3] Walston, born in 1959 in Lynwood, Los Angeles, California, USA (St Francis Hospital). She married Jerry Krueger.

Thomas Scherwerts and Susan Marian Jensen had no children.

*Don and Susie Jensen pose with Cousin Dave Conklin
at Don's house in Palm Springs, 30 Mar 2013.*

3. **DONALD ROY**^{2} **JENSEN** (Mileva^1 Marinković) was born on 27 Jul 1942 in Lynwood, Los Angeles, California, USA as the second child of Arthur Jensen and Mileva Marinković. He had two siblings, namely: Susan Marian, and Robert Arthur. He married Patty Jensen on 23 Jan 1965 in San Mateo CA (Methodist Church).

Children of Donald Jensen and Patty are:

+6.   i.   Karen Janine^5 Jensen was born on 18 Jul 1968 in Houston, Texas, USA. She married Todd Gregory Shields on 06 Jul 1991 in Cincinnati, Hamilton, Ohio, USA.
  7.   ii.   Paul Arthur Jensen was born on 27 Apr 1970 in Houston, Texas, USA.

4. **ROBERT ARTHUR**^{2} **JENSEN** (Mileva^1 Marinković) was born on 19 Aug 1948 in Lynwood, Los Angeles, California, USA as the third child of Arthur Jensen and Mileva Marinković. He had two siblings, namely: Susan Marian, and Donald Roy. Robert Arthur Jensen was also known as Bob, Bobby.

Bob, Susie, and Don Jensen, about 2010 –photo from Don Jensen collection.

Generation 3

5. **GINGER**^{5} **WALSTON** Was born in 1959 in Lynwood, Los Angeles, California, USA (St Francis Hospital). She married Jerry Krueger. She is a travel agent and operates La Dolce Vita Travel.

From left to right: Ginger Walston, her mother Susan Jensen, and Cousin Dave Conklin meet at Susan's home in Banning, California 21 Nov 2015.

Jerry Krueger and Ginger Walston had the following children:

    8.   i.   Corey[6] Krueger was born in May 1987 in San Diego, California, USA (Kaiser Hospital). He does television advertising voice-overs for major companies such as Subaru.

    9.   ii.   Amanda Krueger was born in Jun 1989 in San Diego, California, USA (Kaiser Hospital). She is a sales training manager for a national cosmetics company.

    10.   iii.   Angline Krueger was born in 1993. She is working toward a Master's degree in clinical phycology.

    11.   iv.   Jackson Krueger was born in Feb 1994. He is currently a claims adjuster for Geico Auto Insurance.

6. **KAREN JANINE[5] JENSEN** (Donald Roy[4], Mileva[3] "Millie, Mildred" Marinković, Donald Roy[4], Einar Arthur "Art", John William, Unk) was born on 18 Jul 1968 in Houston, Texas, USA. She married Todd Gregory Shields on 06 Jul 1991 in Cincinnati, Hamilton, Ohio, USA.

Todd Gregory Shields and Karen Janine Jensen had the following children:

    12.   i.   Savanna Jenine[6] Shields was born on 01 Jul 1995 in Fayetteville, Arkansas.

    13.   ii.   Dane Jensen Shields was born on 14 May 1997 in Fayetteville, Arkansas.

Generation 4

12. **SAVANNA "SAVVY" JENINE[6] SHIELDS** was born on 01 Jul 1995 in Fayetteville, Arkansas. In 2016 she won the Miss Arkansas contest and on 12 Sep 2017 she won the Miss America contest when she was 21 years old. Teen Vogue Magazine had this to say about Savvy:

"Savvy dazzled judges, including Olympic gold medalist Gabby Douglas and Shark Tank judge and entrepreneur Mark Cuban, with her talents and worthy platform to be crowned Miss America. The first runner-up was Rachel Wyatt from South Carolina. But there's a lot more to know about Savvy other than the fact that she looks amazing in a crown. Savvy is an art major at the University of Arkansas, and she thinks that deciding to focus on painting in college was a defining moment in her life. "In doing so, I came to realize that there are so many different lifestyles and beliefs other than my own and that they are all equally validated," she said, according to NJ.com."

"While Savvy would love to have an art studio, NJ.com reports that she would like to work at a museum following her reign as Miss America and then get a master's in fine arts. But Savvy's artistic talents don't stop at painting. Savvy wowed judges during the talent portion of the competition, when she danced a jazz routine to "They Just Keep Moving the Line" from the NBC musical series Smash. Our new Miss America is probably a member of the Bey-hive. Before taking the stage for her dance routine, Savvy told judges, "I want to be a backup dancer for Beyoncé. I feel like that's every dancer's secret dream is to be a backup dancer for Beyoncé, especially with her new tour."

"Savvy's a sorority girl. Before the competition, she thanked her Kappa Kappa Gamma sisters in an Instagram outside of her University of Arkansas sorority house. Savvy advocates for healthy eating, and her Miss America platform is "Eat better. Live better." She regularly Instagrams food inspiration on her official Instagram.

"Savvy has some advice for the presidential candidates. When asked about Hillary Clinton during the interview portion of the competition, Savvy instead decided to address Hillary and Donald Trump with the claim that while they have both done well thus far, "they also need to watch what they're doing." During an interview following her win, Newser reports, she continued, "What I want both candidates to focus on is compromise. Our country was founded on compromise. We're in a state now where both parties just seem to be yelling at one another" (Teen Vogue Magazine, 2016).

Don Jensen's granddaughter Savanna Shields being crowned Miss American on 12 Sep 2016 –photo from Teen Vogue.

Chapter 4. Betty Marinković and Charles Conklin

Generation 1

1. **BETTY**[1] **"VUKOSAVA, ZUTA, ELIZABETH" MARINKOVIĆ** was born on 24 Apr 1915 in Salem Ward 3, Columbiana, Ohio, USA (7 Prospect Street) as the third child of Stevan Marinković and Ana Marinković. She had nine siblings, namely: (Boy), Mileva, Mary, Andy, Mary, Mary, Bogdan, Joy, and Dorothy. She died on 06 Aug 1987 (Age 72) in Spokane, Washington, USA (acute pancreatitis). She married (1) WILLIAM DEUTSCH on 04 Jan 1935 in Santa Ana Canyon, Orange, California, USA. He was born in 1912 in Connecticut, USA. She married (2) CHARLES FRANKLIN "CHARLIE, CHUCK" CONKLIN, son of Charles William Conklin and Caroline "Carrie" Lingren, on 08 Nov 1946 in Lynwood, Los Angeles, California, USA (Colonial Wedding Chapel). He was born on 17 Aug 1913 in Marshfield, Coos, Oregon, USA. He died on 23 Mar 2005 in Scottsdale, Maricopa, Arizona, USA.

Betty Marinković lived at 67 Perry Street in Salem, Ohio, USA in 1920 (Age 4; Marital Status: Single; Relation to Head of House: Daughter). She lived in New Castle, Pennsylvania in 1922, and in South Gate, Los Angeles, California in 1930 (Age 15; Marital Status: Single; Relation to Head of House: Daughter). She was described as light complexion, blonde hair, blue eyes, 5ft tall, right-handed in 1950 in Los Angeles, California, USA. She lived at 10414 San Antonio Ave, South Gate, Los Angeles, California, USA in 1930 (Mother's house). She lived at 5236 Tweedy Blvd, South Gate, CA in 1947 (Atlantic Mattress Company), and 10248 Bowman Ave. in 1950. She lived at East 1217 26th Ave in Spokane, WA in 1966. She was buried in August 1987 in Spokane, Washington, USA (Greenwood Memorial Terrace). She was also known as *Vukosava, Zuta*, and Elizabeth. Race: (Serbian).

Right: Marinković family in the late 1930s. From left: Dorothy, Betty, Mileva, widow Ana, Bogdan (Bill). Not pictured: Joy, Mary.

My mom was the second child of the Marinković family in America, born less than two years after mother Ana arrived. She was first named "*Vukosava*" which means "Glory to the Wolf" in Serbian. "*Vuk*" or "*Vukashin*" means wolf. But she said "My mom (Ana) always called me "*Zuta*" because I was the only blonde, blue-eyed child in the family and *zuta kosa* means yellow hair in Serbian (Marinkovic B. , 1980). In about 1921 when she was 6 years old the family moved to a farm near New Castle, Pennsylvania where she started grade school. Since the teachers could not pronounce *Vukosava*, they called her "Sister" so her sister Millie gave her the new name of "Elizabeth" (which she formally adopted later as "Betty") (Marinkovic B. , 1980).

After the family moved to South Gate, California, as a teenager Betty began working with her sisters selling eggs and vegetables from their garden to their neighbors (Marinkovic D. , 2002). then in the summers at a fruit cannery, then as a barmaid at father Steve's Buckeye Beer and Wine Parlor, and finally going to beauty school and becoming a hairdresser at her friend Edna's beauty salon. By 1935 Betty had married William Deutsch, son of German immigrants. However she said he spent more time at the bar then at home after work. He later joined the Army and did a tour in Germany. He also began writing another barmaid at Steve's bar and things led up to his divorce from Betty in 1946. Soon she met and married Charles Conklin, another recent divorcee.

Left to right: Marinković sister beauticians Dorothy, Joy, and Betty in the 1940s.

As soon as Japan surrendered in 1945, Charles quit his job at the Navy Yard and started the Atlantic Mattress Company in South Gate where he had been living since working for General Motors. He soon met Betty Marinković Deutsch at a bar in Newport Beach, who was also a recent divorcee, and they were married in 1946. Soon I was born and I remember our family living in an apartment above the mattress factory that dad built. Betty soon had Rita and was pregnant with Joan when we moved to a larger house on Bowman Avenue. Yet Betty still helped out at the retail store as well as sometimes at the factory sewing mattress ticking. The business grew, celebrating its 17th year in 1962. But by 1966 I was graduating from high school, grandma Ana had passed away, and the mattress workers unionized, driving Charles and Betty out of California. In June of that year we sold all our property and loaded all our belongings and business machines onto two railcars and moved to Spokane, Washington,

Dad retired in 1979 shortly after my sister Joanie died in a plane crash, selling his half of the business to his partner Robert Evanson. Mom and dad bought a winter house in Scottsdale, Arizona and became snowbirds. In 1987 my mom passed away at the age of 72 from acute pancreatitis aggravated by diabetes, high blood pressure, and cigarette smoking.

Left: Betty Conklin in about 1980.

Betty and Charlie were wonderful hosts and all of my high school and college friends loved to visit our house or stay the weekend. She was a funny but down-to-earth person that made you feel at home. There are also many stories about mom and her antics and stories. For one, she could never remember the punchline of her own jokes. For another, she was a terrible cook (probably due to alcoholism more than anything). Of course we kids didn't know any better growing up eating at home. It wasn't until I got married that I began eating toast that wasn't black, oatmeal without lumps, and roast beef that wasn't overcooked to the consistency of cardboard. She was also a first generation driver and we were always repairing the garage door or walls after she parked the Lincoln. Of course as the oldest child and only boy, I was also spoiled by my mom. Since she was a beautician I never paid for a haircut, nor did I do my own laundry until I joined the Army. In fact, I don't think I knew how to comb my hair until I was 12 years old!

Right: Thank you note from Betty after our visit during the second Christmas since her daughter Joan died in a plane crash.

CHARLES FRANKLIN[1] **CONKLIN** was born on 17 Aug 1913 in North Bend, Coos County, Oregon. He died on 23 Mar 2005 in Scottsdale, Maricopa, Arizona (Age 91, atherosclerotic stroke). He married (1) HELEN BAILEY on 21 Jun 1937 in Yuma, Arizona. She was born 16 Dec 1912 in Indiana USA. He married (2) BETTY "VUKOSAVA, ZUTA, ELIZABETH" MARINKOVIĆ, daughter of Stevan "Steve, Stevo" Marinković and Ana Marinković, on 08 Nov 1946 in 12021 Long Beach Blvd, Lynwood, Los Angeles, California (Colonial Wedding Chapel). She was born on 24 Apr 1915 in Salem Ward 3, Columbiana, Ohio (7 Prospect Street). She died on 06 Aug 1987 (Age 72) in Spokane, Washington. He married (3) PAULINE RUTH ZIMMERMAN, daughter of Paul Richard Lewis Zimmerman and Ruth Edna Smith, on 17 Jun 1989 in Spokane, Washington. She was born on 04 May 1918 in Meeteetse, Park County, Wyoming. She died on 11 Aug 2013 (Age 95).

For more information on Charles Franklin Conklin see "Generation 2" in Part I, Chapter 5 Charles William Conklin and Caroline Lingren, beginning on page 61.

Charles Franklin "Charlie, Chuck" Conklin and Betty "*Vukosava, Zuta*, Elizabeth" Marinković had the following children:

+2.   i.   DAVID GENE[3] "DAVE" CONKLIN was born on 03 Nov 1948 in Lynwood, California (St Francis Hospital). He married MARY LAVONNE GUERRA on 22 Nov 1969 in Moscow, Latah, Idaho, USA. She was born on 15 Jun 1949 in Boise, Ada, Idaho.

3.   ii.   RITA MARIE CONKLIN was born on 23 Aug 1950 in Lynwood, California (St Francis Hospital). She married (1) JAMES MACDONALD in Spokane, Washington. She married (2) RODNEY N REEVE in Seattle, King, Washington (Episcopal Church in The Highlands).

+4.   iii.   JOAN LOUISE "JONI" CONKLIN was born on 16 Feb 1952 in Lynwood, California. She died on 04 Aug 1979 in Idaho (died in plane crash in Salmon River, Idaho). She married (1) MICHAEL SCIACCOTTI. She married (2) ROBERT FULTON.

+5.   iv.   LORIE ANN "LORI" CONKLIN was born on 14 Apr 1955 in Lynwood, California (St Francis Hospital). She married JAMES GRAY about 1975. He was born about 1955 in Spokane, Washington.

Generation 2

Information on the Conklin children is found in "Generation 3" in Part I, Chapter 5 Charles William Conklin and Caroline Lingren, beginning on page 69; with Generations 3 and 4 beginning on page 77.

Chapter 5. Mary Marinković and George Wirtz

Generation 1

1. **MARY**[1] **MARINKOVIĆ** was born on 06 Nov 1918 in Salem Ward 3, Columbiana, Ohio, USA as the seventh child of Stevan Marinković and Ana Marinković. She had nine siblings, namely: (Boy), Mileva, Betty, Mary, Andy, Mary, Bogdan, Joy, and Dorothy. She died on 17 Nov 1964 (Age 46) in Los Angeles, California, USA (Buried in St Sava Serbian Cemetery, Los Angeles, CA). When she was 37, she married GEORGE E. WIRTZ on 28 Jul 1956 in Los Angeles, California, USA.

Mary Marinković lived in 67 Perry St Salem, Columbiana, Ohio, USA on 06 Nov 1918. She lived in Salem Ward 3, Columbiana, Ohio, USA in 1920 (Age 1; Age 1 2/12; Marital Status: Single; Relation to Head of House: Daughter). She lived in South Gate, Los Angeles, California, USA in 1930 (Age 11; Marital Status: Single; Relation to Head of House: Daughter). She lived on San Antonio Avenue, Los Angeles, California, USA on 01 Apr 1940 (Age 21; Marital Status: Single; Relation to Head of House: Daughter). Race: (White)

All five Marinković sisters in 1942. Standing from left: Joy, Dorothy, Mary, Mileva. Kneeling: Betty. –from Don Jensen collection.

Mary was actually the fifth girl to be born to the Marinković family, and the third one to live to maturity. According to Ohio birth certificates, two older girls were born, each named Mary, but the family name was spelled differently on each birth certificate. Both had died while toddlers in 1918, possibly due to the Spanish flu epidemic. I recall that Mary herself was always thin and rather sickly looking. We kids thought she would always be a "spinster" but she surprised us when she married George Wirtz in 1956. But Mary died eight years later at the age of 46, and Grandma Ana bought two graves in the Serbian Cemetery so she could be buried next to Mary (Ana died a year later in 1965).

George E. Wirtz was born on 12 May 1911. He died on 15 Sep 1987 in South Gate, Los Angeles, California, USA (Age: 76). When he was 45, he married Mary Marinković, daughter of Stevan Marinković and Ana Marinković, on 28 Jul 1956 in Los Angeles, California, USA. George served in the military on 23 Feb 1942 at Fort Thomas, Newport, Kentucky (Age 31). He lived in Montgomery, Ohio at that time. Race: (White).

George E. Wirtz and Mary Marinković had no children.

Mary Marinković with niece Susan Jensen in 1941 –from Don Jensen collection.

Mary Marinković Wirtz in about 1960.

Mary is buried next to her mother Ana Marinković in the Serbian Cemetery in Los Angeles –photo 18 Feb 2013.

Chapter 6. Bogdan Marinković/Robert Markovic and Florba Grazier

Generation 1

1.   **BOGDAN MARINKOVIĆ**[1] **"BILL, BILLY, ROBERT CROSS" MARKOVIC** was born on 10 Jul 1920 in Salem Ward 3, Columbiana, Ohio, USA (22 Broadway Ave as the eighth child of Stevan Marinković and Ana Marinković). He had nine siblings, namely: (Boy), Mileva, Betty, Mary, Andy, Mary, Mary, Joy, and Dorothy. He died on 10 Apr 1995 (Age 74) in Lynwood, Los Angeles, California, USA. When he was 25, he married **FLORBA MAY GRAZIER**, daughter of Walter Grazier and Rosalie E. Deperieux, on 03 May 1946 in Lynwood, Los Angeles, California, USA (Lynwood Wedding Chapel).

Bogdan Marinković-Robert Markovic lived at 10414 San Antonio Ave, South Gate, Los Angeles, California, USA in 1940. He served in the military between 1942 and 1946 on the USS General JH McRae AP-149 (Electrician's Mate Third Class-PO3). His military serial number was 633-68-03 on 18 Jul 1942 in San Pedro, Los Angeles, California, USA. He lived at 11045 Carson Drive, Lynwood, California in 1948. He was employed as an Electrical Contractor on 05 Mar 1948 in South Gate, Los Angeles, California, USA. He was described as Brown hair, brown eyes, 5ft 11in, 160 lbs. (from CA driver license) in 1984 in Lynwood, Los Angeles, California, USA. He lived at 11045 Carson Drive, Lynwood, CA on 26 Jan 1994. He was buried in Apr 1995 in Rose Hills Memorial Park, Whittier, Los Angeles, California. He was also known as Bill, Billy, and Robert Cross. Race: (Serbian).

Petty Officer 3d Class (PO3) Bill Marinković in 1945 (left) with sisters Betty, Millie and Millie's husband Art Jensen –from Don Jensen collection.

Everyone called him Billy, probably because at school like his older sister *Vukosava* (Betty), they could not pronounce *Bogdan*, the name on his birth certificate, which in Serbian means "gift of God." If you think about it, his father Steve may have chosen his Serbian name after his wife Ana previously had five girls, losing two sons and two daughters in the process. Boban is the Serbian diminutive for Bogdan, but to us kids he was always known as "Uncle Bill" and to his last days always signed his letters to us that way. He enlisted in the Navy in 1942 during World War II and told nephew Don Jensen that he piloted LST landing craft in Morocco early in the war. He also served in the Pacific during the Philippine Liberation. Bill also told his nephew that he was a wild kid back in the 1940's and spent most of his three years in the Navy in the Brig for drinking or fighting (Jensen D. , Don Jensen Family History Interview, 2016). His muster date in San Pedro, CA on the ship General JH McRae was 8 Aug 1944 and his rating was Flc V6 (Electricians Mate).

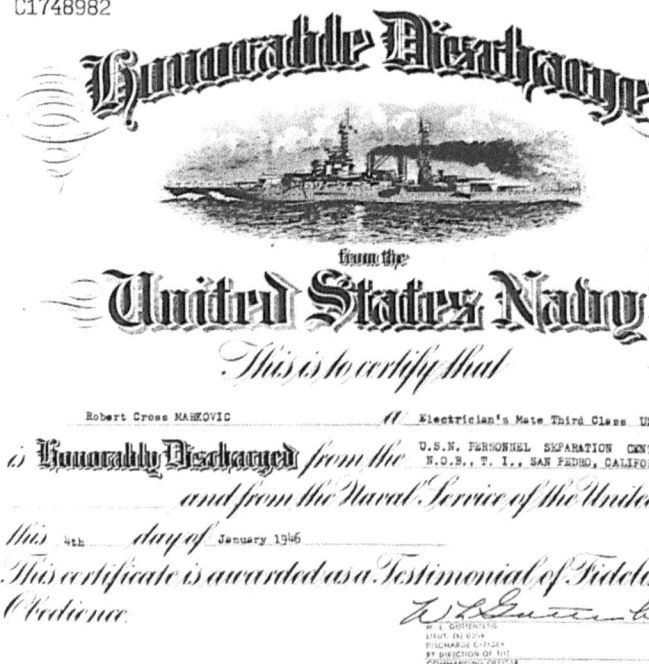

Bill Marinković's 1946 Navy Discharge shows his New name as "Robert Cross Markovic" –from Derek Markovic collection.

Bill Marinković 1942 Navy photo –from Derek Markovic collection.

He joined the Navy as Bill Marinković, but for some reason by the time he was discharged in 1946 his separation papers read "Robert Cross Markovic." His sisters Joy and Dorothy think his future wife Florba had him change his name, but his oldest son Derek said that his name had been changed to Robert Cross Markovic before he left the Navy (Markovic, 2016). Adding to the confusion, a news article (Lynwood Press, 1946) reported on the wedding of "Mr. and Mrs. Bill Marinković," but their marriage license names him as Robert C. Markovic. Nevertheless, Uncle Bill became an electrical contractor after the war and he and his wife Florba raised four children. He was also a scoutmaster and baseball coach in Lynwood, CA. Florba passed away in 1992 and in 1994 he wrote me that he was still living at 11045 Carson Dr, Lynwood, CA 90262 with his youngest son Dennis living in the front house. He was semi-retired and planning to move to Hawthorne, Nevada. That was the last letter I received from my Uncle Bill.

Left: Bogdan Marinković/Robert Cross Markovic is buried in Rose Hills Cemetery, Whittier, CA, next to his youngest son Dennis –photo 21 Nov 2015.

Bogdan Marinković/Robert Cross Markovic and Florba May "Gloria" Grazier had the following children:

2. i.   DEREK WALTER^2 MARKOVIC was born on 26 May 1947 in Lynwood, Los Angeles, California, USA (St Francis Hospital). He married Joyce Etta Rudd on 01 Dec 1984 in Clark, Nevada.

3. ii. DEBBIE MARKOVIC was born on 20 May 1949 in Lynwood, Los Angeles, California, USA (St Francis Hospital). She married Floyd Angus about 1972 in Los Angeles, California, USA.

4. iii. DENISE MAE MARKOVIC was born on 26 May 1951 in Lynwood, Los Angeles, California, USA (St Francis Hospital). She married David P Bright on 08 Nov 1975 in Los Angeles, California, USA. He was born about 1946.

5. iv. DENNIS ROBERT MARKOVIC was born on 14 May 1953 in Lynwood, Los Angeles, California, USA (St Francis Hospital). He died on 31 May 1998 in Lynwood, Los Angeles, California, USA. He married Paula K Dunn on 10 Mar 1972 in Los Angeles City, California, USA. She was born on 20 Jul 1954.

Generation 2

2. Derek Walter^2 Markovic was born on 26 May 1947 in Lynwood, Los Angeles, California, USA (St Francis Hospital) as the first child of Bogdan Marinković-Robert Markovic and Florba May Grazier. He had three siblings, namely: Debbie, Denise Mae, and Dennis Robert. When he was 37, he married Joyce Etta Rudd on 01 Dec 1984 in Clark, Nevada. Derek Walter Markovic lived in Lynwood, California on 01 Dec 1984. He lived in Anaheim, CA in 1993. He was employed as a Real Estate Broker on 26 Jan 1994 in Anaheim, Orange, California, USA. He was employed by Benchmark Realty, Hualapai Way, LV, NV in Jan 2004 as a Real Estate Broker. He began living in Las Vegas, NV in Jan 2004.

Cousins Derek Markovic (left) and Dave Conklin meet again after many years near Derek's home in Las Vegas, Nevada 28 Jan 2016.

3. **Debbie² Markovic** was born on 20 May 1949 in Lynwood, Los Angeles, California, USA (St Francis Hospital) as the second child of Bogdan Marinković-Robert Markovic and Florba May Grazier. She had three siblings, namely: Derek Walter, Denise Mae, and Dennis Robert. When she was 22, she married Floyd Angus about 1972 in Los Angeles, California, USA. Floyd worked for the LAPD on 26 Jan 1994 in Los Angeles, California, USA. She lived in Hacienda Heights, Los Angeles, California, USA on 26 Jan 1994. She lived in Aurora (Marionville), Missouri in 2015.

4. **Denise Mae² Markovic** was born on 26 May 1951 in Lynwood, Los Angeles, California, USA (St Francis Hospital) as the third child of Bogdan Marinković-Robert Markovic and Florba May Grazier. She had three siblings, namely: Derek Walter, Debbie, and Dennis Robert. When she was 24 she married David P. Bright on 08 Nov 1975 in Los Angeles, California, USA. Denise Mae Markovic lived in Downey, CA in 1975. She was employed as a Registered Nurse at St Francis Hospital and Lynwood High School about 1990 in Lynwood, Los Angeles, California, USA. She lived in Marionville, MO in 1991. She lived in Aurora (Marionville), Missouri on 11 Apr 1992 (111 West Locust St.). She lived in Aurora (Marionville), Missouri in 2015.

5. **Dennis Robert² Markovic** was born on 14 May 1953 in Lynwood, Los Angeles, California, USA (St Francis Hospital) as the fourth child of Bogdan Marinković-Robert

Markovic and Florba May Grazier. He had three siblings, namely: Derek Walter, Debbie, and Denise Mae. He died on 31 May 1998 in Lynwood, Los Angeles, California, USA. When he was 18, he married Paula K. Dunn on 10 Mar 1972 in Los Angeles City, California, USA. Dennis Robert Markovic was employed as a California State Pest Control License Inspector. On 26 Jan 1994 he lived at 11045 Carson Drive, Lynwood, CA 90262. He was buried in June 1998 in Rose Hills Memorial Park, Whittier, Los Angeles, California. He lived in Garden Grove, CA.

Chapter 7. Joy Marinković and Sidney Asher

Generation 1

1.   JOY[1] **"JOY RUBY, ZORKA" MARINKOVIĆ** was born on 13 May 1922 in New Castle, Lawrence, Pennsylvania, USA as the ninth child of Stevan Marinković and Ana Marinković. She had nine siblings, namely: (Boy), Mileva, Betty, Mary, Andy, Mary, Mary, Bogdan, and Dorothy. She died on 10 Mar 1973 in Ferndale, Whatcom, Washington, USA (Age 50). She married (1) EDWARD H. "SWAMPY" DAVES, son of Willis E. Daves and Gladys K. Daves, on 12 Jun 1944 in Los Angeles, California, USA. He was born on 10 Oct 1922 in Kingsburg, Fresno, California, CA. He died on 02 May 2014 (Age 91). She married (2) SIDNEY MAURICE ASHER, son of Louis L. Asher and Bessie Pantoskey, about 1945 in Fresno, Fresno, California, USA. He was born on 25 Dec 1897 in Lithuania. He died on 16 Jul 1966 in Fresno, Fresno, California, USA (Age 68). She married (3) THEODORE THOMAS FURBER, son of Arthur Whitney Furber and Madeline Gevelinger, on 16 Nov 1966 in Fresno, Fresno, California, USA. He was born on 04 Aug 1921 in Menlo, Iowa. He died on 09 Apr 1977 in Bellingham, Washington, USA (Age 55).

Right: Joy and her brother Billy (Bogdan) joke with their mother Ana Marinković (on the right) in this photo dated 7 May 1940.

Joy Marinković lived in South Gate, Los Angeles, California, USA in 1930 (Age 7; Marital Status: Single; Relation to Head of House: Daughter). She lived in South Gate, Los Angeles, California, USA in 1935. She lived at 10414 San Antonio, South Gate, CA on 01 Apr 1940 (Age 17; Marital Status: Single; Relation to Head of House: Daughter). She lived in San Jose, Santa Clara, California in 1950. She lived in Modesto, California in 1959. She was cremated and in about 1990 interred in Greenacres Memorial Park, Ferndale, WA (Niche). She was also known as Joy Ruby, Zorka. Race: (Serbian).

Joy's Serbian name was Zorka, a Serbian diminutive of "Zora" from a South and West Slavic word meaning "dawn, aurora." Since she and her sister Dorothy were born on a farm outside of Newcastle, PA neither one had a birth certificate. I remember her sisters always called her Zorka, but in 1942 at age 20 when she was living in California she submitted an affidavit of birth to Pennsylvania using the name Joy Ruby Marinkovich. Also according to her sister Dorothy all the children were given English names by their oldest sister Mileva (Marinkovic D. , 2002).

I remember Joy was always the life of the party. She became a beautician like her sisters Betty and Dorothy. During the 1940s her brother Billy would take his sisters in his car to the dances at the Palladium in Long Beach, CA. I believe that is where she met "Swampy," the Navy test pilot who was the love of her life according to her nephew (Jensen D. , Don Jensen Family History Interview, 2016). Reportedly he survived three plane crashes and later rose to the rank of Lieutenant Commander. He was also said to be related to the famous bank robber Roy Dalton. It is not known if "Swampy" was her first husband Edward Daves. She was only married to him for about a year.

Left: Joy Marinković with her nephew Don Jensen at the Serbian Cemetery during the annual Slav Easter celebration at the adjacent Saint Sava Serbian Church, Los Angeles, about 1946 –photo from Don Jensen collection.

Soon she was introduced to **Sidney Maurice Asher**. Sid was a successful businessman in San Jose who went into the shoe sales business with his two brothers Harvey Asher and William S. Asher (wife Ethel, son Larry). Sid Asher was born on 25 Dec 1897 in Lithuania as the first child of Louis L. Asher and Bessie Pantoskey. He died on 16 Jul 1966 in Fresno, Fresno, California, USA (Age 68). When he was 47, he married Joy Marinković, daughter of Stevan Marinković and Ana Marinković, about 1945 in Fresno, Fresno, California, USA. Sidney Asher lived in Oakland City, Alameda, California in 1900. He lived in Oakland Ward 6, Alameda, California in 1910. He lived in Paterson, Passaic, New Jersey between 1917 and 1918 (Age 21). He lived in Oakland, Alameda, California in 1920. He lived in Oakland, Alameda, California in 1930. He lived in Oakland, Alameda, California in 1935. He lived in Oakland, Alameda, California on 01 Apr 1940 (Age 44; Marital Status: Married; Relation to Head of House: Head). He was employed as Owner of Asher Shoe Co in 1950 in San Jose, Santa Clara, California, USA. He lived in San Jose, Santa Clara, California, USA in 1950. He lived in Modesto, California, USA in 1959. He lived in Sanger in 1966. He was buried in July 1966 in Fresno, CA (Beth-Israel Cemetery).

By 1958 Joy and Sid had moved to Fresno and opened an Asher Brothers Shoe Store there. That is where they adopted a girl and boy in 1959. I first saw my new cousins shortly afterwards at my aunt and uncle' home in Fresno. I remember one visit in particular in 1964. I was sixteen years old and recently got my driver's license. I thought it would be fun to borrow my dad's Lincoln Continental to drive my cousins Steve Schmale, age 10, and Mike Asher, age 5, around Fresno. I borrowed the car and we drove downtown where a cop saw what he thought were three small boys joyriding in a very large car. He turned on his lights and pulled us over. Steve and Mike thought we were all going to jail. After checking my license and car registration he sheepishly let us go, and the boys had a great story to tell their folks how Cousin Dave got stopped by the police.

Joy poses with her mother Ana and her sister Millie's family in 1950. From left to right, Back row: Ana Marinković, Art Jensen, Joy Marinković, Susan Jensen; Front row: Bobby and Donny Jensen

Sid Asher passed away in 1966 and soon Joy married Ted Furber, an ex-convict. They moved from Fresno, CA to Bellingham, WA with the young children. Joy was already a borderline alcoholic and with a little encouragement from Ted, they both pretty much drank themselves to death. In the meantime their adopted children had to grow up in foster homes. Joy died and was cremated in 1973. Later her adopted children interred her ashes at Greenacres Memorial Park in Ferndale, Washington.

Left: Leslye (Asher) O'Shaughnessy in about 2016.

Sidney Maurice Asher and Joy "Joy Ruby, Zorka" Marinković adopted the following children:

   2. i.   GERALDINE EDITH ASHER was born about 1955.

+3. ii.   LESLYE ANN[2] ASHER was born on 15 Jul 1957 in Fresno, California (Adopted daughter). She married Dennis O'Shaughnessy on 25 Sep 2005 in Bellingham, Whatcom, Washington, USA.

+4. iii.   MICHAEL DAVID "MIKE" ASHER was born on 29 Mar 1959 in Downey, Los Angeles, California, USA (Adopted son). He married Paula Marie Blane on 10 May 1981 in Bellingham, Whatcom,

Washington, USA (Laramont Manor). She was born on 17 Jul 1959 in Paisley, Renfrewshire, Scotland.

Generation 2

3. **LESLYE ANN**[2] **ASHER** (Joy[1] "Joy Ruby, Zorka" Marinković, Sidney Maurice, Louis L.) was born on 15 Jul 1957 in Fresno, California (Adopted daughter). She married Dennis O'Shaughnessy on 25 Sep 2005 in Bellingham, Whatcom, Washington, USA.

Leslye Ann Asher had the following child:
  5. i. JEREMIAH[3] ASHER was born on 29 Apr 1980 in Bellingham, Whatcom, Washington, USA.

4. **MICHAEL DAVID "MIKE" ASHER** (Joy[1] "Joy Ruby, Zorka" Marinković, Sidney Maurice, Louis L.) was born on 29 Mar 1959 in Downey, Los Angeles, California, USA (Adopted son). He married Paula Marie Blane on 10 May 1981 in Bellingham, Whatcom, Washington, USA (Laramont Manor). She was born on 17 Jul 1959 in Paisley, Renfrewshire, Scotland.

Michael Asher and wife Paula (Blane) Asher visit Cousin Dave Conklin (center) at Dave's home in Kalispell, Montana 6 Sep 2016.

Michael David "Mike" Asher and Paula Marie Blane had the following female children:
  6. i. LYNDSAY JOY ASHER was born on 14 Nov 1981 in Bellingham, Whatcom, Washington, USA.
  7. ii. NICOLE ANNE ASHER was born on 19 Jan 1986 in Bellingham, Whatcom, Washington, USA.
  8. iii. TAYLOR MARGARET ASHER was born on 25 May 1990 in Bellingham, Whatcom, Washington, USA.

Chapter 8. Dorothy Marinković and Ervin Schmale

Generation 1

1. **DOROTHY**[1] **"DOTTIE, DANTSA, DANITSA, FLORENCE" MARINKOVIĆ** was born on 13 Jun 1923 in New Castle, Lawrence, Pennsylvania, USA as the tenth and youngest child of Stevan Marinković and Ana Marinković. She had nine siblings, namely: (Boy), Mileva, Betty, Mary, Andy, Mary, Mary, Bogdan, and Joy. She died on 16 Oct 2005 in Fresno, California, USA (Age 82). When she was 18, she married Ervin Henry "Smiley" Schmale, son of Henry Schmale and Louise Schmale in 1942. Dorothy Marinković lived in South Gate, Los Angeles, California, USA in 1930 (Age 6; Marital Status: Single; Relation to Head of House: Daughter). She lived in South Gate, California, USA in 1935. She lived ar 10414 San Antonio, South Gate, CA on 01 Apr 1940 (Age 16; Marital Status: Single; Relation to Head of House: Daughter). She lived in Fresno, California in 1958 (2536 E Fedora Ave). She was also known as Dottie, Dantsa, Danitsa, and Dorothy Florence Schmale. Race: (Serbian)

Like her older sister Joy she was born on the farm and did not have a birth certificate. She was given the Serbian name "Dantsa" or "Danitsa" (meaning little Dantsa) which her sister Mileva changed to Dorothy when she started school. But it was not until 1961, long after she was married, that she submitted an affidavit of birth to formally change her name to Dorothy Marinkovich. Dottie said, "I was born in New Castle, PA and we moved to Los Angeles when I was 4 months old. My mother said I lost a bootie during the trip at the Chicago train station." (Marinkovic D. , 2002).

Right: Portrait of Dorothy Marinković taken when she was still in high school and living with her mother Ana in South Gate, California in about 1940.

She only spoke Serbian when she started school in Lynwood, CA. Meanwhile she was her mother Ana's shadow, going to the store, picking vegetables from the garden, and selling eggs door-to-door. "Every Friday night my mother would make Serbian soup with beans, ham hocks, cabbage, onions, garlic and homemade bread. One time she told me to go to the store and get a pound of pig beans. So I asked the man at the store, and he looked at me funny. Finally he says, 'Do you mean PINK beans?' So when I got home I told mama, it's not PIG beans, its PINK beans" (Marinkovic D. , 2002).

Dottie grew up at a unique time in Los Angeles. The feisty Marinković sisters were beauticians—they loved their hairdos and the classy clothes of the 1940s. Dottie and her fun-loving sisters loved dancing and singing to the Big Bands, Jazz, Blues, and later to Rock and

Roll. She always danced like no one was watching! In fact she met her future husband, a sailor they called "Smiley," at a dance with her sisters at the Palladium in Long Beach, California.

Ervin Henry "Smiley" Schmale was born on 22 Mar 1915 in Beemer, Nebraska as the first child of Henry Schmale and Louise Schmale. He had two siblings, namely: Emil, and Louis. He died on 01 Dec 1985 in Fresno (Age 70). When he was 26, he married Dorothy Marinković, daughter of Stevan Marinković and Ana Marinković, in 1942. Ervin Schmale lived in Lodgepole, Cheyenne, Nebraska in 1930 (Age 15; Marital Status: Single; Relation to Head of House: Son). He served in the military (US Navy) in 1936 on the Cruiser USS Chicago (CA-29) (Supply). He served in the military on 19 May 1941 in San Diego, California (Attack transport USS Heywood (APA-6)). He served in the military on 15 Sep 1943 on Escort carrier USS Fanshaw Bay (CVE-70) (Age 28, Battle of Leyte). He served in the military on 01 Jan 1945 (Age 29, Supply Chief Warrant). He lived in Fresno, California, USA in 1955 (Atlantic Mattress Co 3937 N. Arden Dr). He lived in Fresno, California in 1958 (2536 E Fedora Ave). He was also known as Smiley. Race: (German).

Photo # NH 106573 USS Fanshaw Bay (CVE-70) transporting aircraft

Ervin "Smiley" Schmale got his nickname in the Navy, possibly while on the Escort Carrier USS Fanshaw Bay during the largest naval battle in World War II: the Battle of Leyte Gulf, Philippines in Oct 1944 –US Navy photo.

Ervin Schmale with his son Steve in 1955.

Dottie and Smiley were married in 1942 and lived in Navy towns like San Diego, San Pedro, and Long Beach, enjoying their new life in Southern California. In the Navy everyone is known by rating and last name. Ervin's last name Schmale sounded a lot like "Smiley" so the nickname stuck. After the war Smiley became a car salesman before moving to Fresno to open a mattress store for his brother-in-law Charlie. They enjoyed their early life together making memories at the Serbian Church and Hall in Boyle Heights, and mother Ana's house in Lynwood where the family would gather for food, drink, music, dancing, singing and laughter.

Schmale and Conklin family campsite in California's Lassen National Forest, 1955. From left, front row: local reporter, David, Charles, Joan, and Betty Conklin; Susan, Dottie, Steve, and "Smiley" Schmale. back row: Robert Evanson, Rita Conklin, Lois Evanson.

The Schmale and Conklin families used to go tent camping together in the Sierras and northern California every year on the long weekends of Memorial Day, Independence Day, and Labor Day. As a child I looked forward to playing with my cousins on these trips every year. This is where my dad Charlie taught me how to fly fish for trout with a bamboo fly rod in the cold streams of the Sierras. These trips are also the reason my life-long ambition was to be a park ranger. What could be a better life? This is also where I learned not to litter, thanks to my Aunt Dottie. We were returning from camping in our car caravan on a narrow hillside road when we passed a forest ranger. Just before he passed by, Dottie threw an empty peanut can out her car window and down the steep hillside. The ranger stopped the Schmale's car and said, "Lady you can either go pick up your can, or I'll write you up for a littering fine. It's your choice." So we all waited for Dottie to hike down the hill and retrieve her peanut can. I learned from that ranger that littering could be expensive as well as ugly.

In Fresno the Schmales built a house on East Fedora Avenue that Dottie landscaped while sewing clothes for the children. Soon she opened a beauty shop in their garage which she operated for the rest of her life. She loved to meet people (. . . and what's your name?), tell stories, talk sports, politics (a life-long liberal Democrat), and knew everyone in the places she shopped as well as three generations of her neighbors. "I can still remember seeing her tiny head barely visible above the steering wheel of "Dottie's tank," her 1979 Olds Cutlass Supreme," said her daughter Susan. Dottie was independent until the end and passed away in

2005 the way she wanted to, peacefully and in her own home.

Left: *Santa visits with Susan & Steve Schmale (left) with Joan, David, Lorie, and Rita Conklin (right) in Fresno, California in about 1957.*

Ervin Henry "Smiley" Schmale and Dorothy "Dottie" Marinković had the following children:

    2. i. SUSAN[2] "LITTLE SUZIE" SCHMALE was born on 23 Jun 1950 in Lynwood, California (St Francis Hospital).

    3. ii. STEVEN "STEVE, BUSTER" SCHMALE was born on 25 Jul 1953 in Fresno, California.

Generation 2

2. SUSAN[2] "LITTLE SUZIE" SCHMALE was born on 23 Jun 1950 in Lynwood, California (St Francis Hospital) as the first child of Ervin Henry Schmale and Dorothy Marinković. She had one sibling, namely: Steven. Susan Schmale was also known as Little Suzie to differentiate her from her older cousin Susan Jensen. She married Steve "Bosko" Smith.

3. STEVEN "BUSTER" SCHMALE was born on 25 Jul 1953 in Fresno, California as the second child of Ervin Henry Schmale and Dorothy Marinković. He had one sibling, namely: Susan. Steven Schmale was also known as Steve, and "Buster" when he was young, and was named after Dorothy's father Stevan Marinković.

Husband "Bosko" Smith and Suzie at home on 5 Jan 2002.

Suzie poses with a dolphin on one of her trips to the Caribbean.

Appendix 1. Conklin-Marinković Pedigree Chart

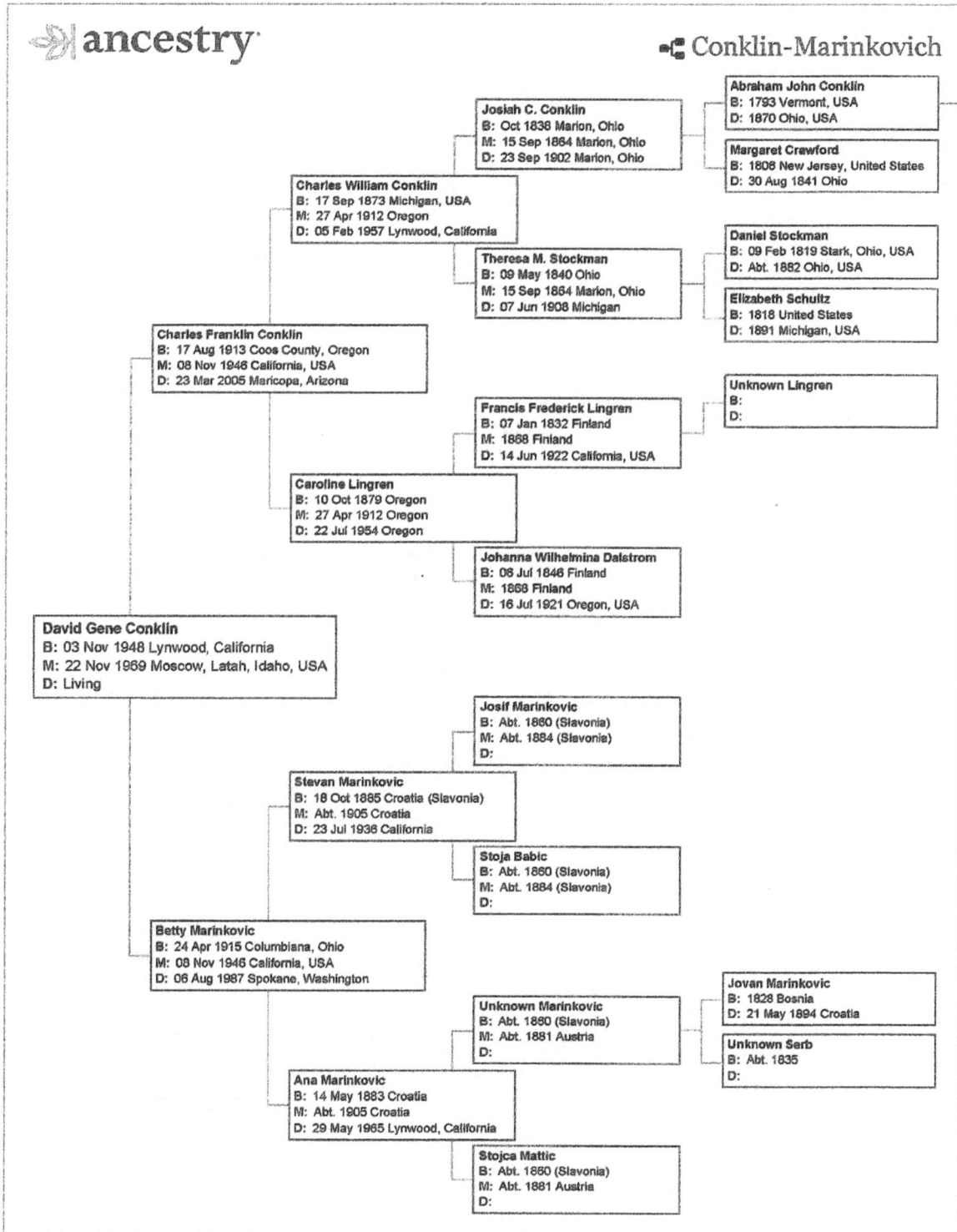

ancestry ‎ ‎ ‎ ‎ ‎ ‎ ‎ ‎ ‎ ‎ ‎ Conklin-Marinkovich

Abraham John Conklin
B: 1793 Vermont, USA
D: 1870 Ohio, USA

Josiah C. Conklin
B: Oct 1838 Marion, Ohio
M: 15 Sep 1864 Marion, Ohio
D: 23 Sep 1902 Marion, Ohio

Margaret Crawford
B: 1806 New Jersey, United States
D: 30 Aug 1841 Ohio

Charles William Conklin
B: 17 Sep 1873 Michigan, USA
M: 27 Apr 1912 Oregon
D: 05 Feb 1957 Lynwood, California

Daniel Stockman
B: 09 Feb 1819 Stark, Ohio, USA
D: Abt. 1882 Ohio, USA

Theresa M. Stockman
B: 09 May 1840 Ohio
M: 15 Sep 1864 Marion, Ohio
D: 07 Jun 1908 Michigan

Elizabeth Schultz
B: 1818 United States
D: 1891 Michigan, USA

Charles Franklin Conklin
B: 17 Aug 1913 Coos County, Oregon
M: 08 Nov 1946 California, USA
D: 23 Mar 2005 Maricopa, Arizona

Unknown Lingren
B:
D:

Francis Frederick Lingren
B: 07 Jan 1832 Finland
M: 1868 Finland
D: 14 Jun 1922 California, USA

Caroline Lingren
B: 10 Oct 1879 Oregon
M: 27 Apr 1912 Oregon
D: 22 Jul 1954 Oregon

Johanna Wilhelmina Dalstrom
B: 06 Jul 1846 Finland
M: 1868 Finland
D: 16 Jul 1921 Oregon, USA

David Gene Conklin
B: 03 Nov 1948 Lynwood, California
M: 22 Nov 1969 Moscow, Latah, Idaho, USA
D: Living

Josif Marinkovic
B: Abt. 1860 (Slavonia)
M: Abt. 1884 (Slavonia)
D:

Stevan Marinkovic
B: 18 Oct 1885 Croatia (Slavonia)
M: Abt. 1905 Croatia
D: 23 Jul 1936 California

Stoja Babic
B: Abt. 1860 (Slavonia)
M: Abt. 1884 (Slavonia)
D:

Betty Marinkovic
B: 24 Apr 1915 Columbiana, Ohio
M: 08 Nov 1946 California, USA
D: 06 Aug 1987 Spokane, Washington

Jovan Marinkovic
B: 1828 Bosnia
D: 21 May 1894 Croatia

Unknown Marinkovic
B: Abt. 1860 (Slavonia)
M: Abt. 1881 Austria
D:

Unknown Serb
B: Abt. 1835
D:

Ana Marinkovic
B: 14 May 1883 Croatia
M: Abt. 1905 Croatia
D: 29 May 1965 Lynwood, California

Stojca Mattic
B: Abt. 1860 (Slavonia)
M: Abt. 1881 Austria
D:

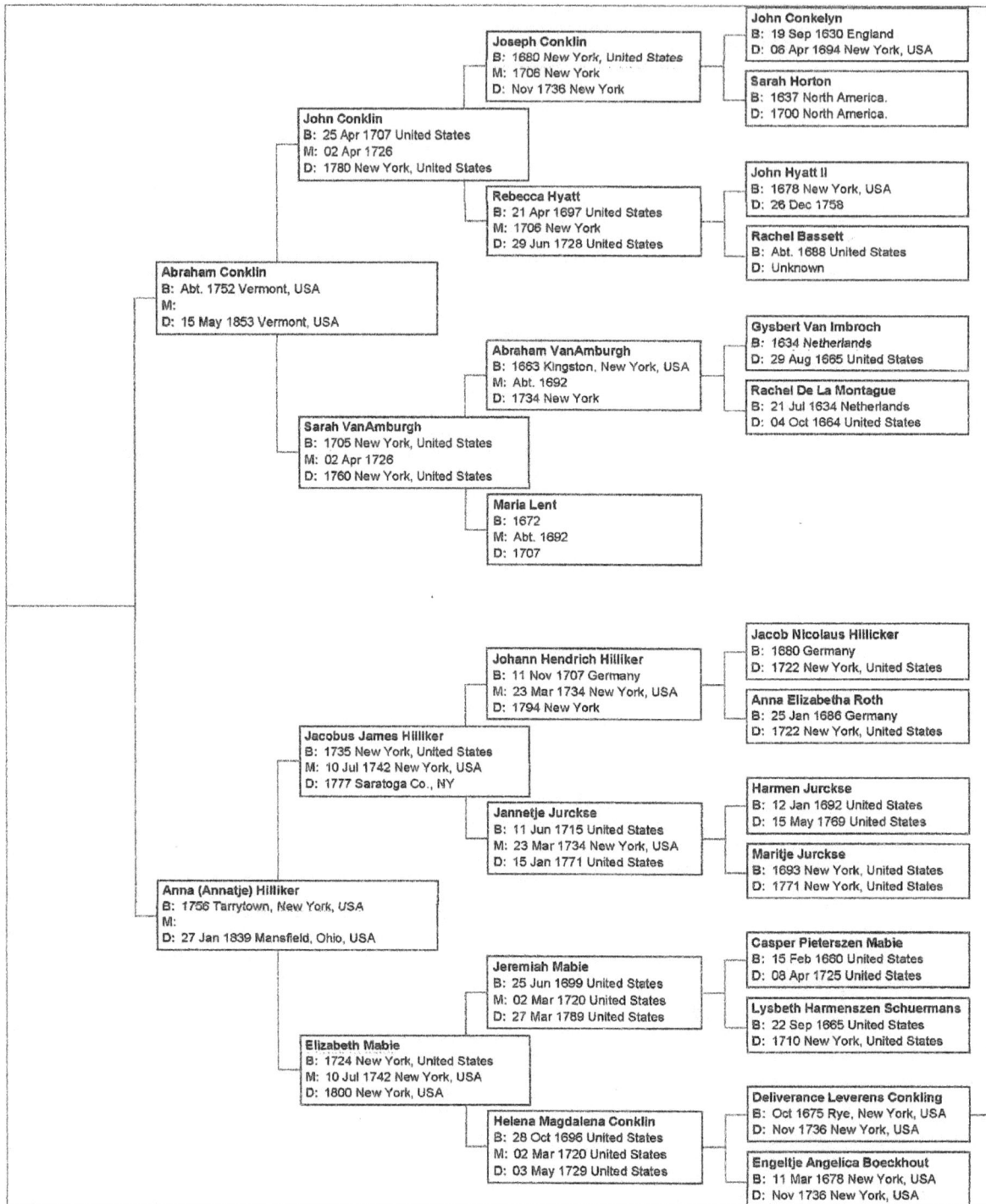

Joseph Conklin
B: 1680 New York, United States
M: 1706 New York
D: Nov 1736 New York

John Conkelyn
B: 19 Sep 1630 England
D: 06 Apr 1694 New York, USA

Sarah Horton
B: 1637 North America.
D: 1700 North America.

John Conklin
B: 25 Apr 1707 United States
M: 02 Apr 1726
D: 1780 New York, United States

Rebecca Hyatt
B: 21 Apr 1697 United States
M: 1706 New York
D: 29 Jun 1728 United States

John Hyatt II
B: 1678 New York, USA
D: 26 Dec 1758

Rachel Bassett
B: Abt. 1688 United States
D: Unknown

Abraham Conklin
B: Abt. 1752 Vermont, USA
M:
D: 15 May 1853 Vermont, USA

Abraham VanAmburgh
B: 1663 Kingston, New York, USA
M: Abt. 1692
D: 1734 New York

Gysbert Van Imbroch
B: 1634 Netherlands
D: 29 Aug 1665 United States

Rachel De La Montague
B: 21 Jul 1634 Netherlands
D: 04 Oct 1664 United States

Sarah VanAmburgh
B: 1705 New York, United States
M: 02 Apr 1726
D: 1760 New York, United States

Maria Lent
B: 1672
M: Abt. 1692
D: 1707

Johann Hendrich Hilliker
B: 11 Nov 1707 Germany
M: 23 Mar 1734 New York, USA
D: 1794 New York

Jacob Nicolaus Hillicker
B: 1680 Germany
D: 1722 New York, United States

Anna Elizabetha Roth
B: 25 Jan 1686 Germany
D: 1722 New York, United States

Jacobus James Hilliker
B: 1735 New York, United States
M: 10 Jul 1742 New York, USA
D: 1777 Saratoga Co., NY

Jannetje Jurckse
B: 11 Jun 1715 United States
M: 23 Mar 1734 New York, USA
D: 15 Jan 1771 United States

Harmen Jurckse
B: 12 Jan 1692 United States
D: 15 May 1769 United States

Maritje Jurckse
B: 1693 New York, United States
D: 1771 New York, United States

Anna (Annatje) Hilliker
B: 1756 Tarrytown, New York, USA
M:
D: 27 Jan 1839 Mansfield, Ohio, USA

Jeremiah Mabie
B: 25 Jun 1699 United States
M: 02 Mar 1720 United States
D: 27 Mar 1789 United States

Casper Pieterszen Mabie
B: 15 Feb 1680 United States
D: 08 Apr 1725 United States

Lysbeth Harmenszen Schuermans
B: 22 Sep 1665 United States
D: 1710 New York, United States

Elizabeth Mabie
B: 1724 New York, United States
M: 10 Jul 1742 New York, USA
D: 1800 New York, USA

Helena Magdalena Conklin
B: 28 Oct 1696 United States
M: 02 Mar 1720 United States
D: 03 May 1729 United States

Deliverance Leverens Conkling
B: Oct 1675 Rye, New York, USA
D: Nov 1736 New York, USA

Engeltje Angelica Boeckhout
B: 11 Mar 1678 New York, USA
D: Nov 1736 New York, USA

William Conkling
B: 1533 Nottinghamshire, England
M: 1595 England
D: 1610 Nottinghamshire, England

John Concklyne
B: 1595 Nottinghamshire, England
M: 24 Jan 1625 England
D: 24 Feb 1684 United States

Richard Hedges
B: 1500 Kent, England
D: 1558

Ruth Hedges
B: 1533 Kent, England
M: 1595 England
D: 1610 Nottinghamshire, England

John Conkelyn
B: 19 Sep 1630 Nottinghamshire, England
M: 02 Dec 1657 New York, United States
D: 06 Apr 1694 Southold, New York, USA

Edward Alseabrook
B: 1582 England
M: 28 Jun 1602 , England
D: 1624 England

Elizabeth Allsaebrook
B: 18 Sep 1608 England
M: 24 Jan 1625 England
D: 26 Mar 1671 United States

Hannah Walker
B: 1586 England
M: 28 Jun 1602 , England
D: 1686 England

William Ellsworth Horton
B: 1551 Yorkshire, England
D: 26 Oct 1640 United States

Joseph Horton
B: Apr 1574 England
M: 1599 Leicestershire, England
D: Apr 1640 United States

Elizabeth Hanson
B: 1562 Leicestershire, England
D: 16 Jul 1660 , England

Barnabas Horton
B: 13 Jul 1600 Mowsley, , England
M: 1629 England
D: 13 Jul 1680 United States

John Schuyler
B: 1550 Mowsley, , England
D: , , , England

Mary Elizabeth Schuyler
B: 1578 Mowsley, , England
M: 1599 Leicestershire, England
D: 1663 Leicestershire, England

Ashley
B: 1555 Mowsley, , England
D: , , , England

Sarah Horton
B: 1637 North America.
M: 02 Dec 1657 New York, United States
D: 1700 Colonial America, North America.

John Langton The Younger
B: 1535 Yorkshire, England
D: 07 May 1583 England

John Langton
B: 11 Mar 1561 England
M: 1606 Leicestershire, England
D: 10 Nov 1616 Lorraine, France

Amy Palmer
B: 1537 Lincolnshire, England
D: 27 Jan 1604 England

Mary Langton
B: 07 Feb 1606 Magna, England
M: 1629 England
D: 22 Oct 1680 United States

Anthony Butler
B: 1532 Lincolnshire, England
D: 05 Sep 1578 England

Katherine Butler
B: 1568 Oxfordshire, England
M: 1606 Leicestershire, England
D: 02 Nov 1635 Louth, Ireland

Margaret Wogan
B: 1536 Oxfordshire, England
D: 03 Mar 1611

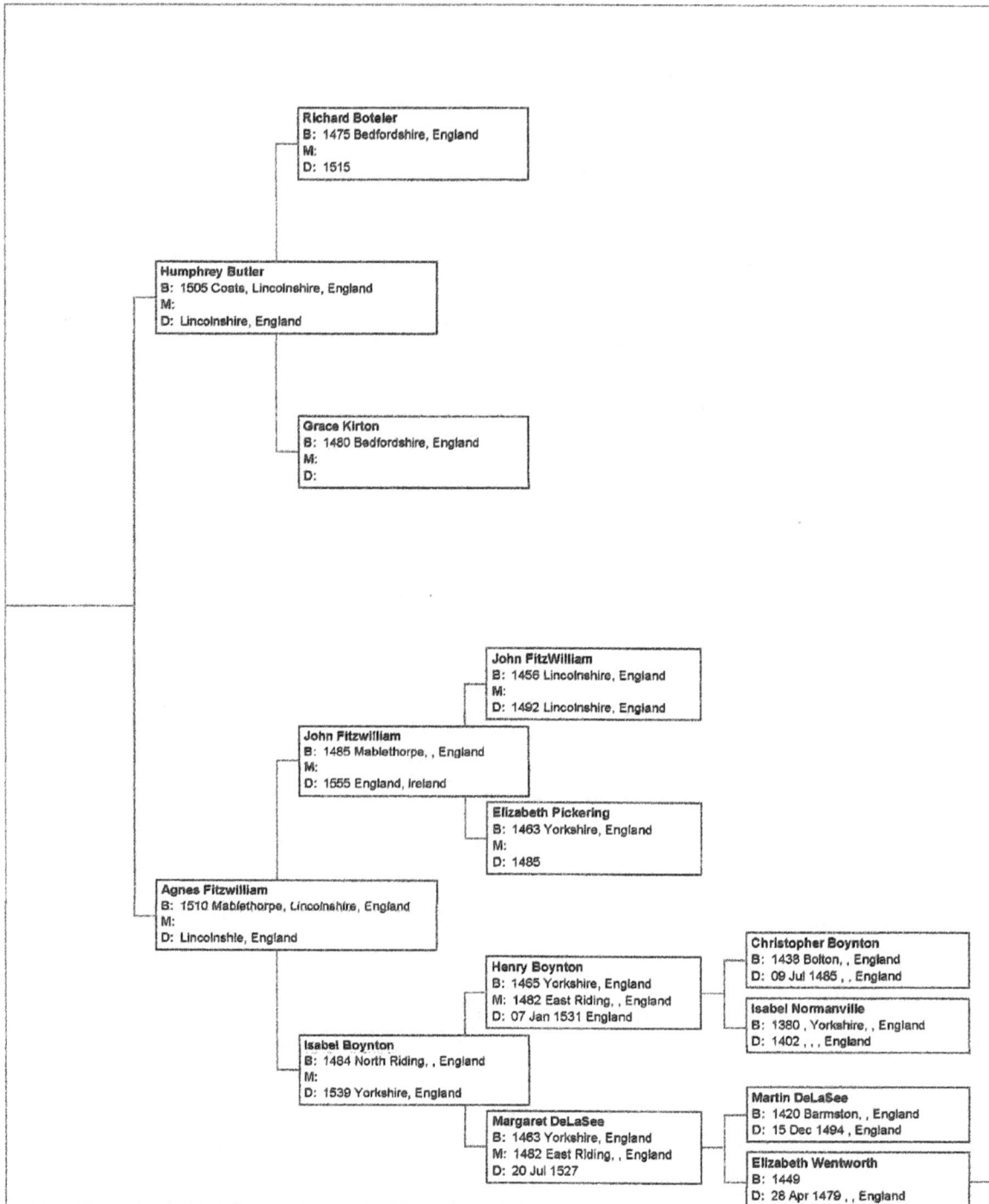

Richard Boteler
B: 1475 Bedfordshire, England
M:
D: 1515

Humphrey Butler
B: 1505 Coats, Lincolnshire, England
M:
D: Lincolnshire, England

Grace Kirton
B: 1480 Bedfordshire, England
M:
D:

John FitzWilliam
B: 1456 Lincolnshire, England
M:
D: 1492 Lincolnshire, England

John Fitzwilliam
B: 1485 Mablethorpe, , England
M:
D: 1555 England, Ireland

Elizabeth Pickering
B: 1463 Yorkshire, England
M:
D: 1485

Agnes Fitzwilliam
B: 1510 Mablethorpe, Lincolnshire, England
M:
D: Lincolnshire, England

Christopher Boynton
B: 1438 Bolton, , England
D: 09 Jul 1485 , , England

Henry Boynton
B: 1465 Yorkshire, England
M: 1482 East Riding, , England
D: 07 Jan 1531 England

Isabel Normanville
B: 1380 , Yorkshire, , England
D: 1402 , , , England

Isabel Boynton
B: 1484 North Riding, , England
M:
D: 1539 Yorkshire, England

Martin DeLaSee
B: 1420 Barmston, , England
D: 15 Dec 1494 , England

Margaret DeLaSee
B: 1463 Yorkshire, England
M: 1482 East Riding, , England
D: 20 Jul 1527

Elizabeth Wentworth
B: 1449
D: 28 Apr 1479 , , England

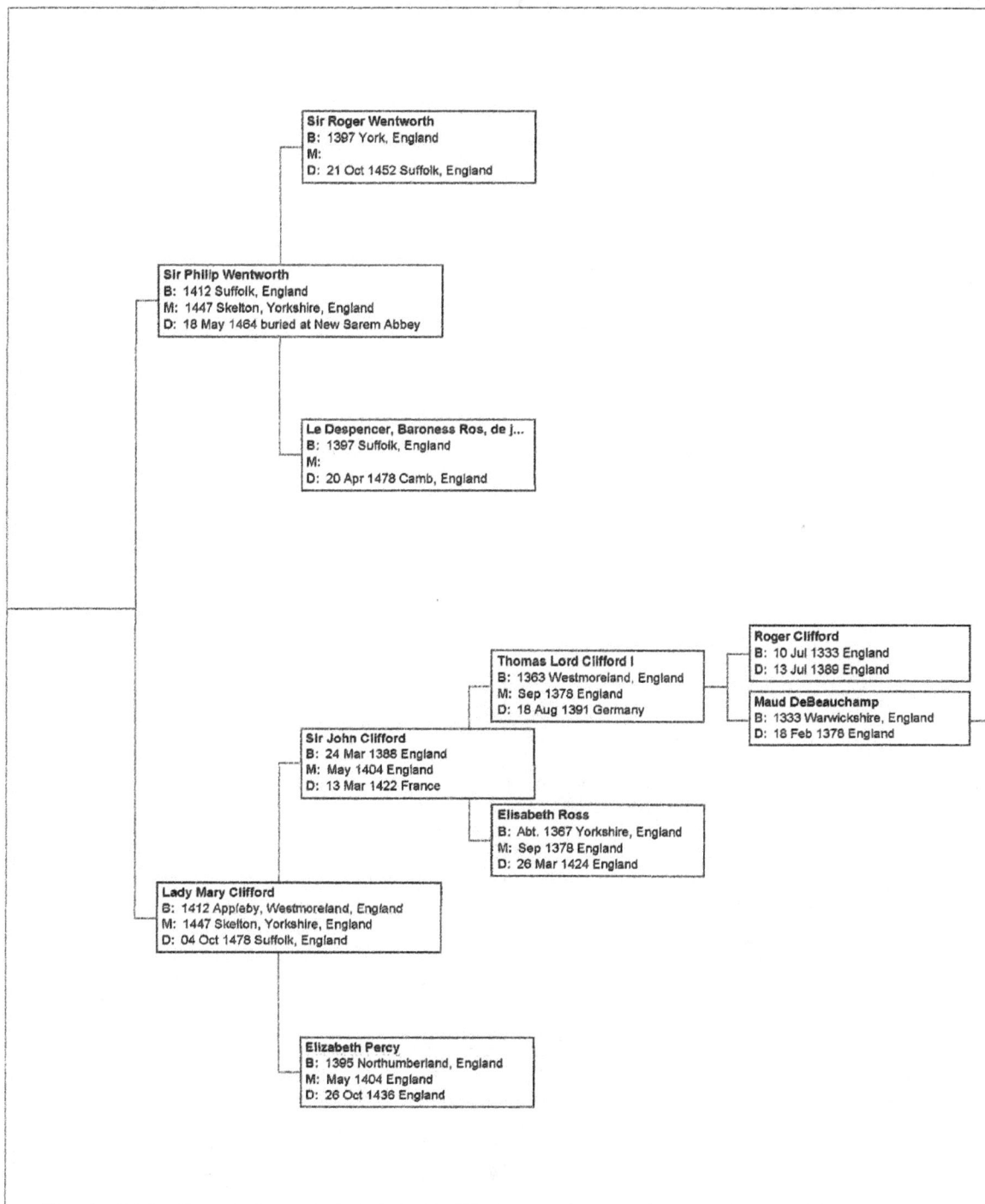

Sir Roger Wentworth
B: 1397 York, England
M:
D: 21 Oct 1452 Suffolk, England

Sir Philip Wentworth
B: 1412 Suffolk, England
M: 1447 Skelton, Yorkshire, England
D: 18 May 1464 buried at New Sarem Abbey

Le Despencer, Baroness Ros, de j...
B: 1397 Suffolk, England
M:
D: 20 Apr 1478 Camb, England

Thomas Lord Clifford I
B: 1363 Westmoreland, England
M: Sep 1378 England
D: 18 Aug 1391 Germany

Roger Clifford
B: 10 Jul 1333 England
D: 13 Jul 1389 England

Maud DeBeauchamp
B: 1333 Warwickshire, England
D: 18 Feb 1378 England

Sir John Clifford
B: 24 Mar 1388 England
M: May 1404 England
D: 13 Mar 1422 France

Elisabeth Ross
B: Abt. 1367 Yorkshire, England
M: Sep 1378 England
D: 26 Mar 1424 England

Lady Mary Clifford
B: 1412 Appleby, Westmoreland, England
M: 1447 Skelton, Yorkshire, England
D: 04 Oct 1478 Suffolk, England

Elizabeth Percy
B: 1395 Northumberland, England
M: May 1404 England
D: 26 Oct 1436 England

Appendix 1. Conklin-Marinković Pedigree Chart   151

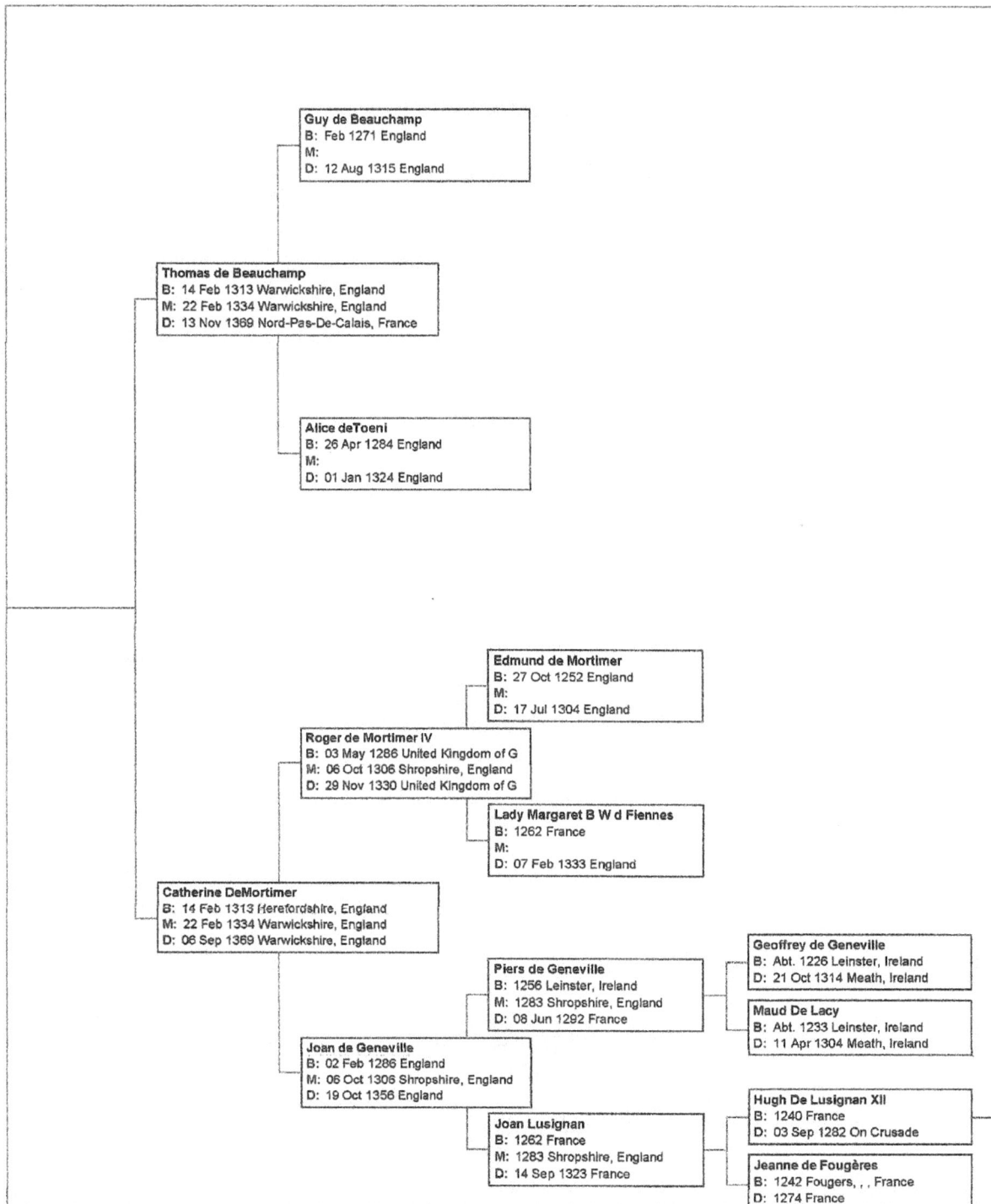

Guy de Beauchamp
B: Feb 1271 England
M:
D: 12 Aug 1315 England

Thomas de Beauchamp
B: 14 Feb 1313 Warwickshire, England
M: 22 Feb 1334 Warwickshire, England
D: 13 Nov 1369 Nord-Pas-De-Calais, France

Alice deToeni
B: 26 Apr 1284 England
M:
D: 01 Jan 1324 England

Edmund de Mortimer
B: 27 Oct 1252 England
M:
D: 17 Jul 1304 England

Roger de Mortimer IV
B: 03 May 1286 United Kingdom of G
M: 06 Oct 1306 Shropshire, England
D: 29 Nov 1330 United Kingdom of G

Lady Margaret B W d Fiennes
B: 1262 France
M:
D: 07 Feb 1333 England

Catherine DeMortimer
B: 14 Feb 1313 Herefordshire, England
M: 22 Feb 1334 Warwickshire, England
D: 06 Sep 1369 Warwickshire, England

Geoffrey de Geneville
B: Abt. 1226 Leinster, Ireland
D: 21 Oct 1314 Meath, Ireland

Piers de Geneville
B: 1256 Leinster, Ireland
M: 1283 Shropshire, England
D: 08 Jun 1292 France

Maud De Lacy
B: Abt. 1233 Leinster, Ireland
D: 11 Apr 1304 Meath, Ireland

Joan de Geneville
B: 02 Feb 1286 England
M: 06 Oct 1306 Shropshire, England
D: 19 Oct 1356 England

Hugh De Lusignan XII
B: 1240 France
D: 03 Sep 1282 On Crusade

Joan Lusignan
B: 1262 France
M: 1283 Shropshire, England
D: 14 Sep 1323 France

Jeanne de Fougères
B: 1242 Fougers, , , France
D: 1274 France

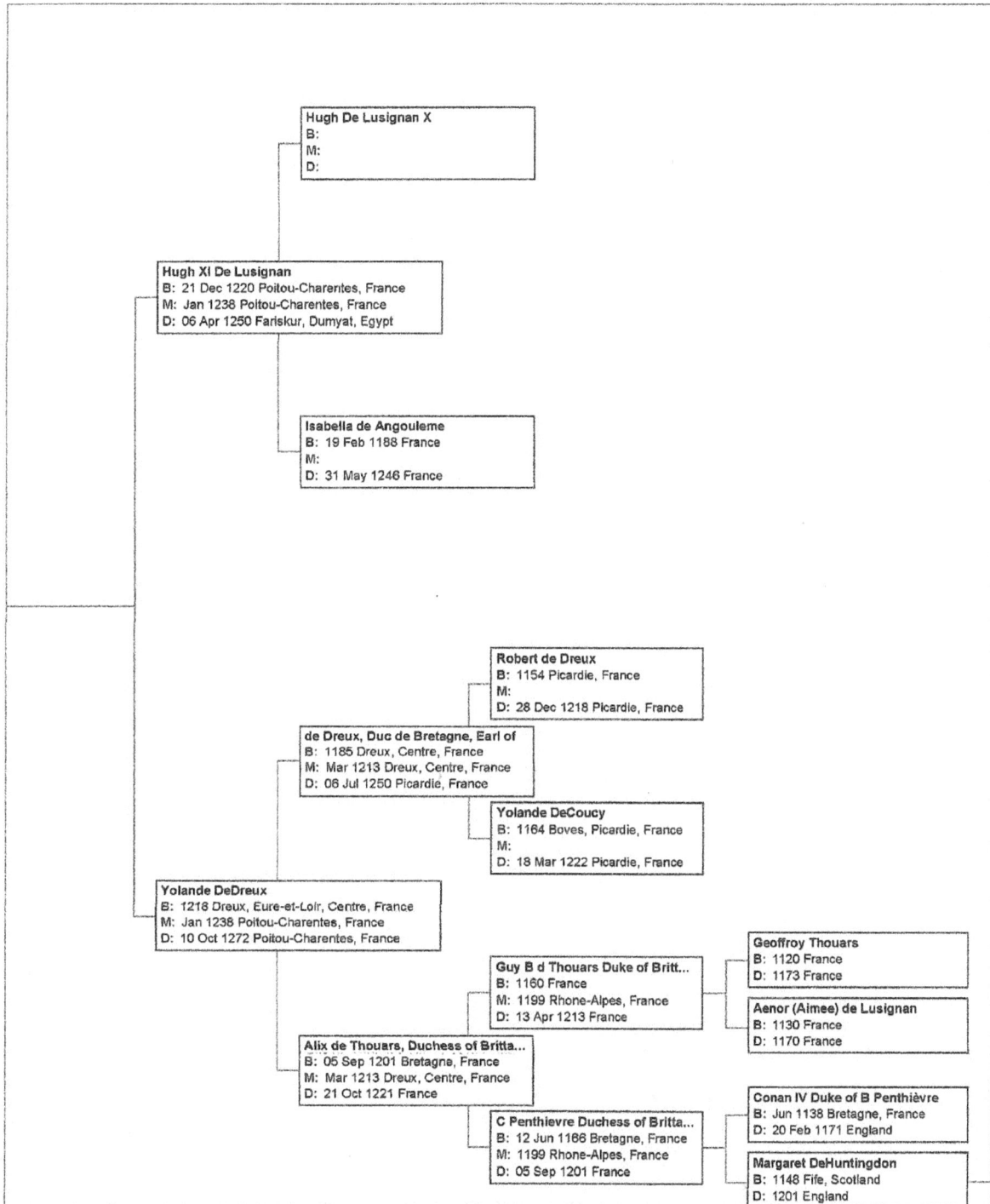

Hugh De Lusignan X
B:
M:
D:

Hugh XI De Lusignan
B: 21 Dec 1220 Poitou-Charentes, France
M: Jan 1238 Poitou-Charentes, France
D: 06 Apr 1250 Fariskur, Dumyat, Egypt

Isabella de Angouleme
B: 19 Feb 1188 France
M:
D: 31 May 1246 France

Robert de Dreux
B: 1154 Picardie, France
M:
D: 28 Dec 1218 Picardie, France

de Dreux, Duc de Bretagne, Earl of
B: 1185 Dreux, Centre, France
M: Mar 1213 Dreux, Centre, France
D: 06 Jul 1250 Picardie, France

Yolande DeCoucy
B: 1164 Boves, Picardie, France
M:
D: 18 Mar 1222 Picardie, France

Yolande DeDreux
B: 1218 Dreux, Eure-et-Loir, Centre, France
M: Jan 1238 Poitou-Charentes, France
D: 10 Oct 1272 Poitou-Charentes, France

Geoffroy Thouars
B: 1120 France
D: 1173 France

Guy B d Thouars Duke of Britt...
B: 1160 France
M: 1199 Rhone-Alpes, France
D: 13 Apr 1213 France

Aenor (Aimee) de Lusignan
B: 1130 France
D: 1170 France

Alix de Thouars, Duchess of Britta...
B: 05 Sep 1201 Bretagne, France
M: Mar 1213 Dreux, Centre, France
D: 21 Oct 1221 France

Conan IV Duke of B Penthièvre
B: Jun 1138 Bretagne, France
D: 20 Feb 1171 England

C Penthievre Duchess of Britta...
B: 12 Jun 1166 Bretagne, France
M: 1199 Rhone-Alpes, France
D: 05 Sep 1201 France

Margaret DeHuntingdon
B: 1148 Fife, Scotland
D: 1201 England

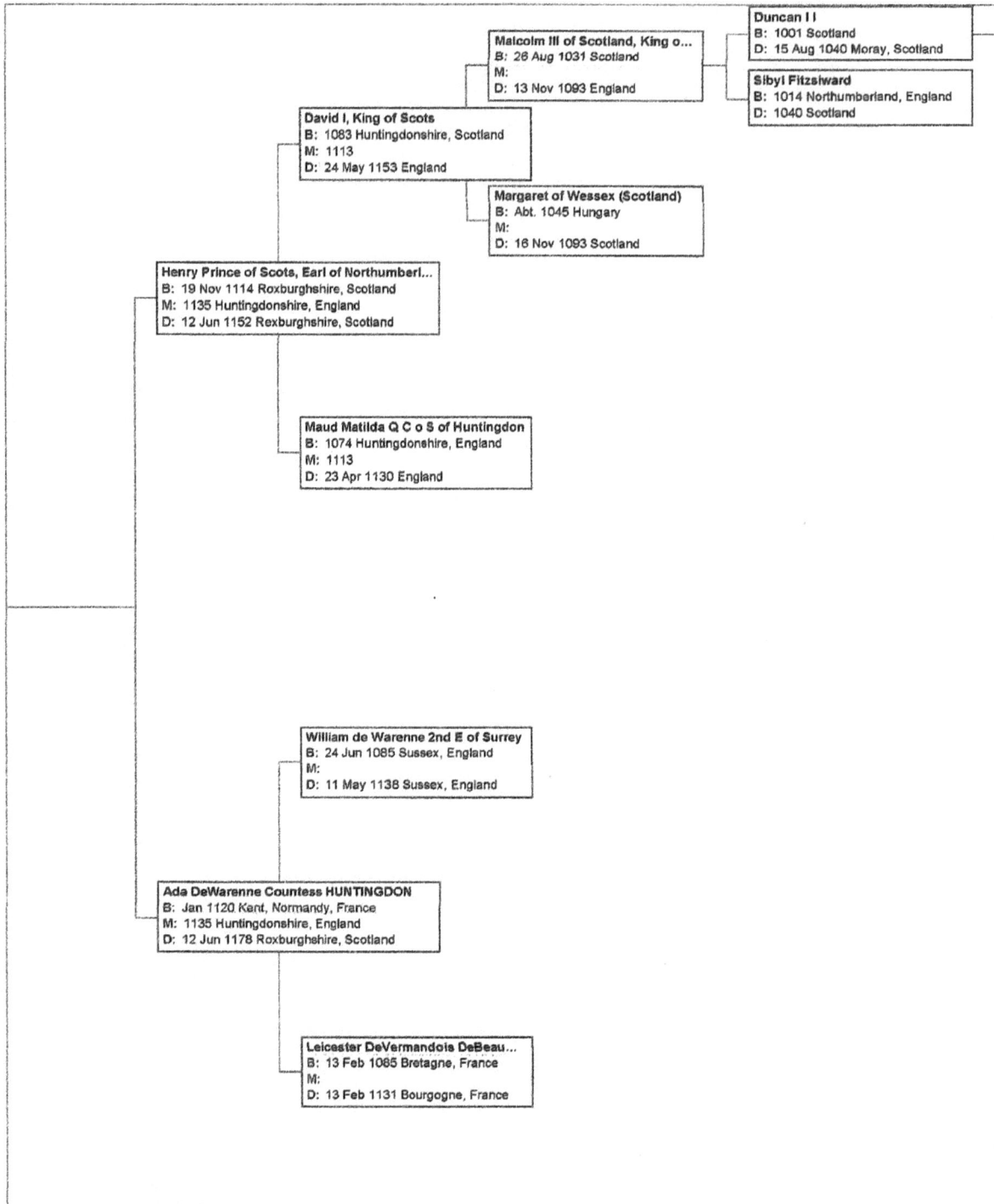

Malcolm III of Scotland, King o...
B: 26 Aug 1031 Scotland
M:
D: 13 Nov 1093 England

Duncan I I
B: 1001 Scotland
D: 15 Aug 1040 Moray, Scotland

Sibyl Fitzslward
B: 1014 Northumberland, England
D: 1040 Scotland

David I, King of Scots
B: 1083 Huntingdonshire, Scotland
M: 1113
D: 24 May 1153 England

Margaret of Wessex (Scotland)
B: Abt. 1045 Hungary
M:
D: 16 Nov 1093 Scotland

Henry Prince of Scots, Earl of Northumberl...
B: 19 Nov 1114 Roxburghshire, Scotland
M: 1135 Huntingdonshire, England
D: 12 Jun 1152 Rexburghshire, Scotland

Maud Matilda Q C o S of Huntingdon
B: 1074 Huntingdonshire, England
M: 1113
D: 23 Apr 1130 England

William de Warenne 2nd E of Surrey
B: 24 Jun 1085 Sussex, England
M:
D: 11 May 1138 Sussex, England

Ada DeWarenne Countess HUNTINGDON
B: Jan 1120 Kent, Normandy, France
M: 1135 Huntingdonshire, England
D: 12 Jun 1178 Roxburghshire, Scotland

Leicester DeVermandois DeBeau...
B: 13 Feb 1085 Bretagne, France
M:
D: 13 Feb 1131 Bourgogne, France

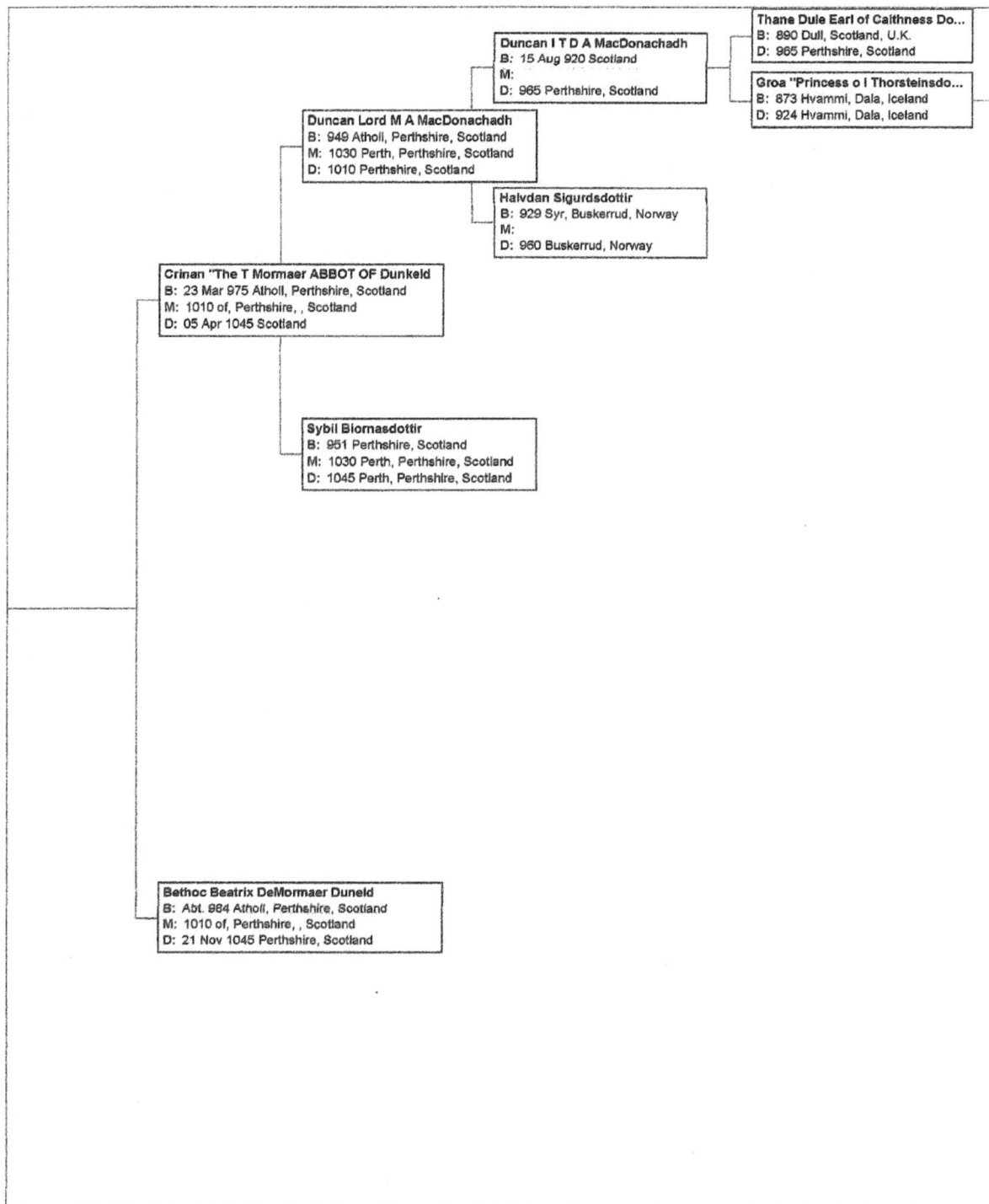

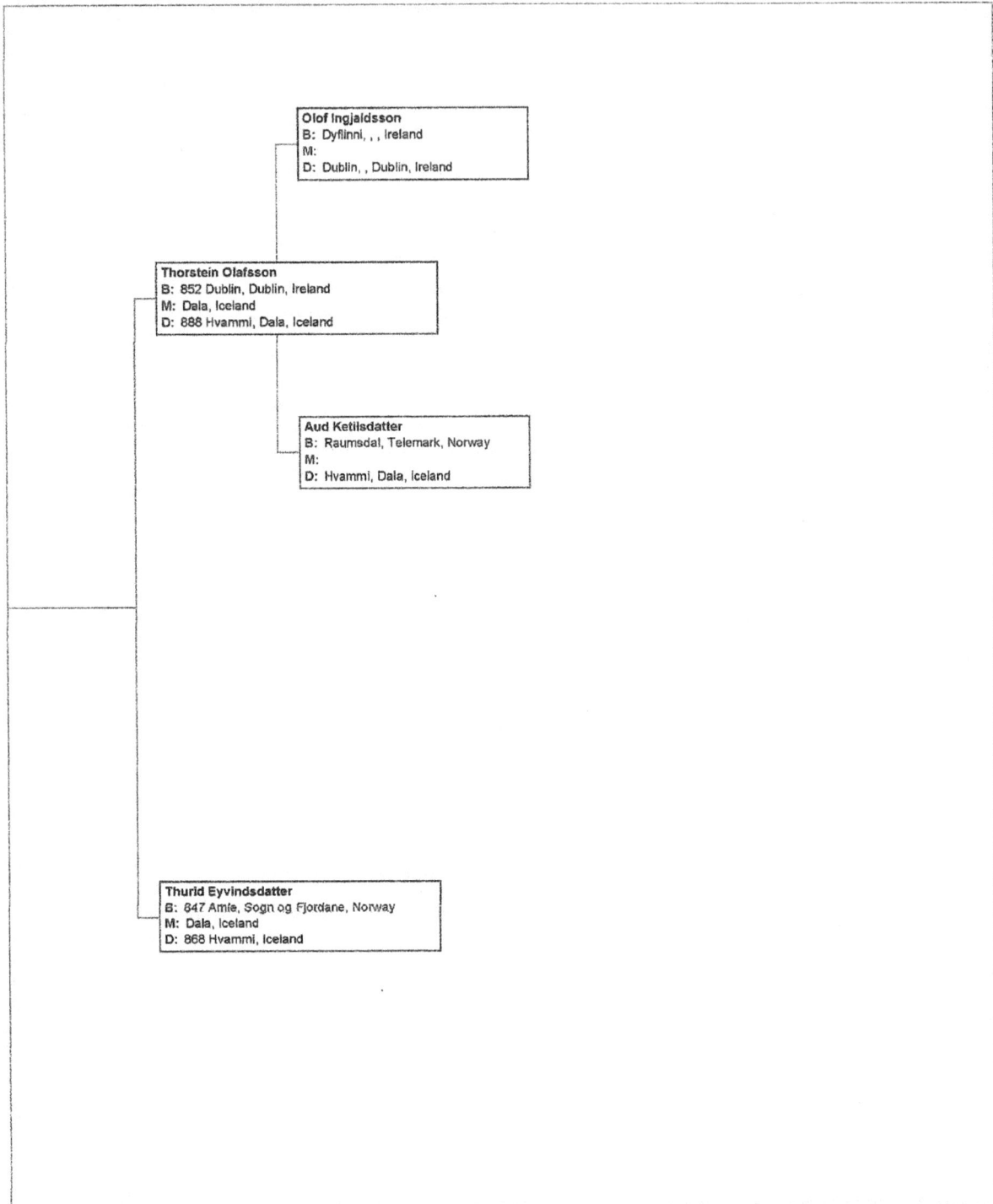

Olof Ingjaldsson
B: Dyflinni, , , Ireland
M:
D: Dublin, , Dublin, Ireland

Thorstein Olafsson
B: 852 Dublin, Dublin, Ireland
M: Dala, Iceland
D: 888 Hvammi, Dala, Iceland

Aud Ketilsdatter
B: Raumsdal, Telemark, Norway
M:
D: Hvammi, Dala, Iceland

Thurid Eyvindsdatter
B: 847 Amfe, Sogn og Fjordane, Norway
M: Dala, Iceland
D: 868 Hvammi, Iceland

Appendix 2. DNA Ethnicity Reports

Introduction to Conklin-Marinković Family DNA Ethnicity Reports

Each of the following DNA ethnicity reports include information on: 1) an Actual *versus* Predicted Relationship to the home person, David Conklin (Ancestry Kit #A858700), based on documentation *versus* DNA analysis; 2) the approximate amount of shared DNA (in centimorgans (cM), a unit used to measure the length of DNA) in the relationship. and 3) a DNA Ethnicity Estimate that graphically shows which regions of the world the approximate percentage of DNA for that person is estimated to be from.

Although the AncestryDNA web page shows that David Conklin currently has 284 4th cousins or closer, only four DNA reports are included at this time. These reports were selected for the following reasons: 1) they all used the same AncestryDNA test kit and results display; 2) they all have separate documentation as to their actual location in the Conklin-Marinković family tree; and 3) they all have given permission to view their reports.

AncestryDNA Match Confidence Score:
When we compare your DNA to the DNA of one of your matches, we calculate a confidence score for you. This score lets you know how much DNA evidence there is for you and your match actually being related.

The confidence score is based on the amount and location of the DNA that you share with your match. We show the shared amount using centimorgans (cM), a unit used to measure the length of DNA. The higher the number, the higher the confidence, and in general, the closer the relationship. Since you can share DNA with your match on one or more segments in different locations in the genome, we show you how many. Note that the number of segments and number of centimorgans that we show reflects only those segments that we believe were inherited from a recent common ancestor (in other words, segments that are likely to be identical by descent).

Confidence Score	Approximate amount of shared centimorgans	Likelihood of a single recent common ancestor	Description
Extremely High	More than 60	Virtually 100%	You and your match share enough DNA to prove that you're both descendants of a common ancestor (or couple)--and the connection is recent enough to be conclusive.
Very High	45—60	About 99%	You and your match share enough DNA that we're almost certain you're both descendants of a recent common ancestor (or couple).

Confidence Score	Approximate amount of shared centimorgans	Likelihood of a single recent common ancestor	Description
High	30—45	About 95%	You and your match share enough DNA that it is likely you're both descendants of the same common ancestor or couple, but there's a small chance the common ancestor(s) are quite distant and difficult to identify.
Good	16—30	Above 50%	You and your match share some DNA, probably from a recent common ancestor or couple, but the DNA may be from distant ancestors that are difficult to identify.
Moderate	6—16	15—50%	You and your match might share DNA because of a recent common ancestor or couple, share DNA from very distant ancestors, or you may not be related.

The amount of centimorgans you share with a match can also help you understand your relationship to them. For example, you'll usually share about 120 centimorgans with a 3rd cousin, but it's possible to share as few as 90 or as many as 200. Be aware that the precise amount of shared DNA can vary beyond the ranges shown in the table below (Ball C. e., Mar 2016).

Approximate amount of shared DNA (in centimorgans)	Possible relationship
3,475	Parent, child, or identical twin
2,400—2,800	Full sibling (including fraternal twins)
1,450—2,050	Grandparent, aunt, uncle, half sibling
680—1,150	1st cousin, great grandparent
200—620	2nd cousin
90—180	3rd cousin
20—85	4th cousin
6—20	Distant cousin: 5th cousin — 8th cousins

AncestryDNA Ethnicity Estimate:
AncestryDNA uses two different processes to determine the regions provided in your DNA Story: a reference panel and Genetic Communities™.

Building a reference panel
One way we create estimates of your genetic ethnicity is by comparing your DNA to the DNA of other people who are native to a region. The AncestryDNA reference panel contains 3,000 DNA samples from people from around the world.

We build the reference panel from a larger reference collection of 4,245 DNA samples collected from people whose genealogy suggests they are native to one region. Many of these samples were originally collected by the Sorenson Molecular Genealogy Foundation. Each panel member's genealogy is documented so we can be confident that their family is representative of people with a long history (hundreds of years) in that region.

Each volunteer's DNA sample from a given region is then tested and compared to all the others to construct the AncestryDNA reference panel. In the end, 3,000 of 4,245 individuals were chosen for the reference panel.

We compare your DNA to the reference panel
We then compare your DNA to the DNA in the reference panel to see which regions your DNA is most like. The ethnicity estimate you see on the web site is the result of this comparison (Ball C. e., Oct 2013).

Ethnicity estimate for David Conklin

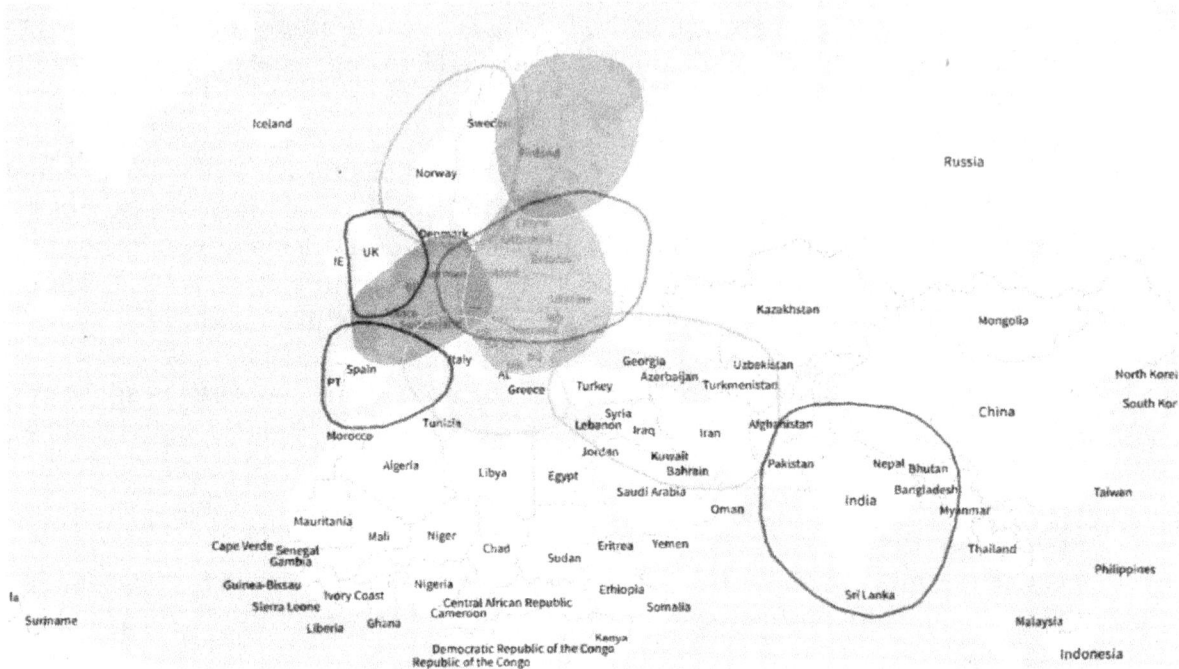

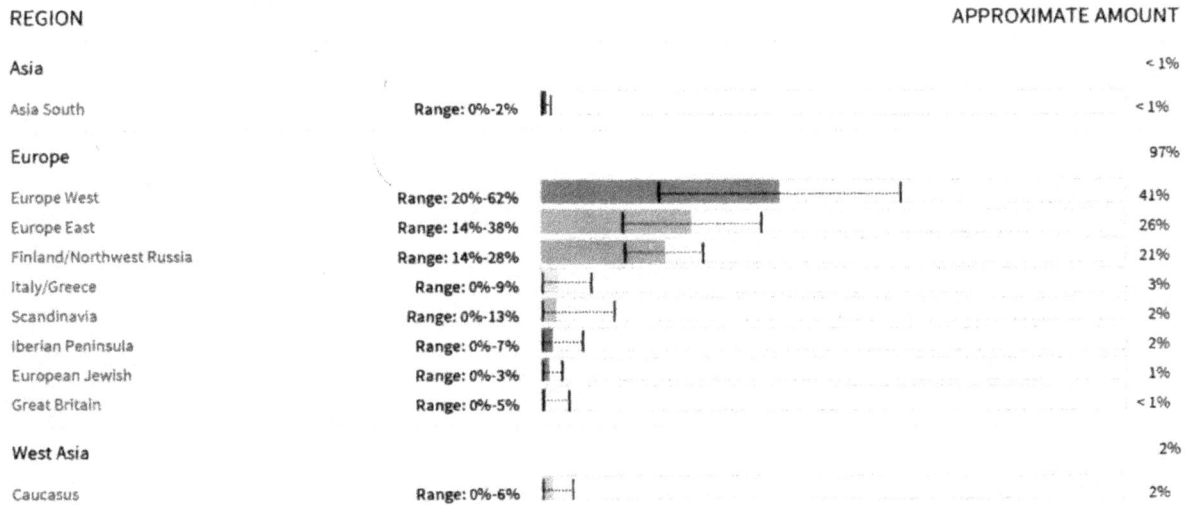

REGION		APPROXIMATE AMOUNT
Asia		< 1%
Asia South	Range: 0%-2%	< 1%
Europe		97%
Europe West	Range: 20%-62%	41%
Europe East	Range: 14%-38%	26%
Finland/Northwest Russia	Range: 14%-28%	21%
Italy/Greece	Range: 0%-9%	3%
Scandinavia	Range: 0%-13%	2%
Iberian Peninsula	Range: 0%-7%	2%
European Jewish	Range: 0%-3%	1%
Great Britain	Range: 0%-5%	< 1%
West Asia		2%
Caucasus	Range: 0%-6%	2%

Ginger Walston Krueger—Maternal 1ˢᵗ Cousin 1x removed (actual)

Amount of Shared DNA: 388 centimorgans shared across 24 DNA segments.
Possible range: 1st - 2nd cousins; 2nd Cousins
Confidence: Extremely High

Relationship Info: 2nd Cousin (Predicted)
Our analysis of your DNA predicts that this person you match with is probably your second cousin. The exact relationship can vary. **It could be a first cousin once removed**, or a great-great aunt.

While there may be some statistical variation in our prediction, it's likely to be a second cousin type relationship – which are separated by 6 degrees or six people. However, the relationship could range from four to seven degrees of separation.

Here are some examples of possible relationships separated by 6 degrees:

1st Cousins (1x removed)
1st Cousins (1x removed) share your great grandparents

Grandparent (Ana Marinković)
2 degrees

Parent (Betty Marinković)
1 degree

Uncle or Aunt (Mileva Marinković)
3 degrees

You (David G. Conklin)
0 degrees

1st Cousin (Susan Jensen)
4 degrees

1st Cousin (1x removed) (Ginger Walston)
5 degrees

Your AncestryDNA Results reveal your unique story —
who your ancestors were and where they came from.

Results as of:
07 Feb 2018

DNA Results Summary
for GINGER KRUEGER

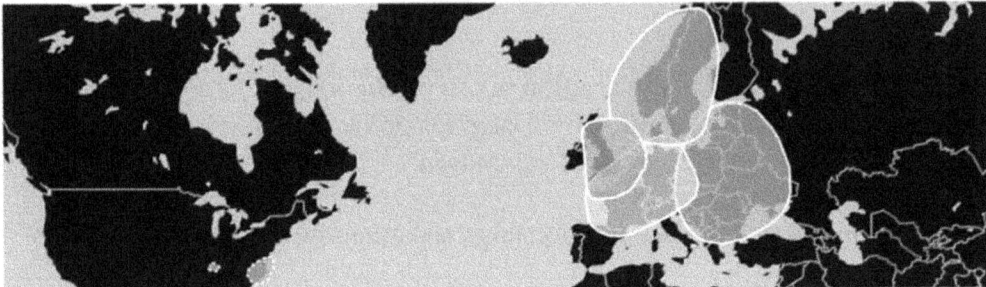

© Mapbox, © OpenStreetMap

Ethnicity Estimate

Europe West	61%	Great Britain 9%
Scandinavia	13%	
Europe East	10%	

Migrations
Eastern North Carolina Settlers

Charlene Elfers McKay—Paternal 2nd Cousin (actual)

Amount of Shared DNA: 146 centimorgans shared across 10 DNA segments
Possible range: 3rd - 4th cousins; 3rd Cousins
Confidence: Extremely High

Relationship Info: 3rd Cousin (Predicted)
Our analysis of your DNA predicts that this person you match with is probably your third cousin. The exact relationship however could vary. **It could be a second cousin** once removed, or perhaps a fourth cousin. While there may be some statistical variation in our prediction, it's likely to be a third cousin type of relationship—which are separated by eight degrees or eight people. However, the **relationship could range from six to ten degrees** of separation.

It's interesting to note that (at this degree of separation) we are accurately able to predict about 98% of the possible relatives that are out there—in other words there is a 2% chance that our DNA analysis can NOT recognize an actual relative of yours. One way to be more certain that the DNA testing captures as many relatives as possible is to have multiple members of your immediate family tested.

Here are some examples of possible relationships separated by eight or ten degrees:

3rd Cousins
3rd Cousins share your great-great grandparents

2nd Cousin
2nd Cousins share your great grandparents:

Great-grandparent (Josiah C. Conklin)
3 degrees

Grandparent (Charles W. Conklin)
2 degrees

Great (Uncle or Aunt) (Eugene L. Conklin)
4 degrees

Parent (Charles F. Conklin)
1 degree

1st Cousin (1x removed) (Myrtle Conklin)
5 degrees

You (David G. Conklin)
0 degrees

2nd Cousin (Charlene Elfers)
6 degrees

Ethnicity estimate for Charlene Elfers Mckay

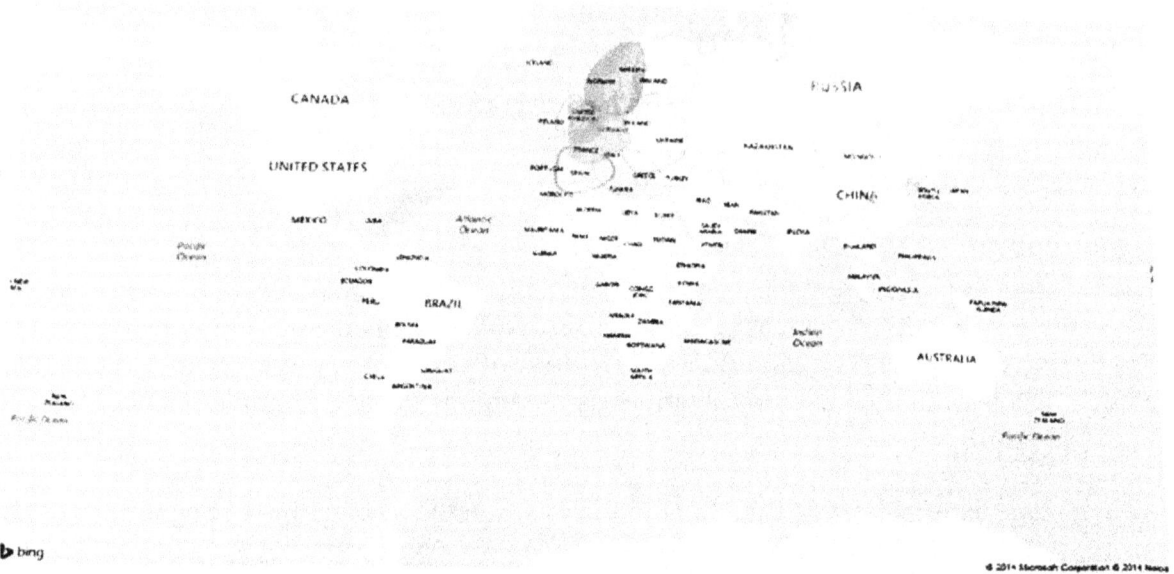

REGION			APPROXIMATE AMOUNT
Europe			100%
Great Britain	Range: 26%-76%		52%
Europe West	Range: 3%-47%		25%
Scandinavia	Range: 0%-27%		9%
Finland/Northwest Russia	Range: 0%-11%		5%
Italy/Greece	Range: 0%-10%		5%
Iberian Peninsula	Range: 0%-8%		2%
Ireland	Range: 0%-6%		1%
Europe East	Range: 0%-3%		< 1%

Savo Marinković—Maternal 4th Cousin

Amount of Shared DNA: 40 centimorgans shared across 4 DNA segments
Possible range: 4th - 6th cousins; *4th Cousins*
Confidence: High
Ancestry Kit #A837671

Relationship Info: 4th Cousin (Predicted)
Our analysis of your DNA predicts that this person you match with is **probably your fourth cousin.** The exact relationship however could vary. It could be a third cousin once removed, or perhaps a fifth or sixth cousin. For relationships this distant from you, there is greater statistical variation in our prediction. It's most likely to be a fourth cousin type of relationship (which are separated by ten degrees or ten people), but the relationship could range from six to twelve degrees of separation.

It's interesting to note that (at this degree of separation) we are accurately able to predict only about 71% of the possible relatives that are out there—in other words there is a 29% chance that our DNA analysis can NOT recognize an actual relative of yours. One way to be more certain that the DNA testing captures as many relatives as possible is to have multiple members of your immediate family tested.
Here are some examples of possible relationships separated by ten or more degrees:
4th Cousins
4th Cousins share your great-great-great grandparents

Great-great-great-grandparent
5 degrees

Great-great-grandparent
4 degrees

Great-great grand (Uncle or Aunt)
6 degrees

Great-grandparent (Josif Marinković)
3 degrees

1st Cousin (3x removed)
7 degrees

Grandparent (Stevan Marinković)
2 degrees

2nd Cousin (2x removed) (Ljubomir Marinković)
8 degrees

Parent (Betty Marinković)
1 degree

3rd Cousin (1x removed) (Nikola Marinković)
9 degrees

You (David G. Conklin)
0 degrees

4th Cousin (Savo Marinković)
10 degrees

Ethnicity estimate for Savo Marinkovic

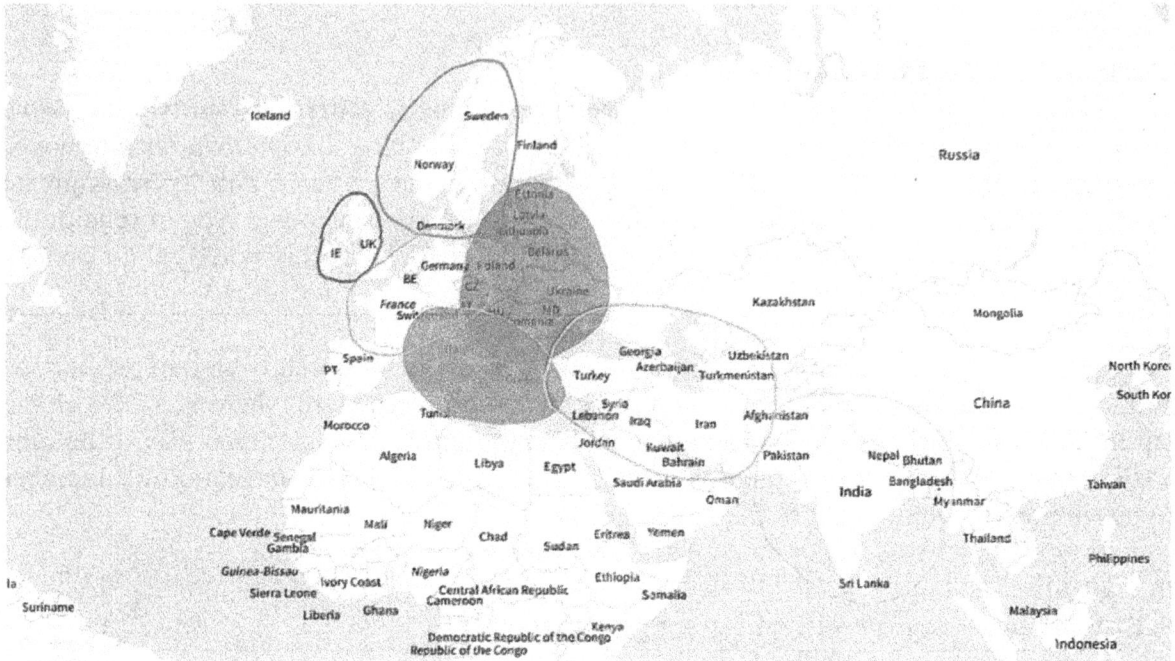

REGION		APPROXIMATE AMOUNT
Asia		1%
Asia South	Range: 0%–4%	1%
Europe		98%
Europe East	Range: 51%–67%	61%
Italy/Greece	Range: 27%–42%	34%
Scandinavia	Range: 0%–8%	2%
Ireland	Range: 0%–4%	< 1%
Europe West	Range: 0%–3%	< 1%
West Asia		1%
Caucasus	Range: 0%–4%	1%

Appendix 3. Conklin-Marinković Grave Locator

Conklin-Marinkovic Grave Locations
Online Find A Grave Memorials (www.findagrave.com)

				as of 10 Feb 2018
NAME				MEMORIAL #
FIRST	MIDDLE	MAIDEN	LAST	
Charles	William		Conklin	179559280
Charles	Franklin		Conklin	155642790
David	Elias		Conklin	171502156
Eugene	Lester		Conklin	180416087
Josiah	C		Conklin	152747718
Louise	Theresa	Conklin	Berg-Boss	184101660
Pauline	Ruth	Zimmerman	Able-Conklin	115539071
Mary	Ann	Bush	Conklin	96065456
Theresa		Stockman	Conklin	183453104
Joan		Conklin	Fulton	184130391
Stevan			Marinkovic	180418725
Ana		Marinkovic	Marinkovic	180418819
Millie		Marinkovic	Jensen	180419026
Betty		Marinkovic	Conklin	155643239
Mary		Marinkovic	Wirtz	180419929
Bogdan/Robert	Cross	Marinkovic	Markovic	99283958
Joy		Marinkovic	Asher	128247103
Caroline		Lingren	Conklin-Wright	165297944
Emma		Jellings	Conklin	84142787
Johanna		Dalstrom	Lingren	104072824
Sylvia		Johnson	Conklin-Edwards	180416284
Florba	May	Grazier	Markovic	99283931
Dennis	Robert		Markovic	99283898
Susan	Marian	Jensen	Walston-Sherwertz	

References

Alburgh, VT. (1796). *First Book of Town Records.* Alburgh, VT.

Ancestry.com Operations, Inc. Lehi, UT, USA. (2016). *Record for John Conklyne.* Retrieved from Colonial Families of the USA, 1607-1775: www.Ancestry.com

Ancestry.com Operations, Inc. Provo, UT, USA. (2011). *Volume: 270. Record for Abram Conklin.* Retrieved from Sons of the American Revolution Membership Applications, 1889-1970: www.Ancestry.com

Ancestry.com Operations, Inc., Provo, UT, USA. (2012). *Record for Daisy Conklin).* Retrieved from Find A Grave Index, 1600s-Current: www.ancestry.com

Ball, C. e. (Mar 2016). *AncestryDNA Matching White Paper.* AncestryDNA. Retrieved from www.ancestry.com

Ball, C. e. (Oct 2013). *Ethnicity Estimate White Paper.* AncestryDNA. Retrieved from www.ancestry.com

Browning, A. J. (2009). *The Descendants of Emory R. Wilder (1889-1967.* Camas, WA: Arnold J. Browning.

Bulatovic, S. (Feb 2016). *Snezana Bulatovic Research in Croatia.* Belgrade, Serbia: Serbian Heritage Tours. Retrieved from http://www.serbianheritagetours.com

Conklin, C. F. (1980, Sep 6). Charles F. Conklin Family History Audio Interview I. (D. G. Conklin, Interviewer)

Conklin, C. F. (1996). Personal History Notes. (P. Abell, Interviewer) unpublished manuscript.

Conklin, C. F. (2001, Nov 23). Charles Conklin Family History Audio Interview II. (D. G. Conklin, Interviewer)

Conklin, D. (1975). *Montana Historic Preservation Plan.* Helena, MT: Montana Dept of Fish, Wildlife & Parks.

Conklin, D. (1999). *Two Years Among the Bulgars.* Kalispell, MT: unpublished manuscript.

Conklin, D. (2002). *Montana History Weekends: Fifty-two Adventures in History.* Guilford, CT: Globe Pequot Press.

Conklin, D. (2005). *Letters from Baghdad.* Kalispell, MT: unpublished manuscript.

Conklin, L. (2002, Jan). Louise Conklin Family History Audio Interview. (D. G. Conklin, Interviewer)

Conklin, L. C. (2002, Jan). Louise & Charles Conklin Family History Audio Interview. (D. G. Conklin, Interviewer)

Conklin, L. (Dec 1997). *Louise Conklin letter to Robert Livingston.* unpublished manuscript.

Conkling, I. B. (1913). *The Conklings in America.* NY: Charles Potter & Co. Retrieved from www.forgottonbooks.com

Daily Signal. (1962, Mar 27). S.G. Girl Picked for Capitol Trip. *Huntington Park Daily Signal.*

Davis, S. (1999, Oct 6). *Abraham & Jacob Conklin.* Retrieved from Roots Web: www.rootsweb.ancestry.com

Dodge, O. (1898). *Pioneer History of Coos and Curry Counties, Oregon, Bio Appendix.* Salem, OR: Capital Printing.

Douthit, N. (1981). *The Coos Bay Region, 1890-1944: Life on a Coastal Frontier.* Coos Bay, OR: Coos County Historical Society.

Field, L. (Ed.). (1948). *Amagansett Lore and Legend.* New York.

Fraser, A. (1904). *Second Report of the Bureau of Archives No. 423.* Prov. of Ontario, Canada, Bureau of Archives. Toronto: Bureau of Archives.

Gerolymatos, A. (2002). *The Balkan Wars.* NY: Perseus Books.

Glenny, M. (1999). *The Balkans: Nationalism, War and the Great Powers 1804-1999.* NY: Viking Books.

Halbert's Family Heritage. (1998). *The New World Book of Conklins.* New York: Halbert's Family Heritage.

Humbolt Standard. (1952, Jun 24). Former Eureka Resident Dead. *Eureka Humbolt Standard, 24 June 1952, p.3)*, p. 3.

Idahonian. (1979, Aug 7). Pilot Tried to Flee Canyon, Then Crashed. *Moscow, Idaho Idahonian*, p. 10.

Ilmoen, S. (1919). *Amerikan Suomalaisten Historia-I.*

Jensen, D. (2016, Oct 21). Don Jensen Family History Interview. (D. G. Conklin, Interviewer)

Jensen, D. (Oct 2017). *Susan Jensen Eulogy.* Beaumont, CA: unpublished manuscript.

Jensen, E. A. (1985, Nov). Art Jensen Family History Audio Interview. (D. Jensen, Interviewer)

Jensen, S. (2015, Nov 21). Susan Jensen Family History Video Interview. (D. G. Conklin, Interviewer)

Kinross, L. (1977). *The Ottoman Centuries.* NY: Morrow Quill.

Leggett Conaway. (1883). *The History of Marion County, Ohio.* Chicago: Leggett Conaway.

Lewis Publishing Co. (1895). *Memorial Record of the Counties of Delaware, Union & Morrow, Ohio.* Chicago: The Lewis Publishing Co.

Livingston, R. (Dec 1997). *Robert Livingston letter to Louise (Conklin) Boss.* unpublished manuscript.

Lynwood Press. (1946, May 3). Pair Wed at Chapel. *Lynwood Press.*

Lyon, J. (2015). *Serbia and the Balkan Front, 1914.* NY: Bloomsbury Publishing.

MacKenzie, G. (n.d.). *Early Families of Philipsburgh, NY.* NY: Westchester County Historical Society.

Mann, C. (1944, Jan). The Family of Conklin in America. *American Genealogist, Vol 21, No 1.*, p. 49.

Mann, C. (1945, Jan). The Line of John Concklyne of Southold and Huntington. *American Genealogist, Vol 21, No 1*, p. 213.

Mann, C. (1950, Jul). John Concklin of Flushing and Rye, New York. *American Genealogist, Vol 26, No 3*, p. 142.

Marinkovic, B. (1980, Sep). Betty Marinkovic Family History Audio Interview. (D. G. Conklin, Interviewer)

Marinkovic, D. (2002, Jan 5). Dorothy Marinkovic Family History Audio Interview. (D. G. Conklin, Interviewer)

Marion Weekly Star. (1902, Apr 17). Mr. Josiah Conklin Dies This Morning. *Marion Weekly Star*, p. 8.

Markovic, D. (2016, Jan 21). Derek Markovic Family History Video Interview. (D. G. Conklin, Interviewer)

Marshfield Sun. (1921, Jul 21). Pioneer Resident Dies. *Marshfield Sun, 21 Jul 1921).*

Mauzey, A. (1981, Apr 8). Alice Mauzey Family History Interview. (D. G. Conklin, Interviewer) unpublished manuscript.

McKay, C. E. (2017, Apr 17). Charlene Elfers McKay Family History Video Interview. (D. G. Conklin, Interviewer)

NARA. (1798-1914). *Registers of Enlistments in the United States Army, 1798-1914.* National Archives and Records Admin, Wash DC.

NARA. (1812). *War of 1812 Pension Application File: Abram Conklin.* Wash DC: National Archives & Records Admin.

NARA. (n.d.). *U.S. Civil War Pension file: Josiah Conklin.* National Archives and Records Administration, Wash DC.

Paxson. Frederic Logan, A. J. (Ed.). (1930). *Dictionary of American Biography*. NY: Charles Scribner's Sons.

Perley, S. (1926). *History of Salem, Vol 2*. Salem, MA.

Rattray, J. (n.d.). *East Hampton History*. New York: Long Island Genealogical Society.

Rutkow, E. (2012). *American Canopy*. New York: Schribner.

Teen Vogue Magazine. (2016, Sep 12). Savanna Shields Crowned Miss America. *Teen Vogue Magazine*.

U.S. Federal Census. (1900). *Record for David E Conklin*. Retrieved from Year: 1900; Census Place: Bear Lake, Manistee, Michigan; Roll: 727; Page: 3B; Enumeration District: 0027; FHL microfilm: 1240727: http://search.ancestry.com/cgi-bin/sse.dll?db=1900usfedcen&h=64630564&indiv=try

U.S. Federal Census. (1900). *Record for Frank Lingren*. Wash DC: Year: 1900; Census Place: North Marshfield, Coos, Oregon; Roll: 1346; Page: 19B; Enumeration District: 0016; FHL microfilm: 1241346.

Vermont. (1820). *Laws of Vermont, Oct Session*.

Guerra, Mary Lavonne, 47, 64, 92, 93

Kunz, Troy Myron, 71

H

Hedges, Richard, 11
Hedges, Ruth, 11
Hilliker, Anna (Annatje), 18, 19, 21
Hilliker, Jacobus James, 18, 19, 20
Hilliker, John, 19
Hohn, Henry, 85, 87
Hohn, Ina (Lingren), 55
Hohn, Larry, 58, 87
Horton, Barnabas, 13, 14, 16
Horton, Sarah, 13, 14, 15
Howell, Austin, 74
Howell, Ladd, 70, 74
Howell, Paige Pilar, 74
Hull, Clarissa, 23
Hull, Samuel, 23
Hundeby, Lisa, 70, 74
Hyatt, John II, 16
Hyatt, Rebecca, 16, 17

J

Jellings, Emma, 27, 35, 36, 37
Jensen, Donald Roy, 111, 117, 118, 119, 121, 123, 129, 130, 131, 132, 138, 168
Jensen, Einar Arthur, 117, 118
Jensen, John William, 117
Jensen, Karen Janine, 122
Jensen, Robert Arthur, 121
Jensen, Susan Marian, 113, 115, 119, 120, 122, 130, 139, 144, 159, 168
Johnson, Christy, 74
Johnson, Donald, 70
Johnson, Frank, 27, 41
Johnson, Stephanie, 71, 74
Johnson, Sylvia, 27, 41, 43

K

Kirkman, Dale Kenneth, 91
Kirkman, Duane Edgar, 91
Kirkman, Ward Alan, 91
Kirkman, William F., 90
Krause, Allen, 70, 74
Krause, Kelby, 74
Krueger, Amanda, 122
Krueger, Angline, 122
Krueger, Ginger (Walston), 122
Krueger, Jackson, 122
Krueger, Jerry, 120, 121, 122
Kunz, Justin Troy, 71

L

Langton, Mary, 13, 14
Laughton, John, 16
Launder, Mary, 12, 13
Lent, Maria, 17, 18
Lindgren, Armas (1874-1929), 80
Lindgren, Astrid, 80
Lingren, Caroline, iii, 3, 8, 49, 50, 53, 54, 77, 78, 89, 94, 109, 125, 128
Lingren, Elizabeth, 85
Lingren, Francis, ii, iii, 27, 49, 75, 77, 78, 79, 81, 82, 84, 85, 170
Lingren, Frank Jr., 85
Lingren, Ina May, 87
Lingren, Johanna (Dalstrom), 77, 85
Lingren, Katherina, 89
Lingren, Mary Bell, 53, 81, 82, 83, 84, 87
Lingren, Wilhelmina, 82, 85, 88
Lingren, William H., 86
Livingston, Dale Leroy, 90
Livingston, Jean Cleo, 78, 92
Livingston, Mary Frances, 93
Livingston, Robert, 81, 82, 83, 87, 90, 93, 168
Livingston, Roy, 87, 90

M

Mabie, Elizabeth, 18, 19
Macomb, Brigadier General Alexander, 24
Marinković, Ana, iii, 55, 89, 91, 97, 98, 100, 105, 106, 109, 113, 114, 116, 117, 118, 125, 127, 129, 130, 131, 137, 138, 139, 141, 142, 159
Marinković, Andy, 109
Marinković, Betty, 9, 59, 98, 125, 126, 159, 163, 169
Marinković, Bogdan, 131, 132, 133, 134, 135
Marinković, Boy, 109
Marinković, Dorothy, 141, 142, 144, 169
Marinković, Josif, iii, 97, 98, 105, 106, 113, 163
Marinković, Joy, 137
Marinković, Mary, 109, 129, 130
Marinković, Mato, 106
Marinković, Mileva, 117, 118, 119, 121, 159
Marinković, Savo, 101, 102, 104, 163
Marinković, Stevan, ii, iii, 55, 89, 91, 95, 97, 98, 105, 109, 110, 111, 112, 113, 114, 115, 117, 118, 125, 127, 129, 130, 131, 137, 138, 141, 142, 144, 163
Marinkovích, Dorothy. *See* Marinković, Dorothy
Marinkovitch, Mary, 109
Marinkovitz, Mary, 109
Markovic, Debbie, 134
Markovic, Denise Mae, 134

Z